Encountering Truth

Meeting God in the Everyday

Jorge Mario Bergoglio
Pope Francis

EDITED AND WITH AN INTRODUCTION BY
Antonio Spadaro

TRANSLATED FROM THE ITALIAN BY
Matthew Sherry

PREFACE BY
Federico Lombardi

IMAGE
NEW YORK

Copyright © 2015 Radio Vaticana, Città del Vaticano
Copyright © 2015 Libreria Editrice Vaticana, Città del Vaticano
Copyright © 2015 RCS Libri S.p.A., Milano

All rights reserved.
Published in the United States by Image,
an imprint of the Crown Publishing Group,
a division of Random House LLC,
a Penguin Random House Company, New York.
www.crownpublishing.com

IMAGE is a registered trademark and the "I" colophon is a trademark
of Random House LLC.

Originally published in Italy as *La Verità è un Incontro: Omelie Da Santa Marta* by
Vaticana, Libreria Editrice Vaticana, Città del Vaticano, and RCS Libri S.p.A.,
Milano in 2014.

Radio Vaticana

These homilies were transcribed by the staff of Vatican Radio and curated in
particular by Sergio Centofanti, Alessandro De Carolis, and Alessandro Gisotti.

Library of Congress Cataloging-in-Publication Data is available upon request.

ISBN 978-1-101-90301-8
Ebook ISBN 978-1-101-90302-5

PRINTED IN THE UNITED STATES OF AMERICA

Book design by Elizabeth Rendfleisch
Jacket photograph: Tiziana Fabi © Getty Images

10 9 8 7 6 5 4 3 2 1

First Edition

Contents

Preface: Truth is an encounter   xiii

Introduction: The homilies from Saint Martha's   xvii

1   God is patient with our weaknesses   1

2   The forgiveness of Jesus   2

3   Those who bad-mouth others are like Judas   3

4   Asking for the grace of tears to see the Risen Christ   4

5   Complaining is bad for the heart   5

6   The amazement of the encounter with Christ generates true peace   7

7   We are not saved by wizards, psychics, or ourselves   8

8   Faith is not up for negotiation   9

9   Christian love is humble or it's not God's love   11

10   Never judge, never bad-mouth   12

11   It is the love of God that saves, not money, power, or vanity   14

12   Listening to God and following the way of Jesus makes us free and happy   16

13   Triumphalism, a temptation for Christians   17

14   We don't have to "sugarcoat" life, but accept good and evil   19

15   Martyrs of the Church   21

16   The anniversary of the Second Vatican Council, work of the Holy Spirit, and moving forward   23

17   May the laity rediscover the responsibility of the baptized   25

18   Faith is believing in a God who is a Person   27

19   May the Church be freed from moralism and ideologies   29

20   Lukewarm Christians build small churches   31

21   Careerists have no faith   33

22   The Church is a love story   35

23   The Christian is not afraid of doing big things   37

24   Faith is not alienation but a journey of truth   39

25   In the Church the Spirit creates open communities and not closed groups   41

26   Being ashamed of our sins is a virtue of the humble   43

27   A "worldly" Church does not bring the Gospel   45

28   It is an unjust society that does not give work or exploits workers   47

29   The Church is a community of the "yes"   49

30   The Church must be courageous   51

31   Be meek and humble to conquer the hatred of the world   53

32   The Holy Spirit, our traveling companion and friend   55

33   A good Christian doesn't complain   57

34   Christians must build bridges, not walls   59

35   Christian joy is not the gladness of a moment   61

36   True prayer brings us out of ourselves   63

37   The Holy Spirit is the unknown quantity of our faith   65

38   He who gives his life for love is never alone   67

39   Pray for priests and bishops that they may be shepherds and not wolves   69

40   The Church needs apostolic fervor   71

41   The problem is not in being sinners   73

42   Gossip in the Church is harmful   75

43   Humble, strong, courageous prayer   77

44   In the Church the only path is service, not power   79

45   The culture of encounter is the foundation of peace   81

46   Without the salt of Jesus we are insipid   83

47   Bearing difficulties with patience and overcoming hardship with love   85

48   Those who approach the Church should find the doors open   87

49   The culture of prosperity and the lure of the transitory   90

50   Following Jesus is not a career   92

51   Triumphalism brings the Church to a standstill   94

52   The Gospel does not move forward with discouraged Christians   96

53   It is the scandal of the Cross that makes the Church   98

54   God weeps for the madness of war   100

55   The corrupt do so much harm to the Church   102

56   Hypocrisy is the language of the corrupt   104

57   The cry of suffering before God is a prayer of the heart   106

58   Let's unmask the idols that keep us from loving God   108

59   Let's allow ourselves to be loved by the tenderness of God   110

60   Let's learn from Mary to interpret life with the Word of God   112

61   To understand the Beatitudes we must open our hearts   114

62   A wealthy Church is a Church that's getting old   116

63   Christians must overcome the temptation to "go backward"   118

64   Let's follow the law of meekness   120

65   If the Christian flees from superficial humility, the power of God is within him   122

66   The Christian takes to the streets to proclaim the peace of Christ   124

67   Jesus is the secret of Christian magnanimity   126

68   Forgiving our enemies makes us like Jesus   128

69   Do not be hypocrites and moralists   130

70   We cannot pray to the Father if we have enemies in our heart   132

71   The treasures that save our hearts   134

72   Let's serve the Word of God, not the idolatry of wealth   136

73   Jesus asks us what he means to us; let's answer with our hearts   138

74   May the Church speak of the word and not of its own ideas   140

75   Being Christian is a call of love   142

76   May priests have the grace of spiritual paternity   144

77   Joyfully build your lives on Jesus the rock   146

78   May the Christian be patient and blameless   148

79   To touch the heart of God, pray   150

80   Let's flee from sin with no looking back   152

81   We meet God in kissing the feet of Jesus in the weakest of our brothers   154

82   We are children of God; no one can steal this identity card   156

83   Mercy: the heart of God's message   158

84   Let's renew the structures of the Church   160

85   We must never kill our neighbors with our tongues   162

86   Jesus doesn't need armies; his power is humility   164

87   Jesus has a promise and a mission for every Christian   166

88   Marriage, an image of the union between Christ and the Church   168

89   May the center be always Jesus   170

90   Christian hope is not optimism, it is Jesus   172

91   Proclaiming Jesus without fear or shame   174

92   If you want to love your enemy, contemplate the Passion of Jesus and the gentleness of Mary   176

93   Gossip kills God and neighbor   178

94   Prayer and tears to glimpse the mystery of the Cross   180

95   Love for the people and humility, necessary virtues for leaders   182

96   The Church is a courageous mother   184

97   No to the idolatry of money   186

98   The gaze of Jesus changes our lives   188

99   A sacrament is not a magic ritual   190

100   Pray incessantly for peace in Syria, Lebanon, and the Middle East   192

101   We can't get to know Jesus in first class   193

102   A Christian must not avoid the Cross   195

103   Asking for the grace not to flee the Cross   197

104   Peace and joy, signs of the presence of God in the Church   199

105   Our work should make us more humble   201

106   The Mass is not a social event   203

107   Someone "far away" can hear God better than someone "near"   205

108   A prayer made with the heart can work miracles   207

109   The true gift is God himself   209

110   Following Jesus means no half measures   211

111   Christians need to leave behind the "Jonah syndrome"   213

112   Let's worship God to keep from being idolaters or hypocrites   215

113   "Ideological Christians" are a grave illness   217

114   Let's not forget about priests and sisters in retirement homes   219

115   Attachment to money destroys persons and families   221

116   God does not save us by decree   223

117   Christian life shouldn't be watered down   225

118   The struggle against evil also means confessing sins   227

119   Jesus continues to pray for us even today   229

120   Hope is dynamic and life-giving   231

121   We are all invited to the feast by the Lord   233

122   God's weakness for love is the joy of mercy   236

123   Corruption destroys dignity   238

124   *Ecclesia semper reformanda*   240

125   No to Christians with a double life   241

126   Even when he scolds us, God caresses us   243

127   The spirit of curiosity pulls us away from the wisdom and peace of God   245

128   Man's prayer is God's weakness   247

129   God save us from the worldly spirit and from uniform thinking   248

130   In the memories of grandparents is the future of our people   250

131   We go to the Temple not to celebrate a ritual but to worship God   252

132   Like the martyrs, Christians must make definitive choices   254

133   The moment belongs to man; time belongs to God   256

134   Faith is not a private affair   258

135   The Christian does not give in to "weak thinking"   260

136   Christmas means letting Jesus encounter us with open hearts   262

137   A Church without joy is unthinkable   264

138   Not putting the Word of God into practice is harmful   266

139   Praying means "bothering" God until he listens to us   268

140   Peace and religious freedom in the Middle East, no more divisions   270

141   The Lord's door is always open   272

142   Approaching Christmas in silence, in order to listen to the tenderness of God   274

143   Christians allergic to preachers are closed off to the Spirit   276

144   Without prophecy you have clericalism   278

145   God became history and walks with us   280

146   Humility makes us fruitful; pride makes us sterile   282

147   Only silence guards the mystery   284

148 At Christmas, let's make room for Jesus   286

149 Putting our hearts to the test to listen to Jesus   288

150 Christian love is not the love of the soap operas   290

151 Half-convinced Christians are Christians defeated   292

152 Our relationship with Jesus saves us from the idolatry of the "god Narcissus"   294

153 God's love straightens our crooked histories   296

154 Faith is not a weight on our shoulders   298

155 Let's give God's people the bread of life   301

156 A Christian does not neglect the Word of God   303

157 Ours is the God of surprises, let's welcome the innovation of the Gospel   305

158 Let's preserve our smallness in order to dialogue with the Lord   307

159 Jealousy, envy, and gossip divide Christian communities   309

160 Always build bridges of dialogue   311

161 Thanks to the many holy priests   313

162 Let's not praise the Lord with coldness   315

163 It is an absurd dichotomy to love Christ without the Church   317

164 If we lose the sense of God, the worst sin seems like no big deal   319

165 A leader does not exploit God and his people   321

166 Even God weeps   323

167 Asking for the grace to die in the Church   325

168 Being Christians is not a privilege   327

169 The mystery of God in the Mass   329

170 Humility can unleash faith   331

171 The Christian must overcome the temptation of becoming a wolf   333

172 It is the patience of the People of God that moves the Church forward   335

173   Temptation: an infection that kills   337

174   In order to know Jesus we must follow him as disciples   339

175   Faith without works is just words   341

176   Following Jesus means having a home, the Church   343

177   The scandal of war   345

178   Inconsistent Christians, a scandal that kills   347

179   Let's not condemn those who fail in love   349

180   Let's free our hearts of idolatry   351

181   There are Christians condemned today because they have a Bible   353

182   There is no Christian style without the Cross and without Jesus   355

183   Fasting is also a caress   357

184   Mercy is the way of peace in the world   359

185   No to hypocrites "gussied up" as saints   361

186   He who trusts in himself and not in the Lord loses his name, meaning everything   363

Preface

Truth is an encounter

In the very first weeks after the election, I thought that the morning Mass at Saint Martha's with a group of faithful and with the homily was one of the most characteristic aspects of the pontificate of Pope Francis. And I continue to think so.

His priestly and pastoral heart manifests itself in a daily relationship with the faithful in a communal Eucharistic celebration that is intense, meditative, and sober, in a certain sense austere without being barren. The personal hearing of the Word of God does not give way even for a moment to erudition or aestheticism, because it is immediately interwoven with the experience of concrete life and is aimed at ordering this according to the will of God, in the spirit of the Gospel.

Personally, every time I have been asked about the features of the pontificate in which I recognize the "Jesuit" spirituality of the pope, I have immediately thought of the Mass at Saint Martha's and his homilies. It was his way of celebrating and reading Scripture to which I related best and most spontaneously.

As Pope Francis explains in his apostolic exhortation *Evangelii Gaudium,* the way in which a priest gives his homilies says a lot about his interior and apostolic qualities, and this continues to hold true when this priest becomes pope. I have always said that I am a great admirer of the homilies of Pope Benedict XVI, especially those given at the big public celebrations. To me they are among the most precious texts of his pontificate; I have often called them sublime because of their harmonious and profound synthesis of theology, spirituality, and teaching of Christian life, their yearning and beauty, the splendor of the truth. A true aid in lifting the eyes and the soul up to God.

The daily homilies of Pope Francis are evidently of a different nature, as Fr. Antonio Spadaro explains in his introduction. They are the homilies of a son of Saint Ignatius, accustomed to "helping souls" to "seek and find the will of God" every day, looking to and following Jesus, who carries his Cross to save us, under the loving eyes of the Father.

For us at Vatican Radio, the homilies from Saint Martha's have been from the beginning an extra job that the new pontificate has required. Not the only one, of course! There are various extra jobs, but the morning homily is the first of these, because the microphones and recording equipment have to be ready in the chapel by 7:00 A.M.

The groups of faithful change every morning, but the engineers of Vatican Radio who accompany the celebration with their friends and colleagues of the Vatican Television Center and with the photographer of *L'Osservatore Romano* are always the same.

After the Mass the recording is sent to the Italian news bureau, which is already working on the morning editions. Attentive ears, expert minds, and quick fingers make a first transcription available around 9:00 A.M. A journalist reads this carefully. I also read the transcription and rapidly compare my impressions with those of the journalist; we identify the main points, the passages most suitable for extracting in audio form for the listeners, and any expressions that may be less clear. The journalist proceeds to write a summary and select three or four audio clips. Sometimes he consults his fellow journalist at *L'Osservatore Romano* who is working on a similar synopsis that will be published in the newspaper that afternoon. The definitive summary is sent to me for a final reading. Sometimes I am able to do this, but often I do not have time. Generally it is not necessary, because the pope's thought is clear and the journalist knows his job.

Around 11:00 A.M. the summary of the homily is published in Italian on the website of Vatican Radio together with the audio clips. The news agencies have been waiting for it and immediately send out their first bulletins. In the meantime the different sections of Vatican Radio begin to translate the summary into their respective languages: English, French, Czech, Slovakian, Hungarian, Chinese, Hindi, Tamil, Swahili . . . about thirty in all. Another journalist requests a video clip from the Vatican Television Center and posts it on the Vatican's YouTube channel.

All of the sections of Vatican Radio say that the homily at Saint

Martha's is one of their most popular features and often the one most visited on their web pages. This means that the homily speaks to the mind and heart beyond cultural differences, to the different peoples on the different continents.

So although it may be an extra job for us, it is a welcome one, an added richness in the service we provide for our listeners, Internet visitors, and readers, setting apart what many call our "service to the voice of the pope."

It is a shared labor in which various persons participate. If this book is being published now, it is because the engineers, secretaries, and journalists have performed this service with commitment and joy in order to spread the word of the pope or, better, so that with the pope's help we may encounter Jesus.

Special thanks go to Sergio Centofanti, Alessandro De Carolis, and Alessandro Gisotti, who took turns preparing with intelligence and attention the texts that we are able to read here.

Federico Lombardi, S.J.
Director General of Vatican Radio

Introduction

The homilies from Saint Martha's

I

Saint Martha's, 6:30 A.M.

A group of persons approach the gate of Saint Martha's House, the "dorm," as Pope Francis calls it. We are expected to arrive at 6:45. The early hour and the chill in the air sharpen our sense of anticipation, but the atmosphere is already meditative. We are all there to attend Mass with the pope. Not a solemn celebration at Saint Peter's but a "down-home" Mass in the little indoor chapel. The gates open. The Swiss Guards help us with our coats and usher us into the chapel. The priests go to a room with a long table and many chairs, which are ordinarily used for holding jackets or purses. Two Vincentian sisters help the concelebrants put on surplices and stoles. There are a few bottles of water and plastic cups: a simple touch, but appreciated. Those who have come for Mass are already in their seats. Then the priests enter and sit down in the front row to concelebrate. The atmosphere is calm, and in fact everything seems completely normal.

Where are we? In the chapel of Saint Martha's House, dedicated to the Holy Spirit. Planning for it began in 1993, and it was designed by the architect Louis D. Astorino of Pittsburgh, Pennsylvania. The chapel was built inside the narrow triangular space between the southern wall of the residence and the ninth-century Leonine Wall: this location discouraged the architect, but then he decided to use triangular forms as the motif for the whole chapel, making immediate reference to the Trinity. Even the floor is based on a pattern of triangles. The faithful see in every part, every decoration, every ornament the triumph of Trinitarian symbolism. This gives it a somewhat "prickly" appearance, but at the same time it is warm, thanks to the marble and the sober interplay of light. The tension of the space is strongly vertical. This detail is not insignificant: the central axis of the chapel lines up perfectly with the axis of the papal altar in Saint Peter's Basilica.

A sober, essential, intense liturgy

The pope enters, immersed in recollection, bows toward the altar, and then makes the sign of the Cross. The first sensation is precisely that of being at Mass. Nothing else. Not of being with the pope, but of participating in morning Mass, like those that are celebrated in every parish. The pope is there, and the white skullcap is the visible evidence of this, but in this moment he is a pastor with his people. Issuing the invitation to prayer, the pontiff looks the people in the eye. Francis does not like abstraction: this celebration is not a relationship between him and God in the presence of spectators but is about living in a truly communal dynamic. "The Lord be with you," the pope says in a placid voice. "And with your spirit," the people respond.

The liturgy is sober, essential, intense. It is accompanied by equally sober songs. The pope usually has two main concelebrants at his side. After the proclamation of the Gospel he goes to the ambo and addresses the faithful. In front of him he has only the lectionary: no papers or other texts, but only the Word of God. After a moment of silence, Francis delves into the readings of the day, grasping their meaning for the people before him.

The duration of the homily is limited: if it lasts too long, Bergoglio wrote in *Evangelii Gaudium,* "it will affect two characteristic elements of the liturgical celebration: its balance and its rhythm" (EG 138). The pope himself says that he finds in the Bible the recommendation for the correct measure: "Be brief, say much in few words" (Sir 32:8).

A celebration that has to stay "in the family"

These brief homilies have drawn the interest of many. Right from the beginning, explains Fr. Federico Lombardi, director of the Holy See's press office, the website of Vatican Radio began receiving requests for video or audio clips of the Mass, or at least the homilies.

And from the beginning summaries have been provided, published every day by *L'Osservatore Romano* and by Vatican Radio. The radio version also contains audio clips of the pope's voice, and the Vatican Television Center (CTV) offers a video clip corresponding to the audio selection broadcast by the radio network. This book uses the radio version and provides readers with a unique opportunity to draw closer to the experience of the faithful who participate in the celebration.

Many have asked for a complete version of the texts, which is not provided. Why not? In order to answer this question it is necessary to understand the significance of what happens at seven o'clock in the morning at Saint Martha's. For the pope, this Mass has a "family" character. As Fr. Lombardi always says, it is not a celebration to be "broadcast" but one to be "shared" in a direct physical manner, not mediated by communications technologies, like many of the other more official celebrations.

It is necessary, therefore, to take into account the character that the Holy Father himself attributes to this morning celebration. The group of faithful present is of medium size—in general around fifty persons—and the pope intends to preserve the distinctive character of this encounter. This is why, in spite of the requests he has received, he explicitly does not want it to be broadcast live. It is recorded in its entirety, however, both audio and video.

Not only that: the pope speaks spontaneously in Italian, a language that he knows very well but that is not his mother tongue. He has no written text to use as a guideline. Publishing his homilies in their entirety would give them an unnatural form: they would have to be revised in some points, becoming something other than what the pope intends them to be. For Francis, the homily is always oral, born in the context of the celebration; it is not a chapter in a book of meditations. Not providing a complete transcription therefore signifies safeguarding its spontaneity and its intimate nature.

What are the homilies at Saint Martha's?

And what is the nature of the homily for Pope Francis? What does it mean to him to celebrate the Mass every morning and give these brief and intense homilies? I touched upon this point while interviewing him for *La Civiltà Cattolica*. He answered by speaking of the balance between dogmatic and moral teaching and the missionary proclamation of the Church: "A beautiful homily, a genuine sermon must begin with the first proclamation, with the proclamation of salvation. There is nothing more solid, deep, and sure than this proclamation. Then you have to do catechesis. Then you can draw even a moral consequence. But the proclamation of the saving love of God comes before moral and religious imperatives. Today sometimes it seems that the opposite order is prevailing . . . The message of the Gospel, therefore, is not to be reduced to some aspects that, although relevant, on their own do not show the heart of the message of Jesus Christ."* In these words I think it is possible to grasp what the homily means for Pope Francis: a proclamation that concentrates on the essential, the necessary, which is also what is most stirring and attractive and makes the heart burn, as for the disciples in Emmaus.

The pope has even said—as in *Evangelii Gaudium*—that the homily is like a litmus test: it is a clear and incontrovertible indicator. In fact, it is the touchstone for calibrating a pastor's closeness and ability to encounter his people. He who preaches must understand the heart of his community in order to seek out where the desire for God is living and ardent. So the homily must not break the bond between a pastor and his people. He who preaches must understand the heart of a community in order to discern the desire for God, which includes drawing upon the inspiration and grace connected to that specific celebration (cf. EG 137).

This necessity gives these homilies a twofold nature and a twofold value: on the one hand they are the densest of messages, appealing to the heart of the Gospel, with no intention of reiterating abstract principles but speaking of mercy; on the other they have a living warmth, a connection with those faces that the pope has in front of him and from which it is not possible to abstract. It is interesting to note that the Vatican Television Center, in its brief video clips available on the Vatican's YouTube channel, focuses not only on the pontiff but also on the faces of those present. This solution serves to

---

* Pope Francis, *La mia porta è sempre aperta: Una conversazione con Antonio Spadaro* (Milan: Rizzoli, 2014), p. 63.

communicate what is happening in the community gathered in that chapel.

So these homilies have a strong symbolic value because they convey the sense of the Gospel proclamation in a unique and unprecedented form. This is why they can be presented as a partial selection of the voice of the pope, instead of being transcribed in their entirety like a sort of official document. And the journalists of Vatican Radio have been equal to their task. With the passing of time, those who have been assigned to publish the summaries have become so attuned to the pope's style that they are able to identify strongly significant messages embedded within the narration.

Who is the preacher of the homilies at Saint Martha's?

Who is the Bergoglio who preaches from the simple ambo of this entirely triangular chapel? In his apostolic exhortation *Evangelii Gaudium,* Pope Francis wanted to encourage and orient the whole Church on a new and dynamic path of evangelization. This is why he decided to deal at length with certain questions that he considers important, "hot." These include the homily (EG 135–144), a topic that Bergoglio has often dealt with in the past. In rereading some of his reflections, it is possible to understand how the preacher for him is a sower, a maternal figure, a communicator.

The pope has always understood the preacher as a good *sower* with a broad and trusting outlook, who bets on the fertility of seed that grows in its own good time. Cardinal Bergoglio said in 2005: "In attending to and weighing within his heart the knowledge and love of the faithful for God's word, the preacher reaps a value that is mature and shows the directions in which it can be put into practice, and at the same time he sows a desire, a new hope, if he finds fertile ground that is suitable for the growth of the seeds."*

When he preaches, Pope Francis sows a desire and provides directions for the journey. It should come as no surprise how rich these homilies are, perhaps even compared to more polished formal discourses. Their nature is, in fact, living thought that arises from direct contact with an assembly that prays.

---

* Pope Francis, *È l'amore che apre gli occhi* (Milan: Rizzoli, 2013), p. 146.

The living character of these homilies can be grasped in many ways, first of all from the pauses. When Francis speaks, in his style, in his rhythm, he is not monotonous. The word is brought forth from silence. Sometimes the beginning of the homily is slow, with the words coming like the blows of a chisel. When the pope reaches a "hot" point, the tension rises and animates his speech, making his gestures dynamic and powerfully expressive. His hands move not only with his words but also with his facial expressions. Francis is physically shaped by the word that he proclaims.

This makes it clear that his words are nourished with a great deal of prayer. These homilies are prepared by his personal prayer before they take shape at the ambo in front of the faithful. "Study, prayer, reflection, and pastoral creativity": these are the four requirements for preparing a good homily (EG 145). But ultimately these are not and must not be a moment of meditation and catechesis. They are neither an exercise of individual meditation nor solely the fruit of the pope's personal prayer. The preparation serves to insert the homily effectively within God's dialogue with his people.

The fact that this dialogue takes place in a chapel makes these homilies truly singular. This is in part because the assembly that Francis has in front of him changes every day. So it is as if this intimate dialogue must in some way overflow into the pastoral activities of the pontiff on a broader scale. And in fact it comes as no surprise that issues presented and elaborated at Saint Martha's later become elements of discourses, speeches, homilies of the pope in more public contexts. So the homily at Saint Martha's, in its way, seems to have become the beating heart of Francis's pastoral practice. And it is the fruit of a discernment that seeks the places where the desire for God is living and ardent.

The "maternity" of the preacher

But in addition to being a sower, the preacher is a *mother.* Bergoglio wants to be maternal because he intends to express the maternity of the Church. He once said: "I maintain that the image of a mother with her child is the one that best clarifies what it means to have to teach someone who already knows. Since the Church is the mother of all of us, it preaches to the people like a parent speaks to his child, trusting that the child, strengthened by the love that generated him, understands that everything the father and mother impart to him is only for his good."* "Moreover, a good mother can recognize everything that God is bringing about in her children, she listens to their concerns and learns from them. The spirit of love which reigns in a family guides both mother and child in their conversations; therein they teach and learn, experience correction, and grow in appreciation of what is good. Something similar happens in a homily" (EG 139).

The awareness of being immersed in a family spirit guides both the one who speaks and those who listen. People appreciate a preacher when he tries to be sincere, when he uses "maternal" language, meaning the original "mother tongue," simple, capable of employing concrete images. Nonetheless, speaking with the heart implies that this language should be not only ardent but also illuminated by revelation in its fullness, by the Word of God and by the journey that this has made in the inmost depths of the Church and of the community of believers over the course of its history. For Bergoglio the heartfelt closeness of the preacher, the warm tone of his voice, his gestures, foster and cultivate the "maternal and ecclesial framework"† in which the dialogue between the Lord and his people is developed. It is impossible to think of the homilies at Saint Martha's without keeping well in mind the maternal significance that preaching has for Bergoglio. He who preaches therefore sows and nourishes with affection, creating an adequate communicative and affective environment so that the Lord may dialogue with his people.

In the homiletic tradition of the Jesuits

It is helpful to remember that a preacher is a communicator. That doesn't mean he's an entertainer. In fact, "the homily cannot be a form of entertainment like those presented by the media, yet it does need to give life and meaning to the celebration." It is a "distinctive

---

* Pope Francis, *È l'amore che apre gli occhi* (Milan: Rizzoli, 2013), pp. 150–51. Cf. EG 139.

† Ibid., p. 151.

genre" (EG 138), or rather more of a context than a genre. The good preacher is not the one who knows how to speak well or knows how to get attention. He is not the preacher-actor or preacher-clown. There are other dynamics that make the homily an effective communicative environment.

Understanding what we mean here may require a bit of extra reflection, even if living it is the most spontaneous and natural thing possible. Bergoglio draws the meaning of the homily from the deepest roots of the *Spiritual Exercises* of Saint Ignatius in a way that may not be evident immediately. Pope Francis does not draw solely upon the classical homiletics of the distinctive tradition of the Society of Jesus. He goes directly and vitally to the radical meaning of the *Exercises,* which are not a testimony of interior life but a guide to spiritual experience, almost like a theatrical plot outline that must be performed or it makes no sense. So the *Exercises* are not some sort of collection of meditations signed by the author: in brief but dense notes the *Exercises* indicate a spiritual itinerary that has been lived by the one who wrote them. They do not, however, resolve the spiritual experience in themselves, and therefore they are by no means intended to say everything. They are not the account of the saint's experience, not a "narration" at all, not a lyrical expression.

What are they then? They represent a "guide" for creating a living language between the person doing the *Exercises* and God. Ignatius compares this relationship to the one between two friends, or between a servant and his master: *así como un amigo habla a otro, o un siervo a su señor* (cf. SE no. 54). But the *Exercises* also allow God to create his own language with which he responds to the participant or *lo mueve y atrae,* stirring him and attracting him to himself (SE no. 175). The *Exercises* generate creative language.

Now, for Bergoglio the homily has a dialogical linguistic structure like that of the *Exercises*: it makes possible a dialogue between God and his people. This is a powerful and original intuition that must be singled out and meditated upon carefully. The pope expresses this dimension of the homily in the warm language of encounter, speaking of the preacher's mission of "bringing together hearts that love each other, that of the Lord and those of his people, who during the time of the homily enclose themselves in silence and allow him to speak."* Therefore its meaning transcends the "communication of a truth": dialogue is much more than this. It is realized through the savor of speech and the good that consists in bringing people together. This is how God unfolds his power through the human word.

The preacher is a unifier, he facilitates the encounter between God and his people. Obviously the Lord and his people "dialogue in a thousand forms, in a direct way, without intermediaries," beyond the space of encounter that is the homily. "Nonetheless in the homily they make use of a mediator who expresses the sentiments of both, in such a way that each one may choose how to continue his personal conversation with God." This is why a purely moralistic or exegetical form of preaching impoverishes the communication between hearts that, for Bergoglio, has an almost sacramental quality, in that "faith comes from what is heard, and what is heard comes through the word of Christ" (Rom 10:17).† If the homily does not create a language between God and his people that allows everyone to develop a personal relationship with God, then it is truly a waste of time.

How does the pope prepare his homilies?

How does Pope Francis prepare his homilies? What are the steps that bring this homily to life as an environment of communication between God and his people? In *Evangelii Gaudium* the pontiff offers some very precise instructions on how to prepare a homily. They do not come from reading manuals of homiletics but from personal and pastoral experience. "The first step, after calling upon the Holy Spirit in prayer, is to give our entire attention to the biblical text, which needs to be the basis of our preaching" (EG 146).

The disposition that Francis asks of every preacher is one of humility and astonished veneration for the word, even a sort of holy fear of manipulating it. And he continues: "To interpret a biblical text, we need to be patient, to put aside all other concerns, and to give it our time, interest, and undivided attention. We must leave

---

* Pope Francis, *È l'amore che apre gli occhi* (Milan: Rizzoli, 2013), p. 152.

† Ibid. (cf. EG 142).

aside any other pressing concerns and create an environment of serene concentration" (ibid.). This takes love: "We only devote peri-
ods of quiet time to the things or the people whom we love; and
here we are speaking of the God whom we love, a God who wishes
to *speak* to us. Because of this love, we can take as much time as we
need, like every true disciple" (ibid.).

The homilies at Saint Martha's are therefore prepared with serene attention and with love for the fact that God speaks to his
people. The Word of God must be approached with a docile and
prayerful heart, so that it may deeply penetrate the thoughts and
feelings (cf. EG 149).* "Whoever wants to preach must be the first
to let the Word of God move him deeply and become incarnate in
his daily life" (EG 150). The word must become flesh in the one
who preaches. And he continues: "Before preparing what we will
actually say when preaching, we need to let ourselves be penetrated
by that word which will also penetrate others, for it is a *living and
active* word, like a sword 'penetrating even between soul and spirit,
joints and marrow, and able to discern reflections and thoughts of
the heart' (Heb 4:12)" (ibid.).

So we know that Bergoglio is well aware that the Word of God
must really pass through him, but not only through his reason:
"Christ's message must truly penetrate and possess the preacher, not
just intellectually but in his entire being" (EG 151). And this is how
he is able to speak "words which he could not find by himself"
(ibid.). So preaching is truly a spiritual experience full of surprise
and mystery for the one who lives it.

The pope's day begins before five o'clock in the morning. His
prayer time opens and closes his day. The readings for the Mass of
the day nourish this, and it is this time of prayer that permits a di-

---

* The text cited is the post-synodal apostolic exhortation of John Paul II *Pastores
Dabo Vobis* (March 25, 1992), 26: AAS 84 (1992), 698. The pope wants every
homilist to be certain that he adequately understands the meaning of the words
he reads. The objective here is not to understand all the little details of the text
but to discover the main message, the one that confers structure and unity on the
text. In order to understand adequately the meaning of the central message of the
text, it is necessary to see it in connection with the teaching of the whole Bible,
as transmitted by the Church.

rect and personal relationship with the text. There are a few specific guidelines in *Evangelii Gaudium* that we would imagine Francis personally follows day after day. These are, in the first place, questions: "Lord, what does this text say to *me*? What is it about my life that you want to change by this text? What troubles me about this text? Why am I not interested in this? Or perhaps: What do I find pleasant in this text? What is it about this word that moves me? What attracts me? Why does it attract me?" (EG 153).

But this is the first step. The second is like the extension of this personal relationship in concentric circles until it reaches the faithful People of God. He who preaches, the pope writes, "also needs to keep his ear to the people and to discover what it is that the faithful need to hear. A preacher has to contemplate the word, but he also has to contemplate his people" (EG 154). In this way the pope, like every preacher, attunes himself to the aspirations and situations of the time by interpreting them in the light of the word. A spiritual sensibility is required in order to be able to read the message of God within events, and this is much more than finding something interesting to say. So the question is this: What does the Lord have to say in this circumstance? It is clear, therefore, that personal prayer on the readings of the day is fundamental for the pope. Preparation for the morning homily becomes an exercise of *evangelical discernment,* in which Francis seeks to recognize—in the light of the Spirit—the appeal that God is making in the historical context, at the moment (cf. EG 154). It therefore has a strong relationship with his action and the development of his ministry. It is like the explicit presentation of a method of action that absolutely cannot do without a daily, living, natural pastoral relationship with the People of God, albeit to a small extent. This is also the reason why since January 2014 the parishes of his diocese, the diocese of Rome, have been invited to participate in the celebration with a group faithful.

What is the rhetorical style and logic of the homilies at Saint Martha's?

It is enough simply to hear them to realize that the Saint Martha's homilies are true homilies, and not speeches. In this sense they take to heart the lessons of style most appropriate to the needs of the faithful People of God. For Pope Francis, according to a classical precept of homiletics, every homily must contain images, simplicity, clarity, and strong messages.

His first effort concerns the use of *images*. In reality, for Francis this is not an effort because his speech naturally generates images, some of which have become famous, starting with that of the Church as a "field hospital" but also that of "god-spray," "*cristiani da pasticceria* [cafeteria Catholics]," "faith milk shake," "insight to go," or "babysitter Church." The pope loves examples, but not those that speak only to reason. In this sense images are for him the most powerful examples. As he writes in his first apostolic exhortation: "An attractive image makes the message seem familiar, close to home, practical and related to everyday life. A successful image can make people savor the message, awaken a desire, and move the will towards the Gospel" (EG 157).

His second effort consists in bringing to life a homily that is "simple, clear, direct, well-adapted."* *Simplicity* has to do with language that is intended to be easily understandable in order to avoid the risk of speaking into a vacuum. The pope knows that often those who have studied theology have learned a precise and technical language, but that the people do not understand it because it is not how they talk. How can the preacher adapt himself to the language of others in order to bring the word to them? The pope replies in *Evangelii Gaudium*: "If we wish to adapt to people's language and to reach them with God's word, we need to share in their lives and pay loving attention to them" (EG 158). The language of the homilies at Saint Martha's is very simple, immediate, understandable to anyone. This ability comes to Francis from his life in constant contact with the people.

But simplicity is not all it takes to be clear, and this is the third characteristic of the homilies at Saint Martha's: *clarity*. The homily, in fact, could be simple in its language but also disorganized, devoid of logic, with too many topics. This is why the morning homily is

---

* Apostolic exhortation of Paul VI, *Evangelii Nuntiandi* (December 8, 1975), 40: AAS 68 (1976), 33.

focused on only one point, one topic: in order to have that clarity which facilitates comprehension.

This is also why the pope uses the characteristic and intrinsic logic of the *Spiritual Exercises* of Saint Ignatius, which is an ascending logic. Let's see in what sense this is the case. Since his first discourse as bishop of Rome, we have been accustomed to the division of his message into three points, three themes, three key words, according to the most deeply rooted rhetorical and spiritual tradition of the Jesuits. In any case the dynamic of Ignatian discourse, which is not linear but spiral, is always present. Even in the span of a few minutes, those who are present realize that the pope is delivering a talk that is circular—repeating expressions, words, images—but also ascending, according to which the talk "mounts," it rises. There is no haste to reach a final point, but the whole argumentation grows within the mind of the listener, becoming full and rich with the passing of a few minutes. This is the upward tension of Francis's preaching.

Finally we note that the homilies at Saint Martha's contain strong messages, often accusations and even specific "warnings." And yet the language is always positive. This is another characteristic of his morning homilies. The pope does not say what we must not do but rather proposes what we could do or do better. His attitude is pro-active, indicating a direction and shaping the future (cf. EG 159). It is forward-looking: it tends to console the mind not by concealing problems but rather by revealing them, always showing the road ahead. And in this he is a shepherd showing his flock the way.

The pope's body language

After the homily there is always a moment of silence. It is interesting to note the pope's posture: we never see a formal pose, there is nothing artificial. There is no rigidity in his movements, which are not followed or guided by a master of ceremonies. If anything his body appears to be almost overbalanced toward the people in front of him, at whom he looks with attention, face by face as it were, while also being marked by the rhythm of his prayerful concentration, which does not stiffen but rather relaxes the posture of his hands, feet, head.

The celebration of the Eucharist proceeds with calm, in its proper rhythm. There are no overlong pauses, no hasty movements. At the end of the Mass, after the blessing, the pope goes back to the sacristy, takes off his liturgical vestments, and goes to sit next to the people for a silent prayer of thanksgiving. Many have been struck to see how close the pope sits to the rest of the people. But by now this is known and accepted as a spontaneous and truly natural action.

After a few minutes, Francis gets up and goes to the atrium of Saint Martha's, where he personally greets, one by one, those who have participated. The hands that have accompanied the word in the homily and that have consecrated the bread and wine on the altar now shake those of all who have participated in the celebration. This farewell gesture is by no means a pure courtesy: it is given time and attention. One often sees the pontiff draw nearer to someone to listen to what he has to say, sometimes with his face lit up by a smile, sometimes breaking out into laughter, sometimes giving a warm embrace or extending his hands in a blessing. In short: his is not a superficial gesture, but the embrace that the pontiff is able to give to a portion of the faithful People of God before beginning his day, even before breakfast.

II

What does the pope say in these homilies?

The risk in reading the homilies of Pope Francis at Saint Martha's is that of imagining that they are paragraphs and chapters of a single talk that can be organized according to themes and topics. We can confidently state that this approach would be mistaken and misguided. The pope follows the readings of the day; he enters into the dynamics of the Liturgy of the Word and does not deliver topical "talks." The only order that can be considered is therefore chronological order. It will become clear, as we have already noted, that there are recurring themes. Grouping the homilies according to theme, however, would kill the vitality characteristic of these reflections: it would reduce them to a fragmentary essay or to pieces in a collection. In this edition we have completely avoided this temptation. The only correct way to proceed is to conduct soundings, construct pathways, make maps to describe a living and dynamic thought that defies systematization because it is guided by two dynamics: that of the spiritual life and that of the liturgy.

In the following reflection I have selected five pairs of words in an attempt to construct a possible, provisory, and certainly nondefinitive framework of interpretation: *struggle and challenge, desire and tenderness, faith and ideology, spirit and organization, way and journey.* I think that these labels could be helpful to readers in forming an idea of the territory explored in Bergoglio's preaching at Saint Martha's. I hope that they may prompt readers to discover others in their own personal meditation.

Struggle and challenge

Pope Francis celebrated his first Mass at Saint Martha's on March 22, 2013, just nine days after his election as bishop of Rome. It was attended by street cleaners and gardeners who work in the Vatican. And the first message was this: "If our hearts are closed, if our hearts are made of stone, the stones find their way into our hands and we are ready to throw them." This strongly visual opening is truly the beginning of a message, the appeal for a heart of flesh, accessible and open. The result of a closed heart is violence, a step that is not to be taken for granted. Here the pope intended to say, beginning the adventure of his daily meditations, that relations with others and with God require an inner transformation, an openness without which the bonds are broken. What hardens the heart shatters it, because it dries out on the inside. It loses life.

Having said this, Francis clarified in his subsequent homilies that this open heart is a gift, it is not a personal achievement. And this inner softness is given by the patience and mercy of God, who attracts us, even with a "caress," without hesitating to enter into our night. And here he distinguished the "night of the sinner" from the "night of the corrupted": in the first the Lord breaks through, in the second there is no room for him. Over the span of a week at Saint Martha's, the pope unfolded the map of his spiritual horizon: the bright and the dark, the contrasts and the shadings. These homilies played a part in making it clear how his is a pontificate of "dramatic" tones, meaning that it takes into account the light and darkness of human life. The pope has an oppositional view of reality, and in this sense we could say he is "militant." This dramatic element comes to him from Saint Ignatius of Loyola and his *Spiritual Exercises*. In the meditation "on the two standards (flags)" (SE nos. 136–148), Ignatius depicts a battlefield in which "Christ, our captain and lord" is pitted against "Lucifer, the mortal enemy of our human nature." For Bergoglio there is an inevitable dimension of belligerence in the Christian modus vivendi. Christian life is a struggle.

And the word "struggle" often appears in these homilies. Pope Francis struggles against worldliness and against the devil, to whom he refers repeatedly, as in the homily of May 4, 2013 (no. 31), when he affirmed: "The path of Christians is the path of Jesus. If we want to be followers of Jesus, there is no path other than the one he showed us. And one of the results of this is hatred; it is the hatred of the world, and also of the prince of this world. The world would love what is its own. 'I have chosen you out of the world.' It is he himself who has ransomed us from the world, who has chosen us: pure grace! With his death, with his Resurrection, he has ransomed us from the power of the world, from the power of the devil, from the power of the prince of this world. And the origin of the hatred is this: we are saved. And that prince who does not want this, who does not want us to be saved, hates." The following October 11 (no. 110) the pope cited the powerful image of Saint Peter: the devil "is like a roaring lion looking for [someone] to devour."

Evoking the devil makes it impossible to "demonize" persons. Never, and in no case. And the pope's struggle always has the consolation of the certainty that the Lord has the last word on the life of the world: he is always present in our history, which he has not left to itself. So for the pope, the Church's task is by no means that of adapting itself to society: this would be "spiritual worldliness." The key experience is instead that of mercy. The Church is a battlefield hospital. Its first "Samaritan" task is to pour oil on the wounds: the rest comes after. But the fight must go on. The oil on the wounds is a bit like the ointment that is applied to a boxer: "And this is the struggle of Christians. It is our struggle every day. And we do not always have the courage to speak as Paul speaks about this struggle.

We are always looking for justification: 'Well, sure, we're all sinners.' That's how we talk, right? This says it dramatically: it is our struggle" (October 25, 2013, no. 118).

So of course one can "fight for power," and this is the work of the evil one; but one can also "fight" with God (May 20, 2013, no. 43), and this is a fight of desire, a necessary fight, an experience of faith, a hand-to-hand combat that "embodies" and imprints the relationship with the Lord in the soul. The relationship with God that emerges from these homilies is indeed a relationship of gentleness, but also of freedom, and therefore of tension and even of "darkness." The pope evokes this darkness in a saint who is most often associated with an image of cheerfulness: "Saint Thérèse of the Child Jesus toward the end of her life said there was a struggle in her soul and that when she thought of the future, of what was waiting for her after death, in heaven, she heard something like a voice that said: 'No, don't be stupid, darkness is waiting for you. All that is waiting for you is the darkness of nothing!' This is what the voice says. It is the voice of the devil, of the demon, who did not want her to entrust herself to God. To die in hope and to die entrusting oneself to God! And to ask for this grace. But entrusting oneself to God begins now, in the little things of life and also in the big problems: to entrust oneself always to the Lord! And so one gets into the habit of entrusting oneself to the Lord and hope grows. To die at home, to die in hope" (February 6, 2014, no. 167).

This struggle involves not only the soul but also the people and their pastors. "Moses is the one who is the head of the People of God; courageous, he fought against their enemies and even fought with God to save the people" (October 18, 2013, no. 114). Every interior struggle takes on a profundity, a three-dimensionality that involves the People of God on its journey.

One powerful element that pervades the message of these homilies is the unmitigated condemnation of corruption, of the corrupt Christian, "of the corrupt layman, of the corrupt priest, of the corrupt bishop, who profits from his situation, from his privilege of faith, from being Christian" (January 14, 2014, no. 154): "A whitewashed putrefaction: this is the life of the corrupted" (November 11, 2013, no. 125). "May the Lord keep us from slipping down this path of corruption," the pope prays (June 3, 2013, no. 55). And his condemnation is aimed at any form of corruption, including that of civil life, that makes some earn "dirty bread" (November 8, 2013, no. 123). His social magisterium is an integral part of the perimeter of the *ring* that Pope Francis defines in preaching from Saint Martha's.

So we must be careful not to read these homilies as a pleasant panorama. For a year the pope has displayed his map of spiritual life and pastoral effort. And this map is not the perimeter of a cafeteria but a boxing ring in which various *bouts* are fought: against the "prince of this world," for power, of the soul with God, of the pastor with the Lord for the sake of his people. The pope does not present only the *ring*: he also offers the rules of the game, the meaning of spiritual discernment. And he has warned us: "There's no dressing this up. This is a fight, and a fight in which our health is at stake, our eternal health, our eternal salvation" (October 11, 2013, no. 110).

In this encounter we experience a "challenge": "Jesus . . . challenges us to prayer" (May 3, 2013, no. 30); "the challenge of God" is "to overcome this, to heal the wounds" (October 22, 2013, no. 116). And this challenge forms the background for Francis's extensive preaching on forgiveness, on the abundant and surprising mercy of God. It is on the foundation of a dramatic and dissonant perception of existence that he builds the perception of the harmony of God's love and patience that heals and gives life, that "consoles," to use a term from the *Exercises* of Ignatius of Loyola.

Desire and tenderness

Feeling and savoring the presence of God brings astonishment, tears, joy, courage, peace. The pope unveils a genuine spiritual phenomenology, certainly not in the form of a treatise but in the form of interior communication. On April 4, 2013 (no. 6), Francis dedicated his homily to this theme: "Amazement is a great grace, it is the grace that God gives us in the encounter with Jesus Christ. It is something that makes us lose our heads a bit out of joy . . . It is wonderful!" He continues. "Perhaps the opposite experience is more common, when human weakness, mental illness, or the devil makes people believe that phantasms and fantasies are the reality; this is not of God. What is of God is this joy that is so great it is beyond belief. And we think: No, this is not real! This is of the Lord. This astonishment is the beginning of the habitual state of the Christian."

And amazement may be only the beginning, but it "leaves its mark on the soul, and spiritual consolation." The "amazement" in these homilies is connected to the encounter with Christ. It marks the moment of the encounter. But then it leaves its effects, which he calls "peace," or better, "consolation," which is "the presence of God in our hearts" (June 10, 2013, no. 61). "This is salvation: living in the consolation of the Holy Spirit, not living in the consolation of the spirit of the world. No, that is not salvation, that is sin. Salvation is moving forward and opening our hearts, so that this consolation of the Holy Spirit, which is salvation, may come to us. But can't we negotiate a bit here and there? Make a bit of a salad, let's say, why not? A little Holy Spirit, a little spirit of the world . . . No! One thing or the other" (ibid.).

It is this consolation that opens the heart and brings life back into play, opening it to new perspectives, making it germinate (June 11, 2013, no. 62). Interior consolation makes it possible for our life to be rethought, restructured, remade. It permits us to start over again: "And the consolation is this remaking of everything not once, but many times, with the universe and also with us" (December 10, 2013, no. 141).

Consolation sets desire, another key word for Bergoglio, in motion. "The Christian is a man, a woman of desire: always desiring more on the road of life" (May 10, 2013, no. 35). Moreover, "the Lord has made us restless so that we will seek him, find him, grow" (June 21, 2013, no. 71). In the homily of October 14, 2013 (no. 111), he presents the figure of the Queen of Sheba, "a restless woman, a woman seeking the wisdom of God." On January 3, 2013, in a homily to the Jesuits, he said, "without restlessness we are sterile," affirming the oxymoron that "only this restlessness brings peace." Certainly not the temptation of "spiritual prosperity" (September 27, 2013, no. 102), which instead is deadening. One person who received a personal note from Pope Francis read this passage to me in a voice trembling with emotion: "God looks for us, God waits for us, God finds us . . . before we look for him, before we wait for him, before we find him. This is the mystery of holiness."

On September 21, 2013 (no. 98), Pope Francis developed a powerful image of the desire that can also smolder beneath the ashes. The gaze of Jesus is able to clear away the ashes that cover it: "And the sinners, the tax collectors and sinners . . . Jesus had looked at them, and that gaze of Jesus upon them I believe was like a breath on the embers, and they felt that there was still fire inside, and that Jesus was lifting them up, restoring their dignity. The gaze of Jesus always makes us worthy; it gives us dignity. It is a generous gaze. 'But look at that Teacher: he eats with the filth of the city!' But under that filth were the embers of desire for God, the embers of God's image in us that needed someone to fan them into flame. And this is what the gaze of Jesus did."

Corresponding to man's desire is the tenderness of God. The term that occurs most frequently in these homilies to express consolation, but from God's point of view, is "tenderness," which has its greatest expression in the "bitter sweetness of the sacrifice of Jesus" (September 14, 2013, no. 94). For Bergoglio this tenderness is above all paternal, it is "the tenderness of God the Father" (December 10, 2013, no. 141).

One hymn of the Argentine breviary that is very dear to Bergoglio is the one for first vespers of the solemnity of Saint Joseph, in which the saint is asked to guard the Church with *ternura de eucaristía,* Eucharistic tenderness. Joseph is the mirror image of the paternal tenderness of God. On June 7, 2013 (no. 59), Pope Francis exclaimed: "Tenderness! The Lord loves us with tenderness. The Lord knows that wonderful science of caresses, that tenderness of God. He does not love us with words. He draws near—nearness—and gives us that love with tenderness. Nearness and tenderness! These are two aspects of the love of the Lord who draws near and gives all his love even with the smallest things: with tenderness. And this is a strong love, because nearness and tenderness show us the strength of God's love."

As we can see, "tenderness" means "nearness." This is why the metaphor of the caress is decisive in Bergoglio's vision. For him being tender is not primarily in the eyes but in physical touch, which means eliminating distances as much as possible, being close enough to touch. And this nearness heals. "The image that comes to me is that of a nurse, of a nurse in a hospital, healing wounds one after another, but with her hands. God gets involved, he intervenes in our misery, he draws near to our wounds and heals them with his hands, and in order to have hands he became man. This is a labor of Jesus, it is personal. A man committed sin, a man comes to heal it. Nearness. God does not save us only by a decree, a law; he saves us with tenderness, he saves us with caresses, he saves us with his life, for us" (October 22, 2013, no. 116). And in fact "Jesus embraced them, he kissed them, he touched them, all of them" (May 25, 2013, no. 48). And this is the response of faith: to open our hearts and allow ourselves to be loved. "To let him get close to us and feel him near. To let him be tender and caress us. That is so difficult, letting him love us" (June 7, 2013, no. 59).

And this tenderness of physical contact permits us to be touched, to be reached. Pope Francis reiterated this on November 12, 2013 (no. 126): "Let's think about the hands of Jesus, when he touched the sick and healed them . . . They are the hands of God; they heal us! I cannot imagine God hitting us! I can't imagine it. Scolding us, yes, I can imagine that, because he does it. But he never, ever hurts us. Never! He caresses us. Even when he has to scold us, he does it with a caress, because he is Father. 'The souls of the righteous are in the hands of God.' Let's think about the hands of God, who created us like a craftsman, who has given us eternal health. They are wounded hands, and they accompany us on the path of life. Let's entrust ourselves to the hands of God, as a child entrusts himself to the hand of his father. That is a sure hand!"

And soon after, on December 10 (no. 141): "Drawing near and giving hope, drawing near with tenderness. But let's think about the tenderness that he had with the apostles, with the Magdalene, with those on the way to Emmaus. He drew near with tenderness: 'Give me something to eat.' With Thomas: 'Put your finger here.'" The tenderness of Christ not only touches us but makes him tangible, "touchable," even in his wounds. Just touching his wounds opens our hearts: "We have to touch the wounds of Jesus, we have to caress the wounds of Jesus, we have to care for the wounds of Jesus with tenderness, we have to kiss the wounds of Jesus, and this literally. Think about what happened to Saint Francis, when he embraced the leper. The same as with Thomas: it changed his life!" (July 3, 2013, no. 81).

The reciprocity of this physical contact between Christ and each one is the relationship of faith. Salvation is the consolation of this encounter, of this embrace.

Faith and ideology

Faith is therefore the gift that is received in the encounter with Christ. It is not an effort of the mind or an abstract idea or adherence to a project. It has to do with the flesh of Christ. God is not an impalpable presence, a nebulous essence that spreads around without knowledge of itself. "But in what God do you believe?" the pope asked the faithful during the Mass of April 18, 2013 (no. 18). And he continued: "A 'diffused god,' a 'god-spray,' that is a little bit everywhere but you don't know what it is. We believe in God who is Father, who is Son, who is Holy Spirit. We believe in Persons, and when we speak with God we speak with Persons; either I speak with the Father, or I speak with the Son, or I speak with the Holy Spirit. And this is the faith." Faith in god-spray leads to a "watered down [faith], a faith without substance" (homily at Saint Peter's, April 23, 2013). Faith in him comes from a living encounter, from an experience. And this encounter cannot be manipulated. The encounter of faith leaves the initiative to God: "When we encounter the Lord on our own, we are—so to speak—the masters of this encounter; but when we allow him to encounter us, it is he who enters within us, it is he who makes us entirely new, because this is the coming, this is what it means when Christ comes: to make everything anew, remake the heart, the soul, life, hope, the journey" (December 2, 2013, no. 136).

In the splendid homily of May 20, 2013 (no. 43), the pope recounts a testimony of openhearted faith that gives "control of things to Jesus": A six-year-old girl in Argentina was sick and the doctors gave her a few hours to live. Her father, an electrician and a "man of faith," seemed to lose his wits and took a bus to the Marian shrine of Luján, forty miles away. "He arrived after nine in the evening, and everything was closed. And he began to pray to the Blessed Mother, with his hands on the iron bars of the gates. And he prayed, and wept, and prayed . . . And he stayed like this all night. Now this man fought: he fought with God, he actually fought with God for the healing of his little girl. Then, after six in the morning, he went to the station and took the bus home, and was at the hospital at around nine. And he found his wife crying. He thought the worst. 'But what's going on? I don't understand, I don't understand! What happened?' 'Well, the doctors came and told me that the fever is gone, she's breathing fine, there's nothing! They're keeping her for two more days, but they don't know what happened!' This still happens, miracles happen!" the pope concludes.

Why did he cite this example? Certainly not to reduce faith to "miracles" but, as he says, to emphasize the faith of that man, his "fight with God," his "courageous" prayer, which was not a mere matter of form, his being a person among "so many people who have faith and with faith they pray, they pray." Prayer, its necessity, its power, its effectiveness are themes present every day in the words of Francis, who also never ceases to ask for prayers for himself.

Prayer is a sign of trusting and courageous faith. The danger of lukewarmness, of a faith that is fleeting or made up of calculation and holding back, is always around the corner. The entire homily of January 10, 2014 (no. 151), is dedicated to the faith that can do everything and that conquers the world: "There are so many Christians with a hope that is watered down, not strong, a weak hope. Why? Because they do not have the strength and courage to entrust themselves to the Lord. But if we Christians believe and confess our faith, guard our faith, and entrust ourselves to God, to the Lord, we will be victorious Christians. And this is the victory that has conquered the world: our faith!"

Next to watered-down faith there is the risk of ideological faith, "and when ideology comes into the Church, when ideology comes into the understanding of the Gospel, nothing makes any sense," the pope said on April 19, 2013 (no. 19). And he continued: "Ideologues falsify the Gospel. Every ideological interpretation, from whatever side it may come—from one side or the other—is a falsification of the Gospel. And these ideologues—we have seen this in the history of the Church—end up being, they become, intellectuals without talent, ethicists without goodness. And let's not talk about beauty, because they don't know a thing about it."

What is the problem with ideology? Faith is a personal encounter, it is not adherence to a program or an idea. Doctrine without trust is hollow. "Christians who think of the faith as a system of ideas" (February 21, 2014, no. 175) instead do not believe in a personal relationship but in a project, in an abstraction. One cannot truly "give" an idea, as good and beautiful as it may be; one cannot "pray" an idea. So "the ideologue does not know what love is, because he does not know how to give himself" (May 14, 2013, no. 38), he does not pray, he remains closed off in his mentality. His knowledge of Jesus turns into an ideological and moralistic knowledge. The faithful or pastor becomes a "scholar of the law" who wants "the door locked and the key in his pocket" (October 17, 2013, no. 113).

In the ideologies—the pope said on October 17, 2013—"there is no room for Jesus . . . : his tenderness, love, meekness. And the ideologies are rigid, always" in their attempt to homogenize, "normalize," interpret, and study the evangelical message. "Paul does not say to the Athenians: 'This is the encyclopedia of truth. Study this and you will have the truth, the truth!' No! The truth does not fit in an encyclopedia. Truth is an encounter; it is an encounter with the supreme truth: Jesus, the great truth. No one is master of the truth. Truth is received in the encounter" (May 8, 2013, no. 34). The truth of faith is only in the personal encounter with Christ, even, at times, in a real "hand-to-hand combat."

And ideology kills true prophecy: "When there is no prophecy, the accent falls on legalism" (December 16, 2013, no. 144), on the formal, superficial aspects. The fire is missing, while the appearances remain, clericalism and functionalism. While ideology is rigid and closed off in its abstractions, "the prophet is aware of the promise and has within his heart the promise of God; he keeps it alive, remembers it, repeats it. Then he looks at the present, looks at his people, and feels the power of the Spirit to speak a word to them that will help them to get up, to continue their journey toward the future" (ibid.). The prophet, a man of faith, has a dynamic relationship with history.

So this is the prayer of Francis: "Let's ask the Lord for the grace of giving all of us the wisdom to trust only in him, not in things, in human strength, only in him" (March 20, 2014, no. 186).

Spirit and organization

Faith lives by the personal encounter with Christ. But while this encounter is always personal, it is never to be considered in an individually private manner. For Bergoglio, interiority always lives within personal and ecclesial relationships. And universality is never an abstract entity with respect to the individual person: "In a people, everyone has a place. The Lord never speaks to the people like that, as a mass, never. He always speaks personally, by name" (January 21, 2014, no. 158).

Bergoglio's ecclesiology emerges with clarity in the homilies at Saint Martha's, his vision of the nature of the Church as "the faithful People of God on the journey," a definition very dear to him. The word "people" is one he uses most often, and is often connected with the word "pastors." For Bergoglio, the Church is "people and pastors" together. The pope's ecclesiology is inclusive, and above all treasures the "rejects." The pope said on September 30, 2013 (no. 104): "The future of a people is right here and here, in the elderly and in the children. A people that does not take care of its elderly and its children has no future, because it cannot have memory and it cannot have promise! The elderly and the children are the future of a people! So often they are left aside, aren't they? The children, pacified with a piece of candy, with a game: 'Do it, do it, go, go.' And the elderly not allowed to speak, no attention paid to their advice: 'They're old, poor things.'" For the pope, the children and the elderly build the future of a people: the children because they will carry history forward, the elderly because they transmit the experience and wisdom of their lives.

It's the same for the Church. The pope dedicated an entire homily (no. 130) to grandparents on November 19, 2013. The message here is simple: a society that does not respect its memory has no future. These accents are reminiscent of World Youth Day in Brazil, which the pope attended at the end of July. On that occasion, in various discourses, he unveiled a genuine ecclesial blueprint, insisting a great deal on inclusivity and on the importance of the elderly and children.

This vision radically rejects organizational functionalism. The Church is not an "organization" that must focus on efficiency: "I understand, the disciples wanted results, they wanted the Church to move forward without problems, and this can become a temptation for the Church: the Church of functionalism! The well-organized Church! Everything in its place, but without memory and without promise! This kind of Church would not work; it would be a Church of power struggles, a Church of jealousy among the baptized and so many other things that come about when there is no memory and no promise" (September 30, 2013, no. 104).

And in the same powerful homily the pope offers an unprecedented view of the Church, founded on the first reading of the day, taken from the prophet Zechariah: "The sign of the presence of God is this, this is what the Lord said: 'Old men and old women will again sit in the streets of Jerusalem, each with staff in hand because of old age. The city will be filled with boys and girls playing in its streets.' Play makes us think of joy: it is the joy of the Lord. And these elderly seated with staff in hand, so tranquil, make us think of peace. Peace and joy: this is the atmosphere of the Church!"

In another homily the pope offers a further image that reiterates the inclusivity of the Church: its ability to prize originality in direct contrast with the risk of conformism. Referring to the Gospel image of salt, he says: "Each one with his own uniqueness receives the salt and becomes better." And he continues: "Christian originality is not uniformity! It takes each one as he is, with his personality, with his characteristics, with his culture, and leaves him with that, because it is precious. But it gives him something more: it gives him savor! This Christian originality is so beautiful, because when we want to make uniformity—everyone salted in the same way—it will be like when the cook puts in too much salt and you taste only the salt and not the flavor of the food seasoned with salt. Christian originality is precisely this: each one as he is, with the gifts that the Lord has given him" (May 23, 2013, no. 46).

The image of the streets with the elderly and children and the image of the salt that enhances the flavor of different dishes also contain the seeds of a constant tension between the spirit and its institutional expression. For the pope, the Church grows "from the bottom up, slowly," like a living organism, not like an organization. On April 24, 2013 (no. 22), in front of a group of faithful including employees of the IOR [the Vatican "bank"], he affirmed: "And when the Church wants to flex its muscles and sets up organizations and offices, becoming a bit bureaucratic, the Church loses its main substance and runs the risk of becoming an NGO [nongovernmental organization] . . . the Church is not an NGO. It is a love story. But then there are bureaucrats who say—sorry, everything is necessary, the offices are necessary . . . okay, fine! But they are necessary to a certain point: as an aid to this love story. But when the organization takes first place, love grows cold and the Church, poor thing, becomes an NGO. This is not the way." And the following June 1 (no. 53) he repeated: "The Church is not an organization of culture, or even of religion, of social work."

And afterward as well, as on January 27, 2014 (no. 161), when he recalled that the bishops are not chosen only to lead an organization called the local church, nor are they the heads of a company or corporation. The more the Church becomes an organization, the more its pastors become "inspectors of the faith," "hypocrites of casuistry," "intellectuals without talent" (June 19, 2013, no. 69), makers of the "pastoral border checkpoint" (May 25, 2013, no. 48). But in this way the Church is also at risk of being reduced to a charitable organization made up of "activist Christians, do-gooder Christians" (June 1, 2013, no. 53). All lacking the fire of faith.

There is always a dialectical tension in the thought of Pope Francis between spirit and organization in the Church; neither of these ever negates the other, but the former must inspire the latter in an efficacious, incisive manner. As he wrote in *Evangelii Gaudium*: "I do not want a Church concerned with being at the center and which then ends by being caught up in a web of obsessions and procedures" (EG 49). And further on, he affirms that the Church is "a people of pilgrims and evangelizers, transcending any institutional expression, however necessary" (EG 111).

Way and journey

The pairings that we have illustrated so far are not to be understood in a static manner. Bergoglio has a very dynamic view of reality.

He grasps the multiplicity and richness of the real, but never in a "cubist" form, so to speak, meaning static although multifaceted. The pope has a "futuristic" vision of the world. He sees it moved by the Spirit, who gives it impulse and direction. Rather than paying attention to objects and facts, he looks at dynamics and trajectories.

It is no coincidence that one of the words he uses most often in these homilies is "way," just as one of his most frequently used verbs is "to go." For Bergoglio, the way is the place where people meet each other, and the pope wants a Church that is capable of being where people are: on the way, with a capacity for accompanying persons on their journey. It is true—he said in an interview—that if we go out onto the street we can get into an accident. But if the Church remains closed off in itself, it is self-referential. And between an accident-prone Church that goes out onto the street and a Church infected with self-referentiality, Bergoglio undoubtedly prefers the former.

In a homily that he gave during the celebration of Palm Sunday at the Basilica of San José de las Flores on March 16, 2008, then-Cardinal Bergoglio had said: "The Church goes out into the streets because today Jesus is the king of the street, as he was on that Palm Sunday in Jerusalem. Today the place of devotion to Jesus, more than the Church, is the street." And therefore: "Today the place of Christ is the street; the place of the Christian is the street. The Lord wants us to be like him: with an open heart, strolling through the streets of Buenos Aires. He wants us to wander through Buenos Aires, bringing his message. He does not want us to keep his word only for ourselves, closed off in our hearts, in our homes, in church, but for us to cast his word out along the street. He wants us to wander."

At Saint Martha's, Pope Francis reiterated: "Christian life does not mean sitting on a corner carving out a path that leads comfortably to heaven, but it is a dynamism that drives us to be 'on the street' to proclaim that Christ has reconciled us with God, becoming sin for our sake" (June 15, 2013, no. 66). It is the path along which the good Samaritan met the suffering traveler, had compassion on him, and cared for his wounds (cf. October 7, 2013, no. 107). So the street evokes mission, "going to the peripheries," as he often says.

But the way is also the life of faith itself: it is the supreme metaphor of "walking every day in the presence of God" (April 12, 2013, no. 13). The pope presents this in many different ways: the way of salvation (April 10, 2013, no. 11), "the way of Jesus" (April 11, 2013, no. 12), the "way of holiness" (April 16, 2013, no. 16), the "way of the Gospel" but also of "love," of "conversion," of "beauty" (April 19, 2013, no. 19), "the way of patience" (May 7, 2013, no. 33), the "way of freedom" (September 9, 2013, no. 90), the "way of the Cross" (September 27, 2013, no. 102), the "way of justice" (October 24, 2013, no. 117), the "way of dialogue in order to make peace" (January 24, 2014, no. 160).

It is in this dynamic sense that the pope very often uses the expression "to go forward." Christian life is not a "state of life" but a forward movement. He said on April 26, 2013 (no. 24): "The whole journey of life is a journey of preparation. Sometimes the Lord must make this in haste, as he did with the good thief; he had only a few minutes to prepare him, and he did it. But ordinarily we have a lifetime to allow our hearts, our hearing, our sight to be prepared to arrive at this homeland, right? Because that is our homeland." The objective of the journey is to "prepare the heart to see the marvelous face of God."

This way is contrasted with the "way of wealth" and the "way of vanity" (May 15, 2013, no. 39), but also the "way of idolatry" (October 15, 2013, no. 112), of "injustice," of "hypocrisy" (October 24, 2013, no. 117), the "way of worldliness" (January 17, 2014, no. 156). The way is also once again a *ring* where holiness and vanity come to blows. The way of Christian life is also a way of temptation (cf. November 11, 2013, no. 125). Temptation has a dynamic aspect; "it grows, it infects, and it justifies itself" (February 18, 2014, no. 173), but in the end it ensnares, "imprisons," the pope says, implicitly citing Saint Ignatius: temptation is a hindrance. Sometimes the only solution is not to fight—which is also a way of dialoguing, of legitimizing temptation—but "to flee" in order to remain on the right path (July 2, 2013, no. 80).

But how can we discern the right path? Bergoglio provides one criterion: it is "the way of Jesus Christ: abasement, humility, even humiliation. If a thought, if a desire leads you on that path of humility, of abasement, of service to others, it is of Jesus. But if it leads you on the path of self-sufficiency, vanity, pride, on the path of an abstract thought, it is not of Jesus" (January 7, 2014, no. 149). For Bergoglio, "the way of the Lord is his service. As he performed his service, we must follow after him, in the path of service" (May 21, 2013, no. 44). The way of the Lord "is a way of 'abasement,' a way that ends in the Cross" (May 28, 2013, no. 50).

And we are not alone on this path. The Lord truly "shows us the way" (May 18, 2013, no. 42) and then sets off on it with us: "our God journeys with us, mingles with us, walks with us" (May 13, 2013, no. 37). Even more, the path is simply Jesus himself.

This creates a radically dynamic dimension in Bergoglio's vision of the spiritual life and the task of the Church. This dynamism is also characteristic of the Church, which is called not to occupy spaces of power in a stationary manner but to accompany the rhythms of cultural, social, and historical processes from within. One of the key principles of Bergoglio's thought is that "time is superior to space" (EG 222–225). For the pope, this means giving preference to actions that generate new dynamisms in society and in the Church, engaging the involvement of persons and groups. Standing on the outside, making critical observations without participation, without direct involvement, or even becoming involved only in condemnation and complaint, means standing outside of life itself, and therefore not living the missionary call in a real way. This would mean being "museum Christians! A salt without savor, a salt that does nothing" (May 23, 2013, no. 46).

One result of the achievement of power is in fact triumphalism, which is so harmful that it "brings the Church to a standstill. Triumphalism in Christians brings Christians to a standstill. It is a triumphalist Church, it is a Church stuck in the middle, a Church that is happy the way it is, well organized—well organized!—with all the offices, everything in place, everything great" (May 29, 2013, no. 51). This is the "babysitter Church that's just trying to get the children to fall asleep" (April 17, 2013, no. 17) and a "religion on a sort of payment system": "I give you glory and you give glory to me" (April 22, 2013, no. 21). Achievement cuts off the ability to walk, to accompany.

And for the pope the spiritual life is also a "journey," as he said from his very first homily of March 14, 2013, during the Mass with the cardinals, immediately after his election: "To journey: our life is a journey and when we stop, it's no good. To journey always, in the presence of the Lord, in the light of the Lord, seeking to live with that blamelessness which God asked of Abraham in his promise." Even the concept of Christian "identity," static in itself, for Bergoglio is not that of an "identity card" but that of belonging to the faithful People of God on its journey in history (homily at Saint Peter's on April 23, 2013). And by "spiritual journey" Bergoglio essentially means the path of continual discernment to do the will of God, which requires the freedom of the Spirit.

This freedom—Bergoglio acknowledges—can also be scary, "because we are afraid of confusing the freedom of the Spirit with another human freedom" (June 12, 2013, no. 63). And so instead of breathing deeply we prefer to stay safe and not go anywhere. When instead "joy is a pilgrim virtue" (May 10, 2013, no. 35). "Go. Walk. That's it: a first attitude of the Christian identity is to walk, and to walk even if there are difficulties, to go beyond the difficulties . . . Saint Augustine says to Christians: 'Go, go forward, sing and walk!' With joy: this is the style of the Christian" (February 14, 2014, no. 171).

The preceding is one of the possible maps for helping readers to navigate the spiritual richness of the homilies of Pope Francis at Saint Martha's. It is drawn from some of the fundamental terms of Bergoglio's spiritual vocabulary. The point of departure is the definition of the field of action as a *ring*. The pope's message is not easy or cheap. His speaking of mercy and forgiveness deeply permeates his dramatic perception of Christian existence as a struggle between the prince of this world and the Lord Jesus, between vanity and holiness. The message is very demanding. Without the perception of this combative tension, Bergoglio's message is not comprehensible in its profundity.

In considering the Christian challenge, one can then understand that this *ring* of life is also the place of encounter between human desire and the consolation of God, who draws near with his caress. Faith is this personal encounter, without which doctrine degrades into rigid and empty ideology: "Our God is the God of the great and the God of the small; our God is personal," he listens to everyone with his heart and "loves with his heart" (June 2, 2013, no. 54).

Thus also the Church, if it is deprived of the spirit of encounter of the People of God with the Lord, becomes a bureaucratic organization obsessed with procedure. And so Pope Francis insists on the dynamic element of the Church. In his homilies he is acting as a teacher of spiritual life, inciting us to move forward, to go to the existential peripheries, on mission. The way becomes the great metaphor of spiritual and ecclesial life. Only on the way is encounter possible. The way is, in this sense, the place of truth.

Antonio Spadaro, S.J.
Director of **La Civiltà Cattolica**
March 25, 2014

Encountering Truth

1

God is patient with our weaknesses

During Holy Week, let's think about the patience that God has with each of us.

God's infinite patience with man is reflected in the infinite patience that Jesus has with Judas. This is shown in the scene of the Gospel in which Judas criticizes the decision of Mary, Lazarus's sister, to anoint the feet of Jesus with three hundred grams of priceless ointment; it would have been better, Judas says, to have sold the ointment and given the proceeds to the poor. John notes in his Gospel that Judas was not interested in the poor but in the money, which he stole. And yet "Jesus did not say to him: 'You are a thief.'"

"He was patient with Judas, seeking to draw him to himself with his patience, with his love. It would do us good to think about the patience of God during this Holy Week, about the Lord's patience with us, with our weaknesses, with our sins."

The passage from Isaiah in the first reading, in presenting "the icon of that 'servant of God,'" also emphasizes the meekness and patience of Jesus. Which is the patience of God himself. "When we think about the patience of God: that is a mystery! How patient he is with us! We do so many things, but he is patient." He is "like that father in the Gospel who saw his son from far off, that son who had gone away with all the money of his inheritance." And why did he see him from far away? "Because every day he went out to see if his son was coming back." This "is the patience of God, this is the patience of Jesus.

"Let's think about a personal relationship, during this week: what has the patience of Jesus meant in my life? Just this. And then only one thing will come from our hearts: 'Thank you, Lord! Thank you for your patience.'"

March 25, 2013   *Isaiah 42:1–7 ✢ John 12:1–11*

2

The forgiveness of Jesus

Opening our hearts to the gentleness of God's forgiveness: this is the theme of the homily for the Mass of Tuesday during Holy Week. Everyone lives through the "night of sin," but Jesus has a "caress" for all.

"When Judas leaves the upper room to betray Jesus, outside—as the evangelist John states—it is night." This remark on the setting leads to a brief reflection that urges us to plumb the depths of the human conscience. The night that envelops Judas is also the night in which his heart is stumbling about. It is the worst night, the "night of the corrupted," a "definitive night, when the heart is closed" in such a way that "it cannot and does not want to come out" from itself. The "night of the sinner" is different; this is a "temporary" night that we all "experience." How many of these nights "have we had," how many "times when the 'night' comes and it is pitch black in the heart . . ." Then hope bursts through and drives us to a new encounter with Jesus. "We are not afraid of this night of the sinner. The most beautiful thing is to speak the name of the sin" in confessing it, and thus have the experience of Saint Paul, who affirmed that "his glory was Christ crucified in his sins. Why? Because in his sins he found Christ crucified, who forgave him."

The reality of forgiveness, "tasting the sweetness of forgiveness," is the second theme of the homily. "In the middle of the 'night,' of the many 'nights,' the many sins that we commit, because we are sinners, there is always that caress of the Lord" that makes us say: "This is my glory. I am a poor sinner, but you are my Savior!" Recalling the gaze with which Jesus forgave Peter after his denial, the invitation is to "open our hearts and taste the sweetness of forgiveness. Let's think about how wonderful it is to be holy, but also how wonderful it is to be forgiven. Let's trust in this encounter with Jesus" and "in the sweetness of his forgiveness."

March 26, 2013   *Isaiah 49:1–6 ✦ John 13:21–33, 36–38*

Those who bad-mouth others are like Judas

The betrayal of Jesus is compared with gossip, with speaking ill of others. This is the reflection on the Gospel that presents the betrayal of Judas for thirty denarii. One of the Twelve, one of Jesus' friends, one of those closest to him speaks with the leaders of the priests, negotiating the price of the betrayal. "Jesus is like a piece of merchandise: he is sold.

"This happens so many times in the marketplace of history as well . . . in the marketplace of our lives when we choose the thirty denarii and leave Jesus aside, we look at the Lord we have sold. And sometimes with our brothers, with our friends, with each other, we do almost the same thing."

This happens "when we gossip about each other." This is selling, and "the person about whom we are gossiping is a piece of merchandise, he becomes merchandise. And how easy it is for us to do this! It is the same thing that Judas did. I don't know why, but there is a dark enjoyment in gossiping." Sometimes we begin with good comments, but then suddenly we come to gossip and begin to "bad-mouth the other." But "every time we gossip, every time we 'bad-mouth' the other we are doing the same thing that Judas did." This, then, is the invitation: "Never speak ill of other persons." When he betrayed Jesus, Judas "had his heart closed, he had no understanding, no love, no friendship." So when we gossip we too have no love, no friendship, everything becomes merchandise: "We sell our friends, our relatives.

"Let's ask for forgiveness because when we do this to a friend, we do it to Jesus, because Jesus is in this friend. And let's ask for the grace not to 'bad-mouth' anyone, not to gossip about anyone."

And if we realize that someone has shortcomings, let's not get justice with our tongues, but let's pray to the Lord for him, saying "Lord, help him!"

March 27, 2013   *Isaiah 50:4–9a* ✤ *Matthew 26:14–25*

Asking for the grace of tears to see the Risen Christ

The Gospel presented by the liturgy for the Tuesday of the Octave of Easter speaks to us of the encounter of the Risen Christ with Mary Magdalene. The scene is the one recounted by the Gospel according to John: the Magdalene is weeping at the tomb because the body of the Teacher is not there anymore. Mary Magdalene is that "sinful woman" who "anointed the feet of Jesus and dried them with her hair," a "woman exploited and also despised by those who believed they themselves were righteous." But she is also the woman "of whom Jesus said that she loved much and because of this her many sins were forgiven her." Nonetheless, this woman had to "face the failure of all her hopes." Jesus, "her love, is not there anymore, and she weeps. It is the dark moment of her soul: the moment of failure." And yet she does not say: "I have failed on this path." Instead "she simply weeps. At times in our life the glasses for seeing Jesus are tears." Now the Magdalene proclaims this message: "I have seen the Lord." She had seen him during his life, and now she bears witness to him: "An example for the journey of our life. All of us, in our lives, have felt joy, sadness, pain.

"In our darkest moments, have we wept? Have we had the gift of tears that prepare our eyes to look, to see the Lord?"

In the face of the Magdalene who is weeping "we too can ask the Lord for the grace of tears. It is a beautiful grace . . . to weep for everything: for the good, for our sins, for graces, even for joy. Weeping prepares us to see Jesus." And the Lord gives all of us the grace to be able to say with our lives: "I have seen the Lord," not because he has appeared to me, but because "I have seen him inside my heart." And this is the witness of our lives: "I live like this because I have seen the Lord."

April 2, 2013   *Acts 2:36–41* ✤ *John 20:11–18*

Complaining is bad for the heart

The Gospel for the Wednesday of the Octave of Easter shows the two disciples of Emmaus leaving Jerusalem after the death of the Teacher. "They were afraid," all the disciples were afraid. But along the road they kept talking about the things they had just experienced "and they were complaining." They wouldn't stop complaining, "and the more they complained, the more they were closed off in themselves; they had no horizon, just a wall in front of them." After so much hope, they felt the failure of everything in which they had believed:

"And they were cooking—so to speak—they were cooking their lives in the broth of their complaints, and they were going on and on with their complaints. I think so many times that when difficult things happen to us, even when we are visited by the Cross, we run this risk of closing ourselves off in complaints. And even in this moment the Lord is close to us, but we do not recognize him. And he is walking with us. But we do not recognize him."

And even if Jesus speaks to us and we feel wonderful things, deep down inside of us we continue to be afraid: it seems "safer to complain! It is like a form of security: this is my truth, failure. There is no more hope."

It is wonderful to see Jesus' patience with the two disciples of Emmaus.

"First he listens to them, then he explains to them slowly, slowly . . . And then, in the end, he shows himself. As he did with the Magdalene, at the tomb, Jesus does the same thing with us. Even in the darkest moments he is always with us, he walks with us. And in the end he lets us see his presence.

"Complaints are bad," not only those against others, but also those against ourselves, when everything seems bitter to us. "They are bad because they take away our hope. Let's not get into this game of living in complaints," but if something is not right let's take refuge in the Lord, confiding in him.

"Let's not eat complaints, because these take away hope, they take away the horizon and close us off behind a wall. And there's no getting out. But the Lord is patient and knows how to get us out of this situation."

As happened for the disciples of Emmaus, who recognized him when he broke the bread.

"Let's have trust in the Lord, he always accompanies us on our journey, even in the darkest hours. The Lord never abandons us: he is always with us, even in the difficult moments. And let's not look for refuge in complaints; they're bad for us. They're bad for the heart."

April 3, 2013   *Acts 3:1–10 ✣ Luke 24:13–35*

The amazement of the encounter with Christ generates true peace

The readings for the Thursday of the Octave of Easter speak to us of amazement: the amazement of the crowd over the healing of the crippled man performed by Peter in the name of Christ, and the amazement of the disciples at the appearance of the Risen Jesus.

"Amazement is a great grace, it is the grace that God gives us in the encounter with Jesus Christ. It is something that makes us lose our heads a bit out of joy . . . It is not mere enthusiasm," like that of sports fans "when their team wins," but "it is something deeper." It is the interior experience of encountering the living Jesus and thinking that this is not possible: "But the Lord helps us to understand that it is reality. It is wonderful!

"Perhaps the opposite experience is more common, when human weakness, mental illness, or the devil makes people believe that phantasms and fantasies are the reality; this is not of God. What is of God is this joy that is so great it is beyond belief. And we think: No, this is not real! But it is. This is of the Lord. This astonishment is the beginning of the habitual state of the Christian."

Of course, "we cannot always live in amazement. No, of course not. But it is the beginning. Then this amazement leaves its mark on the soul, and spiritual consolation." It is the consolation of one who has encountered Jesus Christ.

So after amazement there is spiritual consolation, and at the end, on "the last rung," there is peace. "Even in the most painful trials the Christian need never lose the peace and presence of Jesus" and "with a bit of courage" can pray: "Lord, give me this grace that is the mark of the encounter with you: spiritual consolation and peace." A peace that cannot be lost, because "it is not ours," it belongs to the Lord. True peace "cannot be bought or sold. It is a gift of God," and therefore "let us ask for the grace of spiritual consolation and spiritual peace, which begin with this joyful amazement in the encounter with Jesus Christ."

April 4, 2013   *Acts 3:11–26 ✦ Luke 24:35–48*

We are not saved by wizards, psychics, or ourselves

The readings for Friday of the Octave of Easter remind us with Saint Peter that it is only in the name of Jesus that we are saved: "There is salvation in no one else." Peter, who had denied Jesus, now with courage, in prison, gives his testimony in front of the Jewish leaders, explaining that it is through the invocation of the name of Jesus that a crippled man has been healed. It is "that name which saves us"; Peter does not pronounce that name on his own, but "filled with the Holy Spirit.

"We cannot confess Jesus, we cannot speak of Jesus, we cannot say anything about Jesus without the Holy Spirit. It is the Spirit who urges us to confess Jesus or speak of Jesus or trust in Jesus. Jesus, who is on our journey of life, always. There was a man who worked in the chancery of Buenos Aires, a humble man, he had been working there for thirty years, the father of eight children. Before going out, before going to do his thing, he always said: 'Jesus' and one time I asked him: 'Why do you always say "Jesus"?' 'Well . . . When I say "Jesus," this man told me, 'I feel strong, I feel like I can work, and I know that he is beside me, that he's taking care of me.' This man never studied theology, he had only the grace of Baptism and the power of the Spirit. And this testimony did me so much good."

Because it reminds us that "in this world that offers us so many saviors" it is only the name of Jesus that saves. So many go to psychics or sorcerers to resolve their problems. But only Jesus saves, "and we must give witness to this! He is the only one."

Finally, the invitation is to stay with Mary: "The Blessed Mother always takes us to Jesus," as she did in Cana when she said: "Do whatever he tells you." And so, entrusting ourselves to the name of Jesus, let's invoke the name of Jesus, allowing the Holy Spirit to urge us "to make this trustful prayer in the name of Jesus . . . It will do us good!"

April 5, 2013   *Acts 4:1–12* ✦ *John 21:1–14*

Faith is not up for negotiation

Bearing witness with courage to the entirety of the faith: this is what the readings for the Saturday of the Octave of Easter invite us to do. The first sees Peter and John bearing witness to the faith in front of the Jewish leaders, in spite of the threats, while in the Gospel the Risen Jesus criticizes the incredulity of the apostles, who do not believe those who say they have seen him alive.

"How is our faith? Is it strong? Or is it a bit watered down at times?" When difficulties come our way, "are we courageous like Peter, or a bit lukewarm"? Peter was not silent on the faith. He did not descend to compromise, because "faith is not up for negotiation. There has always been, in the history of the People of God, this temptation to cut a piece off of the faith," the temptation to do "what everybody else does, not to be so very rigid. But when we start to cut up the faith, to negotiate the faith, to sell it to the highest bidder, we start down the road of apostasy, of unfaithfulness to the Lord.

"The example of Peter and John helps us, it gives us strength," but in the history of the Church there are many martyrs continuing right down to our own day.

"We don't have to go to the catacombs or the Colosseum to find martyrs; the martyrs are here now, in many countries. Christians are being persecuted for their faith. In some countries they cannot wear the Cross; if they do they are punished. Right now, in the twenty-first century, our Church is a Church of martyrs."

Martyrs who say, like Peter and John: "We cannot be silent about what we have seen and heard." And this "gives strength to us, who at times find our faith a bit weakened." It gives us the strength to bear witness with our lives to the "faith that we have received, this faith that is the gift that the Lord gives to all peoples.

"But we cannot do this on our own; it is a grace. The grace of faith. We must ask for it, every day: 'Lord, . . . protect my faith, make it grow, make it strong, courageous, and help me in the moments in which—like Peter and John—I must make it public. Give me the courage.' This would be a wonderful prayer for our time: that the Lord may help us to protect the faith, to carry it forward, to be, ourselves, men and women of faith."

April 6, 2013   *Acts 4:13–21 ✤ Mark 16:9–15*

9

Christian love is humble or it's not God's love

A road that keeps rising the more it descends: this is the way of Christian humility, which rises toward God the more its witness is able to "abase himself" to make room for charity. This is the reflection suggested by the liturgical feast of the Annunciation.

The road that Mary and Joseph take to Bethlehem, in obedience to the imperial census order, is a road of humility. Mary is humble, she "does not understand" but "leaves her soul to the will of God." Joseph is humble, he "abases" himself in order to take up the "great responsibility" of his wife, who is expecting a child. "This is always the way it is with God's love, which, in order to come to us, takes the path of humility." This is the way he preferred in order to express his love to men, unlike the "powerful idols," who "make themselves heard, who say: 'I'm in charge here.'" Our God, instead—who is "not a fake God, not a God of wood, made by men—prefers to go this way, by the path of humility." Which is the same one that Jesus followed, a path that lowered itself to the Cross. For the Christian, "this is the golden rule," this is "moving forward, advancing and lowering ourselves. There is no other path for us. If I do not lower myself, if you do not lower yourself, you are not a Christian."

Nonetheless, "being humble does not mean going down the path" with "our eyes lowered." That was not the humility of Jesus, his Mother, or Joseph. Setting off on the path of humility brings "all the charity of God to this path, which is the only one that he chose; he did not choose another." Even the "triumph of the Resurrection" follows this route; "the triumph of the Christian" takes the "way of self-abasement." Let's ask for "the grace of humility," because "if there is no humility, love is at a standstill, it cannot go."

April 8, 2013   Isaiah 7:10–14; 8:10 ✠ Hebrews 10:4–10 ✠ Luke 1:26–38

10

Never judge, never bad-mouth

May the Spirit bring peace to Christian communities and teach their members to be meek, not bad-mouthing others.

What the first Christian community was able to be in the first year of the Church is an unsurpassed and unsurpassable model for the Christian community today. They were of one heart and one mind, thanks to the Spirit, who had brought them to be born again to a "new life." In the Gospel dialogue between Jesus and Nicodemus, the latter does not immediately grasp the way in which a man can be "born again." "Again" means by the Holy Spirit, "it is the new life that we have received in Baptism." A life that "must be developed; it does not come automatically." We must "do all that we can so that this life may develop into the new life; it is a laborious journey," which "mainly depends on the Spirit." Along with each one's capacity to open himself to the breath of the Spirit.

And this is exactly what happened to the first Christians. They had the "new life," which expressed itself in living with one heart and one mind. They had "that unity, that unanimity, that harmony of sentiment in love, mutual love . . ." A dimension to be rediscovered today: for example, the aspect of "meekness in community," a virtue "that is a bit forgotten." Meekness has "many enemies," and the first of these is gossip.

"When we prefer to gossip, to gossip about the other, to beat up on the other a little—these are things we go through every day, they happen to everyone, even to me—these are temptations of the evil one, who does not want the Spirit to come to us and make this peace, this meekness in Christian communities.

"There are always these struggles": in the parish, in the family, in the neighborhood, among friends. "And this is not the new life," because when the Spirit comes "and brings us to birth in a new life, he makes us meek, charitable."

So here is the correct behavior for Christians. First, "do not judge anyone" because "the only judge is the Lord." Next, "zip it," and if you have to say something, say it directly to the persons concerned, to "someone who can remedy the situation," but "not to the whole neighborhood. If with the grace of the Spirit we are able never to gossip, this will be a big step forward" and "will be good for everyone."

April 9, 2013   *Acts 4:32–37 ✢ John 3:7b–15*

11

It is the love of God that saves, not money, power, or vanity

God so loved the world that he gave his only-begotten Son, so that everyone who believes in him might not perish but might have eternal life"; this is what Jesus says in the Gospel.

"The Lord saves us with his love; he does not save us with a letter, with a decree, but he has saved us with his love." A love so great that it drives him to send his Son, who "became one of us, he walked with us . . . And this saves us." But "what does it mean, this salvation? What does it mean to be saved?" It means getting back from the Lord "the dignity that we lost," the dignity of being children of God. It means getting hope back.

This dignity continues to grow "until the definitive encounter with him. This is the path of salvation, and this is wonderful. Only love does this. We are worthy, we are women and men of hope. This means being saved by love." The problem is that sometimes we want to save ourselves "and we think we can do it," basing our security on money, for example, and we think: "I'm set, I have money, everything . . . There's no problem . . . I have dignity, the dignity of a rich person.

"This is not enough. We think of the parable in the Gospel, about the man who had his granary full to the very top and said: 'I will make another so that I will have more, and then I will sleep soundly.' And the Lord says to him: 'Fool! Tonight you will die.' That salvation is no good, it is a temporary salvation, even a false salvation!"

Other times "we think we will save ourselves with vanity, with pride, right? We think we're powerful . . . That's no good either. We disguise our poverty, our sins with vanity, pride . . . All of that comes to an end." But "true salvation" lies in the dignity that God restores to us, in the hope that Christ has given us in Easter.

"Let's make an act of faith today: 'Lord, I believe. I believe in your love. I believe that your love has saved me. I believe that your love has given that dignity which I did not have. I believe that your love gives me hope.'"

And "only the love of God" can give true dignity and true hope.

"It is wonderful to believe in love, this is the truth. It is the truth of our lives. Let's make this prayer: 'Lord, I believe in your love.' And let's open our hearts so that this love may come, may fill us and impel us to love others."

April 10, 2013   *Acts 5:17–26 ✢ John 3:16–21*

12

*Listening to God and following the way of
Jesus makes us free and happy*

Listening to God sets us free and gives us the happiness that can never be guaranteed by "what the world has to offer."

"Obeying God means listening to God, having our hearts open to travel down the path that God points out for us. Obedience to God means listening to God. And this sets us free."

Obeying the Lord means listening to his voice, as Peter did when, addressing the Pharisees and scribes, he said: "I do what Jesus tells me, not what you want me to do." "In our lives we also hear things that do not come from Jesus, that do not come from God. Our weaknesses sometimes lead us down that road" or down another path where we come to a fork, with "what Jesus says" in one direction and "what the world tells us" in the other. But what happens when we listen to Jesus? Sometimes those who offer the other choice, the things of the world, "become infuriated," and the road ends in persecution. Many listen to what Jesus asks of them, and so often they are persecuted. The lives of many bear witness that they want to obey God, to travel the road that Jesus points out for them.

This is the goal toward which the Church urges us today: "Go the way of Jesus." This means not listening to what the world proposes, "proposals of sin" or of compromise that draw us away from the Lord. "This will not make us happy." The help we need to travel the road pointed out by Jesus and to obey God is to be found in the Holy Spirit. "It is the Holy Spirit who gives us the strength to go on," to continue on this journey. Our Father "gives us the Spirit, without measure, so that we can listen to Jesus and go the way of Jesus." But we must be courageous in this, and ask "for the grace of courage," the courage to say: "Lord, I am a sinner, sometimes I obey worldly things, but I want to obey you. I want to go your way." Let's ask for the grace always to go the way of Jesus. And when we don't, let's ask for forgiveness. "The Lord forgives us, because he is so good."

April 11, 2013   *Acts 5:27–33 ✢ John 3:31–36*

Triumphalism, a temptation for Christians

Following Christ means walking with perseverance and without triumphalism. When God touches a person's heart, he gives a grace that lasts a lifetime; he doesn't do a "magic trick" that's over in a moment.

In the climate of agitation immediately following the death of Jesus, the behavior and preaching of the apostles became the focus of the Pharisees and scholars of the law. The Acts of the Apostles present the words of Gamaliel, a Pharisee who warned the Sanhedrin against putting the disciples of Christ to death, because in the past the uproar created by false prophets had quickly dissolved together with their proselytes. Gamaliel's suggestion is to wait and see what will happen with the followers of the Nazarene. This "is good advice for our lives as well, because time is God's messenger. God saves us in time, not in the moment. Sometimes he works miracles, but ordinarily he saves us in time," he saves us "in history," in the "personal history" of each one. The Lord does not behave "like a fairy with a magic wand. No." On the contrary, he "gives us grace and says, as he said to all those he healed: 'Go, walk.' He says the same thing to us: 'Walk in your life, give witness to all that the Lord does with us.'

"A great temptation" is lurking in Christian life, "that of triumphalism. It is a temptation that the apostles also faced." Peter faced it when he solemnly pledged that he would not deny his Lord. Or the people after they witnessed the multiplication of the loaves.

"Triumphalism is not of the Lord. The Lord came to the earth humbly; he lived his life for thirty years, he grew up as a normal child, he went through the trial of work, and even the trial of the Cross. Then, in the end, he rose."

So "the Lord teaches us that life is not all magical, that triumphalism is not Christian." The life of the Christian is characterized by normalcy, but one that is lived with Christ, every day.

"This is the grace that we must ask for: perseverance. To persevere in the way of the Lord, right to the end, every day. May the Lord save us from triumphalist fantasies. Triumphalism is not Christian, it is not of the Lord. Walking every day in the presence of God, that is the way of the Lord."

April 12, 2013   *Acts 5:34–42 ✠ John 6:1–15*

14

We don't have to "sugarcoat" life, but accept good and evil

Confronted with life's problems, the Christian does not take shortcuts but always entrusts himself to God, who does not leave him without his help. This is the message that can be drawn from the liturgy of the Mass for Saturday of the second week of Easter.

Life must not be "sugarcoated" when things go wrong, because this means that we do not trust in God, who is the Lord of life. A Christian must instead be able to accept what happens to him. This is the profound life lesson that we find in the reading from the Acts of the Apostles, which the liturgy presents in the days after Easter, focusing on events in the first Christian community. The situation in the biblical passage sees the new brothers in faith discussing among themselves—Greeks against Jews—on account of certain practical necessities, like assistance for widows, that are seen as being neglected. "The first thing they do is to murmur; they are bad-mouthing each other.

"But this does not lead to any solution, this does not bring a solution. The apostles, with the help of the Holy Spirit, did the right thing: they gathered the group of disciples and talked. And that is the first step: when there are difficulties, we must take a good look at them, get a grip, and talk about it. Never hide them."

And that is what the apostles do. They do not hide, but they evaluate and decide, without hesitating. Having understood that their first duty is "prayer in the service of the word," they choose deacons to help them with the other services. And here—linking this episode in the life of the first Christians with the reading of the Gospel that sees Jesus reassuring the disciples on the stormy lake—we can observe: "When there are problems we must take hold of them, and the Lord will help us to resolve them.

"We must not be afraid of problems. Jesus himself says to his disciples: 'It is I. Do not be afraid. It is I.' Always. With life's difficulties, with problems, with new things that we have to face: the Lord is there. We might make mistakes, sure, but he is always close to us and says: 'You made a mistake, get back on the right path.' . . . It's no good to sugarcoat life, to dress life up. No, no. Life is what it is, it is reality. It is what God wants it to be or allows it to be, but it is what it is, and we must take it as it is. And the Holy Spirit will give us the solution to our problems.

"Do not be afraid, it is I!" This "is the word of Jesus, always," in difficulties, "in moments when everything is dark" and "we don't know what to do." Therefore "let's take things as they come, with the Spirit of the Lord and the help of the Holy Spirit. And in this way we will move forward, sure that we are on the right path.

"Let's ask the Lord for this grace: not to be afraid, not to sugar-coat life, to take life as it comes and seek to resolve problems as the apostles did, and also to seek the encounter with Jesus, who is always beside us, even in the darkest moments of life."

April 13, 2013   *Acts 6:1–7 ⚜ John 6:16–21*

15

Martyrs of the Church

"Calumny destroys the work of God in people." Even today so many martyrs are falsely accused, persecuted, and killed out of hatred for the faith.

Stephen, the first martyr of the Church, was a victim of calumny. And calumny is worse than a sin; calumny is a direct expression of Satan. The reading from the Acts of the Apostles presents Stephen, one of the deacons appointed by the disciples, who was brought before the Sanhedrin because of his witness to the Gospel, accompanied by extraordinary signs. And in front of the Sanhedrin—the text states—"false witnesses" appear to accuse Stephen. Since "fair fighting wasn't going well, a fight between good men," Stephen's enemies decided "to fight dirty, with calumny.

"We are all sinners, all of us. We have sinned. But calumny is something else. It is a sin, sure, but it is something else. Calumny wants to destroy the work of God; calumny arises from something very evil. It arises from hatred. And the one who makes hatred is Satan. Calumny destroys the work of God in persons, in souls. Calumny uses lies to get what it wants. And let's have no doubt about this: where there is calumny there is Satan, none other than he."

Stephen does not repay lies with lies, "he does not want to save himself that way. He looks to the Lord and obeys the law," remaining in the peace and truth of Christ. And this is "what happens in the history of the Church," because from the first martyr until today there have been so many examples of those who have borne witness to the Gospel with extreme courage.

"But the time of martyrs is not over. Even today we can say, in truth, that the Church has more martyrs than during the first centuries. The Church has so many men and women who are calumniated, who are persecuted, who are slain out of hatred for Jesus, out of hatred for the faith. This one is slain because he teaches catechism, this one is slain because he wears the Cross. Today, in so many countries, they calumniate them, they persecute them . . . These are our brothers and sisters who are suffering today, in this time of martyrs."

Ours is an era of "such spiritual turmoil" that it calls to mind the image of an ancient Russian icon, that of the Blessed Mother covering the People of God with her mantle.

"We pray to the Blessed Mother that she may protect us, and during times of spiritual turmoil the safest place is under the mantle of the Blessed Mother. She is the mom who takes care of the Church. And in this time of martyrs, she is the protagonist of protection: she is the mom . . . Let's say this with faith: 'Under your protection, Mother, is the Church. Take care of the Church.'"

April 15, 2013   *Acts 6:8–15* ✤ *John 6:22–29*

16

The anniversary of the Second Vatican Council, work of the Holy Spirit, and moving forward

The first reading of the day speaks to us of the martyrdom of Saint Stephen, who before he was stoned proclaimed the Resurrection of Christ, admonishing those present in strong words: "You stiff-necked people . . . you always oppose the Holy Spirit." Stephen recalls how many have persecuted the prophets. Jesus also scolds the disciples on the way to Emmaus: "Foolish, and slow of heart to believe all that the prophets have said! Always, even among us, there is this resistance to the Holy Spirit.

"To put it simply: the Holy Spirit bothers us. Because he moves us, he makes us walk, he pushes the Church to go forward. And we are like Peter at the Transfiguration: 'Ah, how wonderful it is to be here like this, all together!' . . . But don't bother us. We want the Holy Spirit to doze off . . . we want to domesticate the Holy Spirit. And that's no good. Because he is God, he is that wind which comes and goes and you don't know where. He is the power of God, he is the one who gives us consolation and strength to move forward. But: to move forward! And this bothers us. It's so much nicer to be comfortable."

Today it seems that "we are all happy" about the presence of the Holy Spirit, but "that's not true. This temptation still exists today. Just one example: think about the Council.

"The Council was a beautiful work of the Holy Spirit. Think about Pope John. He was a good pastor, and he was obedient to the Holy Spirit, and he did that. But after fifty years, have we done everything that the Holy Spirit told us in the Council? In that continuity of the growth of the Church which was the Council? No. We celebrate this anniversary, we make a monument, but don't let it bother us. We don't want to change. There are even some who want to go back. This is called being stiff-necked, this is called wanting to domesticate the Holy Spirit, this is called becoming foolish and slow of heart."

The same thing happens "in our personal lives"; in fact, "the Spirit is pushing us to take a more evangelical path," but we resist. "Do not resist the Holy Spirit. It is the Spirit who sets us free, with that freedom of Jesus, with that freedom of the children of God!

"Do not resist the Holy Spirit. This is the grace that I would like all of us to ask of the Lord: docility to the Holy Spirit, to that Spirit who comes to us and moves us forward on the way of holiness, that beautiful holiness of the Church. The grace of docility to the Holy Spirit."

April 16, 2013   *Acts 7:51–8:1a ✛ John 6:30–35*

17

May the laity rediscover the responsibility of the baptized

The power of Baptism impels Christians to have the courage to proclaim Christ even without safety, even amid persecution.

In the reading from the Acts of the Apostles, the first Christian community of Jerusalem is living in peace and love, but immediately after the martyrdom of Saint Stephen a violent persecution breaks out. "This is the way life is for the Church: between the peace of charity and persecution." This is what has always happened in history, "because it is the style of Jesus." With persecution many of the faithful flee to Judea and Samaria, and here they proclaim the Gospel, even though they are alone, without priests, because the apostles have remained in Jerusalem.

"They left their homes, perhaps they took a few things with them; they had no security, but went from place to place proclaiming the word. They brought with them the wealth that they had: their faith. That wealth which the Lord had given them. They were ordinary faithful, just baptized a year ago or a little more, perhaps. But they had that courage to go and proclaim. And they believed in him! And they worked miracles!"

These first Christians had only "the power of Baptism" that "gave them this apostolic courage, the power of the Spirit.

"I think about us, the baptized. If we have this power. And I think: But we, do we believe in this? That Baptism is enough, is sufficient for us to evangelize? Or do we hope that the priest will say it, that the bishop will say it? . . . And what about us? Then the grace of Baptism is a bit closed off, and we are fenced in behind our thoughts, our concerns. Or maybe sometimes we think: No, we are Christians. I have received Baptism, I have received Confirmation, First Communion . . . the identity card is in place. So you sleep easy. You are Christian. But where is this power of the Spirit that carries you forward?"

We have to be "faithful to the Spirit to proclaim Jesus with our lives, with our witness, and with our words.

"When we do this, the Church becomes a Mother Church who bears children, children, children, because we, children of the Church, bear witness. But when we don't do it, the Church becomes not a mother but a babysitter Church that's just trying to get the children to fall asleep. It is a coddled Church. Let's think about our Baptism, about the responsibility of our Baptism."

We remember the persecutions in Japan during the seventeenth century, when the Catholic missionaries were driven out and the Christian communities remained without priests for two hundred years. When they came back, the missionaries found "all the communities in place, everyone baptized, everyone catechized, everyone married in church." Thanks to the work of the baptized.

"There is a great responsibility for us, the baptized: to proclaim Christ, to carry the Church forward, this fruitful maternity of the Church. Being Christian does not mean making a career in an office, to become a Christian lawyer or doctor. No. Being Christian . . . is a gift that moves us forward with the power of the Spirit in the proclamation of Jesus Christ."

During the persecution of the first Christians, Mary "prayed so much" and encouraged the baptized to move forward with courage.

"Let's ask the Lord for the grace to become baptized persons who are courageous and sure that this Spirit that we have in us, received in our Baptism, is always driving us to proclaim Jesus Christ with our lives, with our witness, and also with our words."

April 17, 2013   *Acts 8:1b–8 ✢ John 6:35–40*

18

Faith is believing in a God who is a Person

Faith is a gift that begins in encountering Jesus, a real Person and not a "god-spray." Not an impalpable presence, a nebulous essence that spreads around without anyone knowing quite what it is. God is a concrete "Person," he is a Father, and therefore faith in him comes from a living encounter, a tangible experience.

The passage from the Gospel of John in which Jesus tells the crowd that "whoever believes has eternal life" is the occasion for an examination of conscience. "How many times" do so many people say that deep down they believe in God? "But in what God do you believe?" is the direct question, with which we are confronted with the evanescence of certain convictions concerning the concreteness of a true faith.

"A 'diffused god,' a 'god-spray,' that is a little bit everywhere but you don't know what it is. We believe in God who is Father, who is Son, who is Holy Spirit. We believe in Persons, and when we speak with God we speak with Persons; either I speak with the Father, or I speak with the Son, or I speak with the Holy Spirit. And this is the faith."

In the passage from the Gospel, Jesus also affirms that no one can come to him "unless the Father . . . draw him." These words demonstrate that "going to Jesus, finding Jesus, knowing Jesus is a gift" that God bestows on us. A gift like the one given to the official of the queen of Ethiopia described in the reading from Acts, when Christ sends Philip to explain the Old Testament to him in the light of the Resurrection. That official was not "an ordinary man" but a royal finance minister, and for this reason "we can think that he was a bit attached to money, a careerist." And yet, when this individual hears Philip talking to him about Jesus, "he feels that this is good news, he feels joy," to the point of having himself baptized in the first place where there is water.

"He who has faith has eternal life, he has life. But faith is a gift, and it is the Father who gives it to us. We must remain on this path.

But if we travel down this road, still with our own affairs—because we are all sinners and we always have some things that are no good, but the Lord forgives us if we ask for his forgiveness—and if we keep moving forward on the road without getting discouraged, the same thing will happen to us that happened to that finance minister."

What will happen is what the Acts of the Apostles says about that official after he discovered the faith: he "continued on his way rejoicing.

"This is the joy of faith, the joy of having encountered Jesus, the joy that only Jesus gives us, the joy that gives peace: not that which the world gives, that which Jesus gives. This is our faith. Let's ask the Lord to make us grow in this faith, this faith that makes us strong, makes us joyful, this faith that always begins with the encounter with Jesus and always continues in life with the little daily encounters with Jesus."

April 18, 2013   *Acts 8:26–40 ♣ John 6:44–51*

19

May the Church be freed from moralism and ideologies

The Word of God must be welcomed with humility because it is a word of love; it is only in this way that it enters into our hearts and changes our lives.

The conversion of Saint Paul and Jesus' words in the synagogue of Capernaum are the biblical readings centered on Jesus who speaks. He speaks to Saul, who is persecuting him; he speaks to Ananias, who is called to welcome Saul; and he also speaks to the scholars of the law, telling them that he who does not eat his flesh and drink his blood will not be saved. The voice of Jesus "passes through our minds and goes to our hearts. Because Jesus is seeking our conversion." Paul and Ananias respond with perplexity, but with open hearts. The scholars of the law respond in a different way, discussing among themselves and harshly contesting the words of Jesus.

"Paul and Ananias respond like the greats of the history of salvation, like Jeremiah, Isaiah. Even Moses had his difficulties: 'But, Lord, I do not know how to speak, how will I go to the Egyptians to say this?' And Mary: 'But, Lord, I am not married!' This is the response of humility, of the one who welcomes the Word of God with his heart. The scholars of the law, instead, respond only with their heads. They do not know that the Word of God goes to the heart, they do not know conversion."

Who are those who respond only with their heads?

"They are the great ideologues. The word of Jesus goes to the heart because it is a word of love, it is a beautiful word, and it brings love, it makes us love. These others cut off the path of love: the ideologues. And also that of beauty. And they began to discuss it bitterly among themselves: 'How can this man give us his flesh to eat?' A completely intellectual problem! And when ideology comes into the Church, when ideology comes into the understanding of the Gospel, nothing makes any sense."

These are the ones who walk only "on the path of duty"; it is the moralism of those who presume to accept the Gospel only so far as they can understand it. They are not "on the path of conversion, that conversion to which Jesus calls us.

"And these, on the path of duty, load everything onto the shoulders of the faithful. Ideologues falsify the Gospel. Every ideological interpretation, from whatever side it may come—from one side or the other—is a falsification of the Gospel. And these ideologues—we have seen this in the history of the Church—end up being, they become, intellectuals without talent, ethicists without goodness. And let's not talk about beauty, because they don't know a thing about it.

"The way of love, instead, the way of the Gospel is simple; it is the way that the saints knew.

"The saints are those who carry the Church forward! The way of conversion, the way of humility, of love, of the heart, the way of beauty . . . Let's pray to the Lord for the Church today: that the Lord may free it from any ideological interpretation and open the heart of the Church, of our Mother Church, to the simple Gospel, to that pure Gospel which speaks to us of love, brings us to love, and is so beautiful! And it also makes us beautiful, with the beauty of holiness. Let's pray for the Church today!"

April 19, 2013   *Acts 9:1–20 ✢ John 6:52–59*

20

Lukewarm Christians build small churches

Lukewarm Christians are those who want to build a church to the size that suits them, but it is not the Church of Jesus. The first Christian community, after the persecution, was living a moment of peace, establishing itself, walking and growing "in the fear of the Lord, and with the consolation of the Holy Spirit." This is the air in which the Church lives and breathes, being called to walk in the presence of God and in a blameless way.

"It is a style of the Church. To walk in the fear of the Lord gives us the sense of adoration, the presence of God, doesn't it? This is how the Church walks, and when we are in the presence of God we do not do ugly things or make ugly decisions. We stand before God. And with joy and happiness: this is the comfort of the Holy Spirit, meaning the gift that the Lord has given us—this comfort—that makes us move forward."

In the Gospel presented by the liturgy of the day, many of the disciples think Jesus' words are too tough, and they grumble and are scandalized and ultimately leave the Teacher.

"These withdrew, they went away, because they said, 'This man is a bit unusual; he is saying things that are tough. It's too big a risk to go down this path. Let's be sensible. Let's hang back a bit and not get so close to him.' These, perhaps, had a certain admiration for Jesus, but from a distance. Don't get too mixed up with this man; he says things that are a bit strange . . .'"

These Christians "do not establish themselves in the Church, they do not walk in the presence of God, they do not have the comfort of the Holy Spirit, they do not help the Church to grow.

"They are perfectly sensible Christians, and that's all; they keep their distance. We could call them 'satellite' Christians, with a little church built just the way they like it; to put it in the words of Jesus in Revelation, 'lukewarm Christians.' The lukewarmness that comes into the Church . . . They walk only in the presence of their own good sense, of common sense."

Let's think of the many Christians "who in this moment are giving witness to the name of Jesus, even to the point of martyrdom." These are not "satellite Christians," because "they go with Jesus, on the path of Jesus.

"These know perfectly well what Peter says to the Lord when the Lord asks him: 'Do you also want to leave, to be "satellite Christians"?' Simon Peter answers him: 'Master, to whom shall we go? You have the words of eternal life.' So from a large group they become a slightly smaller group, but of those who know perfectly well that they cannot go anywhere else, because only he, the Lord, has the words of eternal life."

So let us lift up this prayer:

"Let's pray for the Church, that it may continue to grow, to be firm, to walk in the fear of God and with the comfort of the Holy Spirit. May the Lord free us from the temptation of so-called good sense, from the temptation to grumble against Jesus, because he is too demanding, and from the temptation of scandal."

April 20, 2013   *Acts 9:31–42 ✤ John 6:60–69*

21

Careerists have no faith

The Gospel of the Good Shepherd, with Jesus calling himself "the gate for the sheep" is at the center of this reflection. In this passage of the Gospel, Jesus tells us that anyone who does not enter into the sheepfold by the gate is not the shepherd. The only door for entering into the Kingdom of God, for entering into the Church, is Jesus himself: "Anyone who does not enter into the sheepfold by the door, but climbs in another way, is a thief or a brigand." He is "someone who wants to make profits for himself," he is one who "wants to climb.

"Even in Christian communities there are these climbers, right? Who are looking out for themselves . . . And consciously or unconsciously pretend to enter but are thieves and brigands. Why? Because they steal glory from Jesus; they want their own glory, and this is what he said to the Pharisees: 'You give glory to one another . . .' A religion on a sort of payment system, isn't it? I give you glory and you give glory to me. But these have not entered through the true door. The door is Jesus, and anyone who does not enter by this door is wrong. And how do I know that the true door is Jesus? How do I know that this door is that of Jesus? Well, take the Beatitudes and do what the Beatitudes say. Be humble, be poor, be meek, be righteous . . ."

But "Jesus is not only the door; he is the path, he is the way. There are so many paths, some of them perhaps seeming to get us there more quickly," but these are "deceptive, they are not true; they are false. The only way is Jesus.

"But some of you will say: 'Father, you are a fundamentalist!' No, this is simply what Jesus has said: 'I am the door,' 'I am the way' to give us life. Simply this. It is a beautiful door, a door of love; it is a door that does not deceive; it is not false. It always speaks the truth. But with tenderness, with love. But we always have that which was at the origin of original sin, don't we? We want to have the key for interpreting everything, the key and the power to make our own path, whatever it may be, to find our own door, whatever it may be.

"Sometimes we have the temptation of being too much our own masters and not humble children and servants of the Lord.

"This is the temptation of seeking other doors or other windows for entering into the Kingdom of God. We enter only by the door named Jesus. We enter only by that door which leads us to the way called Jesus and leads us to the life called Jesus. All those who do anything else—says the Lord—who climb up to enter through the window, are 'thieves and brigands.' He is simple, the Lord. The things he says are not complicated. He is simple."

Let's ask for "the grace always to knock at that door.

"Sometimes it is closed. We are sad, we are devastated, we have trouble knocking, knocking on that door. Do not go looking for other doors that seem easier, more comforting, closer to hand. Always that: Jesus. And Jesus never lets us down, Jesus does not deceive us. Jesus is not a thief, he is not a brigand. He has given his life for me. Each of us must say this: 'And you who have given your life for me, please open, so that I may come in.'"

April 22, 2013   *Acts 11:1–18 ✤ John 10:1–10*

22

The Church is a love story

The Church is not a bureaucratic organization, it is a love story. This is what is suggested by the readings of the day, which recount the events of the first Christian community that grows and multiplies its disciples. This is a good thing, but it can lead to striking "deals" in order to have "more members in this enterprise.

"Instead, the way that Jesus wanted for his Church is completely different: the way of difficulties, the way of the Cross, the way of persecutions . . . And this makes us think: But what is this Church, this Church of ours, because it seems that it is not a human enterprise."

The Church is "something else." It is not the disciples who make the Church; they have been sent, sent by Jesus. And Christ is sent by the Father.

"So we can see that the Church begins there, in the heart of the Father, who had this idea . . . I don't know if he had an idea, the Father; the Father had love. And this love story began, this love story that has been going on for such a long time and is not yet finished. We, women and men of the Church, we are in the middle of a love story. Every one of us is a link in this chain of love. And if we do not understand this, we understand nothing about what the Church is."

The temptation is that of making the Church grow without going the way of love.

"But the Church does not grow by human strength. And then, some Christians have been mistaken for historical reasons; they have mistaken the way, they have made armies, they have made wars of religion. That is another story, which is not this love story. We too must learn from our mistakes how this love story goes. But how does it grow? Jesus said it plainly: like the mustard seed, it grows like the leaven in the dough, without noise."

The Church grows "from the bottom up, slowly.

"And when the Church wants to flex its muscles and sets up organizations and offices, becoming a bit bureaucratic, the Church loses its main substance and runs the risk of becoming an NGO. [As I said a few weeks ago] the Church is not an NGO. It is a love story. But then there are bureaucrats who say—sorry, everything is necessary, the offices are necessary . . . okay, fine! But they are necessary to a certain point: as an aid to this love story. But when the organization takes first place, love grows cold and the Church, poor thing, becomes an NGO. This is not the way."

A head of state once asked how big the pope's army was. The Church does not grow "with a military" but with the power of the Holy Spirit. Because the Church is not an organization.

"No: it is a Mother. It is Mother. What would a mom feel like if someone said: 'So you're the organizer at your house'? 'No: I'm the mom!' And the Church is Mother. And we are in the middle of a love story that moves forward with the power of the Holy Spirit, and we, all of us together, are a family in the Church, who is our Mother."

May the Blessed Mother "give us the grace of joy, of the spiritual joy of walking in this love story."

April 24, 2013   *Acts 12:24–13:5a ✢ John 12:44–50*

23

The Christian is not afraid of doing big things

The Christian style of proclamation is humble, but at the same time it is not afraid of doing big things.

At the center of the reflection is the passage from the Gospel of Saint Mark in which the Ascension of Jesus is recounted. The Lord, before going up to heaven, sent the apostles to proclaim the Gospel: "to the ends of the earth," not only in Jerusalem or Galilee.

"No: all over the world. The horizon . . . the grand horizon . . . And as we can see, this is the missionary nature of the Church. The Church moves forward with this preaching to all, to the whole world. But it does not go forward on its own; it goes with Jesus. So 'they went forth and preached everywhere, while the Lord worked with them.' The Lord works with all those who preach the Gospel. This is the magnanimity that Christians must have. A weak-willed Christian does not understand this: this magnanimity belongs to the Christian vocation, ever more, ever more, ever more, ever forward."

The first letter of Saint Peter defines the Christian style of preaching, which is that of humility:

"The evangelical style of preaching takes this attitude: humility, service, charity, fraternal love. 'But . . . Lord, we have to conquer the world!' That word, 'conquer,' is no good. We must preach in the world. Christians must not be like soldiers who, when they win the battle, make a clean sweep of everything."

Some time ago, "a wise bishop," an Italian, said that sometimes we get confused and think that our evangelical preaching must be a salvation of ideas and not a salvation of souls. "But how do we get to the salvation of souls? With humility, with charity."

The Christian "proclaims the Gospel with his witness, more than with his words." And with a twofold disposition, as Saint Thomas Aquinas says: a great heart that is not afraid of big things, of going forward toward endless horizons, and the humility to take little things into account. "This is divine, it is like a tension between the big and the small," and "Christian missionary activity" proceeds "along this path."

The Gospel of Saint Mark ends with "a wonderful phrase" where it says that Jesus acted with the disciples, confirming "'the word through accompanying signs.'"

"When we go forward with this magnanimity and humility, when we are not afraid of big things, of that horizon, but also take up the little things—humility, everyday charity—the Lord confirms the word. And we move forward. The triumph of the Church is the Resurrection of Jesus. But first there is the Cross. Let's ask the Lord today to make us missionaries in the Church, apostles in the Church, but with this spirit: a great magnanimity and also a great humility."

April 25, 2013   *1 Peter 5:5b–14 ✠ Mark 16:15–20*

24

Faith is not alienation but a journey of truth

The journey of faith is not alienation, but to prepare the heart to see the marvelous face of God. The Gospel of the day brings back to us the words of Jesus to his disciples: "Do not let your hearts be troubled."

"These words of Jesus are wonderful words. In a moment of farewell, Jesus speaks to his disciples, but from his heart. He knows that his disciples are sad, because they realize that things are not going well. He says: "Do not let your hearts be troubled.' And he begins to talk like that, like a friend, even with the attitude of a pastor. I say: the music of these words of Jesus is the attitude of the pastor, like the shepherd with his lambs, right? . . . 'Do not let your hearts be troubled. You have faith in God; have faith also in me.' And he begins to talk about what? About heaven, about our definitive homeland. 'Have faith also in me.' I am always faithful, it's like that's what he's saying, right? . . . With the figure of the engineer, of the architect he tells them what he is going to do: 'I am going to prepare a place for you.' 'In my Father's house there are many dwelling places.' And Jesus goes to prepare a place for us.

"What is that place like? What does it mean 'to prepare a place'? To rent a room up there? 'Preparing a place' means preparing our possibility of enjoyment, the possibility—our possibility—of seeing, of feeling, of grasping the beauty of what awaits us, of that homeland toward which we are walking.

"And the whole Christian life is a work of Jesus, of the Holy Spirit to prepare a place for us, to prepare our eyes to be able to see . . . 'But, Father, I see just fine! I don't need glasses!' That's another kind of vision . . . Let's think about those who have cataracts and have to get an operation for cataracts; they see, but after the operation what do they say? 'I never thought I could see like this, without glasses, so clearly!' Our eyes, the eyes of our soul need, they have to be prepared to look at that marvelous face of Jesus. To prepare the hearing to be able to hear beautiful things, beautiful words. And in the first place to prepare the heart: to prepare the heart to love, to love more."

In the journey of life the Lord prepares our hearts "with trials, with consolations, with tribulations, with good things.

"The whole journey of life is a journey of preparation. Sometimes the Lord must make this in haste, as he did with the good thief; he had only a few minutes to prepare him, and he did it. But ordinarily we have a lifetime to allow our hearts, our hearing, our sight to be prepared to arrive at this homeland, right? Because that is our homeland. 'But, Father, I went to a philosopher and he told me that all of these thoughts are alienation, that we are alienated, that life is this, the concrete, and nobody knows what is on the other side . . .' Some people think that way. But Jesus tells us that it's not true, and he tells us: 'Have faith also in me.' What I am telling you is the truth. I'm not tricking you, I'm not fooling you.

"Preparing ourselves for heaven means starting to hail it from a long way away. This is not alienation; this is the truth, this is allowing Jesus to prepare our hearts, our eyes for that great beauty. This is the way of beauty" and "the way of the return to the homeland." Let's pray that the Lord may give us "this strong courage," the courage and also the humility to allow the Lord to prepare the place, "the definitive place, in our hearts, in our eyes, and in our hearing."

April 26, 2013   *Acts 13:26–33 ✦ John 14:1–6*

25

In the Church the Spirit creates open communities and not closed groups

Looking at Jesus, who sends us to evangelize, to proclaim his name with joy." We must not "be afraid of the joy of the Spirit," the way to overcome being closed off "in ourselves.

"It seemed that this happiness would never be defeated." This might remind us of how the first disciples entrusted themselves to Christ, gathered in Antioch to listen to the word of the Lord, as recalled in the Acts of the Apostles. But then why was the "closed off" community of the Jews, "a little group, good people," so full of jealousy in seeing the multitude of Christians that they began to persecute them?

"Simply because their hearts were closed, they were not open to the newness of the Holy Spirit. They believed that everything had been said, that everything was as they thought it should be, and therefore they felt like defenders of the faith and started to speak against the apostles, to calumniate . . . Calumny . . . And they went to the pious women among the nobility, who had power, and they filled their heads with ideas, with things, with things, and they pushed them to speak with their husbands so that they would oppose the apostles. This is an attitude of this group and of all groups in history, closed groups: to make deals with those in power, to resolve difficulties, but 'among ourselves' . . . Like they did on the morning of the Resurrection, when the soldiers went to tell them: 'We have seen this' . . . 'Shut up! Here, take this . . .' And they covered everything up with money.

"This is precisely the attitude of this closed religious devotion that does not have the freedom to open itself to the Lord.

"Their community life to defend the truth always—because they believe they are defending the truth—is always calumny, gossip . . . They are truly gossipy communities, bad-mouthing, destroying others, and looking inside, always inside, shut up behind their walls. But the free community, with the freedom of God and of the Holy

Spirit, went forward, even in persecutions. And the word of the Lord spread throughout the whole region. That's just what the community of the Lord is like, moving forward, spreading itself, because it's the right thing to do: Keep reaching out! The good is not supposed to stay shut up inside. This is one criterion, a criterion of the Church, and for our examination of conscience too: what are our communities like, our religious communities, parish communities? Are they communities open to the Holy Spirit, that are always moving forward to spread the Word of God, or are they closed communities, with all the commandments just right, loading so many commandments onto the shoulders of the faithful, as the Lord said to the Pharisees?

"Persecution begins for religious reasons and out of jealousy," but not only were "the disciples full of the joy of the Holy Spirit," they were "speaking beautifully, opening pathways.

"By contrast the closed community, sure of itself, seeking the assurance that comes from dealing with power, with money, speaks with harmful words: insults, condemnation . . . This is precisely their attitude. Maybe they have forgotten about the caresses of their mothers, when they were little. These communities know nothing about caresses; they know about duty, about action, about closing themselves off in superficial observance. As Jesus had said to them: 'You are like a tomb, like a sepulcher, white, beautiful, but nothing more.' Let's think about the Church today, so beautiful: that Church which moves forward. Let's think about our many brothers who are suffering for this freedom of the Spirit and suffering persecutions, right now, in so many places. But these brothers, in suffering, are full of joy and of the Holy Spirit.

"Let's look to Jesus, who sends us to evangelize, to proclaim his name with joy, full of joy." We must not be "afraid of the joy of the Spirit," so that we do not "close ourselves off within ourselves."

April 27, 2013   *Acts 13:44–52* ✛ *John 14:7–14*

26

Being ashamed of our sins is a virtue of the humble

Being ashamed of our sins is the virtue of the humble that prepares us to receive God's forgiveness.

The first letter of Saint John, in which it says that "God is light, and in him there is no darkness," prompts us to think that "all of us have darkness in our lives," moments "in which everything, even in our conscience, is dark," but this does not mean walking in darkness.

"Walking in darkness means being satisfied with ourselves, being convinced that we have no need of salvation. That is darkness! When someone starts off on this path of darkness, it is not easy to turn back. That is why John continues, because perhaps this way of thinking made him reflect: 'If we say, "We are without sin," we deceive ourselves, and the truth is not in us.' Look at your sins, at our sins. We are all sinners, all . . . This is the point of departure. But if we confess our sins, he is faithful, he is so just that he forgives our sins and purifies us from all iniquity. And John presents us— doesn't he?—with that Lord who is so good, so faithful, so just that he forgives us.

"When the Lord forgives us, he works justice," in the first place for himself, "because he came to save and forgive us," welcoming us with the tenderness of a father for his children. "The Lord is tender toward those who fear him, toward those who go to him," and with tenderness "he always understands us," he wants to give us "that peace which comes only from him. This is what happens in the sacrament of Reconciliation," even if "many times we think that going to confession is like going to the dry cleaners" to clean the dirt off of our clothing.

"But Jesus in the confessional is not a dry cleaner; this is an encounter with Jesus, with this Jesus who is waiting for us, but waiting for us as we are. 'But, Lord, listen, this is how I am . . .' We are ashamed to tell the truth: 'I have done this, I have thought this.' But shame is a true Christian virtue, and also a human virtue . . . The ability to be ashamed: I don't know if you say this in Italian, but where I come from those who cannot be ashamed of themselves are called *sin vergüenza,* shameless: this guy is 'shameless' because he does not have the capacity to be ashamed of himself, and being ashamed of oneself is a virtue of the humble, of the man or woman who is humble."

We have to have trust, because when we sin we have a defender before the Father: "Jesus Christ, the just one." And he "supports us before the Father" and defends us in the face of our weaknesses. But we have to place ourselves before the Lord "with our truth as sinners, with trust, and also with joy, without disguising ourselves . . . We must never disguise ourselves before God!" And shame is a virtue: "blessed shame. This is the virtue that Jesus asks of us: humility and meekness.

"Humility and meekness are like the capstone of a Christian life. A Christian always walks like this, in humility and meekness. And Jesus is waiting for us, to forgive us. We can ask him a question: So going to confession is not like going to a torture session? No! It is going to praise God, because I, a sinner, have been saved by him. And is he waiting to beat me up? No, with tenderness to forgive me. And if I do the same thing tomorrow? Go again, and go and go and go . . . He is always waiting for us. This tenderness of the Lord, this humility, this meekness . . ."

This trust "lets us breathe. May the Lord give us this grace, this courage always to go to him with the truth, because the truth is light, and not with the darkness of half-truths or lies in front of God. May he give us this grace!"

April 29, 2013   *Acts 14:5–18 ✚ John 14:21–26*

27

A "worldly" Church does not bring the Gospel

When the Church becomes worldly" it becomes a "weak Church." It is in prayer, it is within the close bond with the salvific action of Christ that we find the way of protection and entrustment to the Lord for "the elderly, the sick, children, young people," for the whole Church. "May the Lord make us strong so that we do not lose faith, do not lose hope.

"We can protect the Church, we can take care of the Church, and we must do this with our work. But the most important thing is what the Lord does: he is the only one who can look the evil one in the face and overcome him. The 'prince of the world' is coming, against me he can do nothing. If we do not want the prince of this world to get hold of the Church, we must entrust it to the only one who can overcome the prince of this world. And here the question arises: We pray for the Church, but do we pray for the whole Church? For our brothers whom we do not know, everywhere in the world? It is the Church of the Lord; in our prayers let us say to the Lord: 'Lord, protect your Church . . . It is yours. Your Church, and our brothers.' This is a prayer that we should make from our hearts, always more and more."

It is easy to pray, to ask for a grace from the Lord, "to give thanks," or when "we need something." But it is fundamental to pray to the Lord for all, for those who have "received the same Baptism," saying "they are yours, they are ours, protect them.

"Entrusting the Church to the Lord is a prayer that makes the Church grow. It is also an act of faith. We cannot do anything, we are poor servants—all of us—of the Church: he is the one who can move it forward and protect it and make it grow, make it holy, defend it, defend it from the prince of this world and from what he wants the Church to become, more and more worldly. This is the greatest danger! When the Church becomes worldly, when it has within itself the spirit of the world, when it has that peace which is not of the Lord—that peace when Jesus says, 'Peace I leave with you;

my peace I give to you. Not as the world gives'—when it has that worldly peace, the Church is a weak Church, a Church that will be defeated and incapable of carrying the Gospel, the message of the Cross, the scandal of the Cross . . . It cannot carry it forward if it is worldly.

"Entrusting the Church to the Lord, entrusting the elderly, the sick, children, young people . . . 'Protect your Church, Lord': it is yours! With this attitude he will give us, in the midst of tribulations, that peace which only he can give. That peace which the world cannot give, that peace which cannot be bought, that peace which is a true gift of the presence of Jesus in the midst of his Church. Entrusting the Church, which is in tribulation: there are great tribulations, persecution . . . They are there. But there are also the little tribulations: the little tribulations of sickness or family problems . . . Entrust all of this to the Lord: protect your Church in tribulation, that it may not lose faith, that it may not lose hope.

"May the Lord make us strong so that we may not lose faith, not lose hope": this must always be the heart's request to the Lord.

"Making this prayer of entrustment for the Church will do us good and will do the Church good. It will bring great peace to us and great peace to the Church. It will not take our tribulations away, but it will make us strong in tribulations."

April 30, 2013   *Acts 14:19–28 ✠ John 14:27–31a*

28

It is an unjust society that does not give work or exploits workers

S ociety is not just if it does not offer everyone a job or exploits
   workers. In the Gospel, Jesus is called "the carpenter's son." Joseph was a laborer, and Jesus learned to work with him. God works
to create the world. This "icon of God the laborer tells us that work
is something more than earning our bread.

"Work gives us dignity! He who works is worthy, he has a special
dignity, a dignity as a person: the man and woman who work are
worthy. But those who do not work do not have this dignity. But
there are many who want to work and cannot. This is a weight on
our conscience, because when society is organized in this way, that
not everyone has the possibility to work, to be united by the dignity
of work, that society is not okay: it is not just! It is going against God
himself, who has wanted our dignity to begin from here.

"Dignity does not come from power, money, culture, no! We get
dignity from work!" And worthy work, because today so many "social, political, and economic systems have made a choice that means
exploiting the person.

"Not to pay what is right, not to give work, because I am looking
only at the bottom line, at the company bottom line; I'm looking only at what I can gain. That goes against God! How many
times—so many times—have we read in *L'Osservatore Romano* . . .
One headline really hit me on the day of the tragedy in Bangladesh,
LIVING ON FIFTY DOLLARS A MONTH: this was the pay of these people
who died . . . And this is called slave labor! And today in this world
there is this slavery that is built on the most beautiful thing that
God has given to man: the capacity to create, to work, to make this
his dignity. How many brothers and sisters in the world are in this
situation because of these economic, social, political attitudes? . . ."

In the Middle Ages a rabbi told his Jewish community the story of
the Tower of Babel. At the time bricks were very expensive. "When
a brick fell by mistake there was a tremendous problem, a scandal:
'Look what you have done!' But if one of those building the tower

fell: 'Rest in peace!' And they left him alone . . . A brick was more important than a person. This was what that medieval rabbi was talking about, and it's happening now! Persons are less important than the things that make profits for those who have political, social, economic power. What have we come to? To the point that we are unaware of this dignity of the person, this dignity of work. But today the figures of Saint Joseph, of Jesus, of God, who work—these are our models—show us the way to dignity."

Today we can no longer say what Saint Paul said: "He who does not work, let him not eat," but we must say: "He who does not work, he has lost his dignity!" Because "he does not find the possibility for work." More than that: "Society has stripped this person of dignity!" It would be good for us today to listen to "the voice of God when he spoke to Cain" saying to him: "Where is your brother Abel?" Today, instead, we hear this voice: "Where is your brother who does not have work? Where is your brother who is under slave labor? Let's pray, let's pray for all these brothers and sisters who are in this situation."

May 1, 2013   *Acts 15:1–6 ⚜ John 15:1–8*

29

The Church is a community of the "yes"

The Church is a community of the "yes" because it is born from the love of Christ. When Christians do not let the Holy Spirit work, then divisions begin in the Church.

Let's think of the first steps of the founders of the Church who, after Pentecost, went out to the "peripheries" to proclaim the Gospel. The Holy Spirit does two things: "first he pushes" and even creates "problems," and then "he makes harmony in the Church." So in Jerusalem, among the first disciples, "there were many opinions" on welcoming pagans into the Church. There were some who said no and some who were open:

"There was a Church of 'no, we can't; no, no, we must, we must, we must,' and a Church of 'yes, but . . . let's think about it, open ourselves, there is the Spirit who opens the door for us.' The Holy Spirit had to do the second part of his work: make harmony from these positions, the harmony of the Church, between those in Jerusalem and between them and the pagans. It is a wonderful work that he always does, the Holy Spirit, in history. And when we don't let him work, divisions begin in the Church, sects, all of these things . . . Because we are closed to the truth of the Spirit."

So what is the key word in this dispute over the origins of the Church? Let's remember the inspired words of Peter, who emphasizes how we must not place on the necks of the disciples a yoke that the fathers themselves were not capable of bearing:

"When the service of the Lord becomes such a heavy yoke, the doors of Christian communities are closed: no one wants to come to the Lord. We believe instead that we are saved by the grace of the Lord Jesus. First this joy of the charism of proclaiming the grace, then let's see what we'll do. This word, 'yoke,' comes to my heart, comes to my mind."

But what does it mean today, in the Church, to bear a yoke? Jesus asks all of us to remain in his love. So it is precisely from this love that the observance of his commandments is born. This is "the

Christian community of the 'yes' " that remains in the love of Christ and sometimes says no "because there is that yes." It is this love that "leads us to fidelity to the Lord . . . Because I love the Lord, I will not do this" or that.

"It is a community of the 'yes,' and the 'nos' are a result of this 'yes.' Let's ask the Lord that the Holy Spirit may always help us to become this community of love, of love for Jesus, who has loved us so much. A community of this 'yes.' And this 'yes' leads to the fulfillment of the commandments. A community with open doors. And that he may defend us from the temptation of perhaps becoming puritan, in the etymological sense of the word, from seeking a para-evangelical purity, a community of the 'no.' Because Jesus first asks us for love, love for him, and to remain in his love."

So "when a Christian community lives in love, it confesses its sins, worships the Lord, forgives offenses." And also "has charity for others" and "the manifestation of love" and thus "feels the obligation of fidelity to the Lord, to fulfill his commandments."

May 2, 2013   *Acts 15:7–21* ✠ *John 15:9–11*

30

The Church must be courageous

All Christians have the duty to transmit the faith with courage. Jesus invites us to have courage in prayer as well, and has urged Christians not to be lukewarm.

"May the Lord give all of us" the "grace of courage" and "perseverance" in prayer. All of us Christians who have received the faith "must transmit it, we must proclaim it with our lives, with our words." But then what is this fundamental faith? It is "faith in Jesus Risen, in Jesus, who has forgiven our sins with his death and has reconciled us with the Father.

"And transmitting this requires us to be courageous, to have the courage of transmitting the faith. A courage that is sometimes simple. Pardon me, but let me tell a personal story: When I was a child, my grandma took us to the candlelight procession every Good Friday, and at the end of the procession there came Christ lying lifeless, and my grandma had us kneel down and said to us, to us children: 'Look, he is dead, but tomorrow he will be risen!' This is how faith came in: faith in Christ dead and risen. In the history of the Church there have been many, so many who have wanted to blur this powerful certainty and speak of a spiritual resurrection. No, Christ is alive!

"Christ is alive," and he is "also alive among us!" Christians must have the courage to proclaim his Resurrection, the Good News. But there is also another courage that Jesus asks of us.

"Jesus—to put it a little more strongly—challenges us to engage in prayer and says this: 'Whatever you ask in my name, I will do, so that the Father may be glorified in the Son.' If you ask for anything in my name, I will do it . . . This is big! Let's have the courage to go to Jesus and ask him: 'But you said you would do this, do it! Make faith move forward, make evangelization move forward, resolve this problem that I have . . .' Do we have this courage in prayer? Or do we pray however, as we can, spending a little time in prayer? But that courage, that candor even in prayer . . ."

In the Bible we read that Abraham and Moses have the courage to "negotiate with the Lord." A courage "on behalf of others, on behalf of the Church," that is also needed today:

"When the Church loses courage, the atmosphere of lukewarmness enters the Church. The lukewarm, lukewarm Christians, without courage . . . That does so much harm to the Church, because lukewarmness turns us inward, and problems begin among us; we do not have horizons, we do not have courage, not even the courage of prayer to heaven and not even the courage to proclaim the Gospel. We are lukewarm . . . And we do not have the courage to deal with our little things, our jealousies, our envy, our careerism, in moving forward egotistically . . . In all these things, but this is not good for the Church. The Church must be courageous! We must all be courageous in prayer, challenging Jesus."

May 3, 2013   *1 Corinthians 15:1–8* ✠ *John 14:6–14*

31

Be meek and humble to conquer the hatred of the world

Humility and meekness are the weapons that we have to defend ourselves from the hatred of the world. This homily is centered on the struggle between the love of Christ and the hatred of the prince of the world. The Lord tells us not to be afraid because the world will hate us as it hated him.

"The path of Christians is the path of Jesus. If we want to be followers of Jesus, there is no path other than the one he showed us. And one of the results of this is hatred; it is the hatred of the world, and also of the prince of this world. The world would love what is its own. 'I have chosen you out of the world.' It is he himself who has ransomed us from the world, who has chosen us: pure grace! With his death, with his Resurrection, he has ransomed us from the power of the world, from the power of the devil, from the power of the prince of this world. And the origin of the hatred is this: we are saved. And that prince who does not want this, who does not want us to be saved, hates."

So the hatred and persecution of the early Church continue today. There are "so many Christian communities that are persecuted in the world at this time, more than in the early years: today, now, in these days and in this hour." Why is this? Because "the spirit of the world hates." And this leads to a warning that is always relevant.

"With the prince of this world there is no dialogue: let this be clear! Today dialogue is necessary among us, it is necessary for peace. Dialogue is a habit; it is precisely an attitude that we must have among ourselves in order to hear each other, to understand each other . . . That must continue always. Dialogue arises from charity, from love. But with that prince of this world there is no dialogue, only responding with the Word of God, which defends us, because the world hates us. And what it did with Jesus it will do with us. 'But look, do this, it's just cutting corners a little . . . It's nothing, it's a little thing . . .' And it begins to take us down a way that is not quite right. This is a seductive lie: 'Do it, do it, there's no problem,' and it starts small, that's always the way it is, right? And: 'But you're good, you're sharp, you can do it.' It flatters us, and with flattery it butters us up. That's what it does. And then we fall into the trap."

The Lord asks us to remain lambs, because if we stop being lambs, then we do not have "a shepherd who defends us, and we fall into the hands of these wolves.

"You can ask this question: Father, what is the weapon for defending us from these seductions, from these fireworks that the prince of this world puts on? From this flattery? The weapon is the very weapon of Jesus: the Word of God—not dialogue, but always the Word of God and then humility and meekness. Let's think about Jesus, when they strike him: what humility, what meekness! He could have insulted them, right? Just a question, meek and humble. Let's think of Jesus and his Passion. His prophet says: Like a sheep led to the slaughter. He does not cry out, nothing: humility. Humility and meekness. These are the weapons that the prince of the world and the spirit of the world do not tolerate, because their offerings are offerings of worldly power, offerings of vanity, offerings of dishonest wealth, offerings like that."

Today "Jesus makes us think of this hatred that the world has against us, against the followers of Jesus." It hates us "because he has saved us, he has ransomed us." And let's think of the "weapons to defend ourselves": to remain always lambs, "because in this way we have a shepherd, and being lambs, let us be meek and humble." Finally, let us invoke the Blessed Mother so that "she may help us to become humble and meek in the way of Jesus."

May 4, 2013   *Acts 16:1–10 ✝ John 15:18–21*

32

The Holy Spirit, our traveling companion and friend

The Holy Spirit is our friend and traveling companion, and tells us where Jesus is. The Holy Spirit is "God, the Person God, who gives witness to Jesus Christ in us" and protects us. "Jesus calls him the Paraclete, meaning the one who defends us," who "is always by our side to support us.

"Christian life cannot be understood without the presence of the Holy Spirit; it would not be Christian. It would be a religious life of pagan piety that believes in God but without the vitality that Jesus wants for his disciples. And what gives vitality is the Holy Spirit, present."

The Spirit "gives witness" to Jesus "so that we can give it to others."

"There is something beautiful in the first reading: that woman who listens to Paul, named Lydia. It is said that the Lord opened her heart so that she could respond to Paul's words. This is what the Holy Spirit does: he opens our hearts to know Jesus. Without him we cannot know Jesus. He prepares us for the encounter with Jesus. He takes us along the way of Jesus. The Holy Spirit acts in us throughout the whole day, during our whole life, as a witness who tells us where Jesus is."

Prayer is the way to have, at "every moment," the grace of the "fecundity of Easter," a richness that is possible thanks to the Holy Spirit. And the examination of conscience, "which Christians make over the day they have lived," is an "exercise" that "is good for us because it means making ourselves truly aware of what the Lord has done in our hearts.

"Let's ask for the grace to accustom ourselves to the presence of this traveling companion, the Holy Spirit, of this witness of Jesus who tells us where Jesus is, how to find Jesus, what Jesus is telling us. To have a certain familiarity: he is a friend. Jesus said it: 'No, I am not leaving you alone, I am leaving you Him.' Jesus leaves him to us as a friend. Let's get into the habit of asking ourselves, before the end of the day: 'What has the Holy Spirit done in me today? What testimony has he given me? How has he spoken to me? What has he suggested to me?' Because he is a divine presence who moves us forward in our life as Christians. Let's ask for this grace, today. And this will mean that, as we have asked in prayer, at every moment we have present the fecundity of Easter."

May 6, 2013   *Acts 16:11–15* ✤ *John 15:26–16:4a*

33

A good Christian doesn't complain

Even in tribulations Christians are joyful, and never sad. Paul and Silas, called to confront imprisonment and persecution in order to bear witness to the Gospel, were joyful because they were following Jesus on the way of his Passion. A way that the Lord travels with patience.

"Entering into patience: this is the way that Jesus also teaches to us Christians. Entering into patience . . . This does not mean being sad. No, no, it is something else! It means enduring, bearing the weight of difficulties on our shoulders, the weight of contradictions, the weight of tribulations. This Christian attitude of endurance: entering into patience. What the Bible says with a Greek word that is so rich, *hypomoné,* enduring life's labor day after day: the contradictions, the tribulations, all of this. They—Paul and Silas—endured tribulations, they endured humiliations. Jesus endured these, he entered into patience. This is a process—allow me to use the word 'process'—a process of Christian maturation, through the way of patience. A process that takes time, that is not accomplished overnight; it takes a whole lifetime to come to Christian maturity. It is like a good wine."

So many martyrs were joyful, as for example the martyrs of Nagasaki who helped one another, "waiting for the moment of death." It is said of some martyrs that "they went to martyrdom" as to a "wedding banquet." This attitude of endurance is the normal attitude of the Christian, but it is not a masochistic attitude. It is instead an attitude that leads us "along the way of Jesus."

"When difficulties come, so many temptations arrive as well. For example, complaining: 'But look at what's happening to me' . . . a complaint. And a Christian who continually complains gives up being a good Christian; he is Mr. Whiner or she is Mrs. Whiner, right? Because they're always complaining about everything, right? Silence in endurance, silence in patience. That silence of Jesus: Jesus in his Passion did not speak anymore, only two or three necessary words . . . But it is also not a sad silence; the silence of enduring the Cross is not a sad silence. It is sorrowful, so often it is very sorrowful, but it is not sad. The heart is in peace. Paul and Silas prayed in peace. They had sorrows, because it is said that the jailer washed their wounds—they had wounds—but they endured them in peace. This way of enduring deepens our Christian peace; it makes us strong in Jesus."

So the Christian is called to endure as Jesus did, "without complaints, enduring in peace." And this "going in patience renews our youth and makes us younger.

"The patient person is the one who, in the long run, is younger! Think of the elderly in retirement homes, those who have endured so much in their lives. Look into their eyes; they have young eyes, they have a young spirit and a renewed youth. This is what the Lord is calling us to: to this Paschal youth that has been renewed by the way of love, of patience, of enduring tribulations, and also—allow me to say this—of bearing with one another. Because we must also do this with charity and love; because if I must bear with you, I am sure that you are bearing with me, and thus we go forward in the journey on the path of Jesus. Let's ask the Lord for this grace of Christian endurance that gives us peace, this enduring with the heart, this joyful enduring in order to become ever younger, like good wine: younger with this renewed Paschal youth of the spirit."

May 7, 2013   *Acts 16:22–34 ✢ John 16:5–11*

34

Christians must build bridges, not walls

Evangelization does not mean proselytism. The Christian who wants to proclaim the Gospel must dialogue with all, knowing that no one possesses the truth, because the truth is received in the encounter with Jesus.

Christians today must be like Paul, who, speaking to the Greeks in the Areopagus, built bridges to proclaim the Gospel without condemning anyone. Paul's "courageous" attitude "draws closer to the heart" of the one listening to him, "seeking dialogue." This is why the Apostle of the Gentiles was truly a "pontiff, a builder of bridges," and not a "builder of walls." This makes us think of the attitude that a Christian must always have.

"A Christian must proclaim Jesus Christ in such a way that Jesus Christ is accepted, received, not rejected. And Paul knows that he must sow this evangelical message. He knows that proclaiming Jesus Christ is not easy, but that it does not depend on him. He must do all he can, but proclaiming Jesus Christ, proclaiming the truth, depends on the Holy Spirit. Jesus tells us in the Gospel today: 'When he comes, the Spirit of truth, he will guide you to all truth.' Paul does not say to the Athenians: 'This is the encyclopedia of truth. Study this and you will have the truth, the truth!' No! The truth does not fit in an encyclopedia. Truth is an encounter; it is an encounter with the supreme truth: Jesus, the great truth. No one is master of the truth. Truth is received in the encounter."

But why did Paul act this way? In the first place, because "this is the way" of Jesus, who "spoke with all," with sinners, tax collectors, the scholars of the law. So Paul "is following the attitude of Jesus.

"The Christian who wants to bear the Gospel must go by this path: to listen to everyone! Now is a good time in the life of the Church: these past fifty years, sixty years have been a good time, because I remember when I was a boy we were told in our Catholic families, in my family: 'No, we can't go to their house, because they were not married by the Church!' It was a sort of exclusion. No, you couldn't go! Or because they are socialists or atheists, we can't go. Now—thanks to God—no, we don't say that, do we? We don't say that! There was a sort of defense of the faith, but with walls; the Lord made bridges. First: Paul has this attitude, because it was the attitude of Jesus. Second: Paul is aware that he must evangelize, not make proselytes."

The Church, as Benedict XVI often reiterated, "does not grow through proselytism" but "grows through attraction, through witness, through preaching." And Paul has precisely this attitude: he proclaims, he does not proselytize. And he succeeds in acting this way because "he did not doubt his Lord. Christians who are afraid of bridges and prefer to build walls are Christians who are not sure of their faith, not sure of Jesus Christ." Christians instead should do as Paul did, and begin "to build bridges and move forward.

"Paul teaches us this way of evangelizing, because this is what Jesus did, because he is well aware that evangelization is not proselytism; it is because he is sure of Jesus Christ and has no need to justify himself and seek reasons to justify himself. When the Church loses this apostolic courage, it becomes a stationary Church, well organized, beautiful, everything beautiful, but without fecundity, because it has lost the courage of going to the peripheries, where there are so many people who are victims of idolatry, of worldliness, of weak thinking, . . . so many things. Let's ask Saint Paul today to give us this apostolic courage, this spiritual fervor, of being sure. 'But, Father, we might make mistakes' . . . 'Keep going. If you make a mistake, get up and keep going: that is the way.' Those who do not move because they are afraid of making a mistake, they are making a more serious mistake."

May 8, 2013   *Acts 17:15, 22–18:1* ✤ *John 16:12–15*

35

Christian joy is not the gladness of a moment

"The Christian is a man or woman of joy." But the joy of the Christian is not the gladness that comes from temporary conditions, it is a gift of the Lord that fills us inside. May the Christian be a witness of the true joy, that which Jesus gives.

"The Christian is a man or woman of joy. This is what Jesus is teaching us, what the Church is teaching us at this time in a special way. What is it, this joy? Is it having fun? No, it is not the same thing. Having fun is good, enjoying ourselves is good. But joy is something more, it is something else. It is something that does not come from temporary conditions, from the conditions of the moment; it is something more profound. It is a gift. If we try to have fun all the time, it becomes frivolous, superficial, and it also deprives us of Christian wisdom; it makes us a bit stupid and naïve, doesn't it? Everything is fun . . . No. Joy is something else. Joy is a gift of the Lord. It fills us up inside. It is like an anointing of the Spirit. And this joy is in the confidence that Jesus is with us and with the Father."

The joyful person is a confident person. Confident that "Jesus is with us, that Jesus is with the Father." But can we "bottle this joy a bit, to have it always with us?

"No, because if we want to have this joy only for ourselves, in the end we get sick and our hearts become a bit worn out, and our faces do not transmit that great joy but a nostalgia, a melancholy that is not healthy. Sometimes these melancholy Christians have faces more like pickled peppers than those of joyful people with a beautiful life. Joy cannot stand still; it has to move. Joy is a pilgrim virtue. It is a gift that walks, that walks on the path of life, walks with Jesus: preaching, proclaiming Jesus, joy, lengthening the road and widening the road. It is precisely a virtue of the great, of those greats who are above trivialities, who are above this human pettiness, who do not let themselves get caught up in the little things inside the community, the Church; they're always looking to the horizon."

Joy is a "pilgrim. The Christian sings with joy, and walks, and carries this joy." It is a virtue of the journey, or rather more than a virtue, it is a gift.

"It is the gift that leads us to the virtue of magnanimity. The Christian is magnanimous, he cannot be pusillanimous; he is magnanimous. And magnanimity is a virtue of vitality, it is a virtue of always moving forward, but with that spirit full of the Holy Spirit. It is a grace that we must ask from the Lord, joy. In these days in a special way, the Church invites us to ask for joy and also for desire. That which carries forward the life of the Christian is desire. The greater your desire is, the greater your joy will be. The Christian is a man, a woman of desire: always desiring more on the road of life. Let's ask the Lord for this grace, this gift of the Spirit: Christian joy. Far from sadness, far from simple fun . . . it is something else. It is a grace to be asked."

May 10, 2013   *Acts 18:9–18 ✤ John 16:20–23*

36

True prayer brings us out of ourselves

Trunk rue prayer brings us out of ourselves and opens us to the Father and to our needy brothers and sisters. In the Gospel, Jesus says: "Whatever you ask the Father in my name he will give you." "There is something new here, something that has changed; it is something new in prayer. The Father will give us everything, but always in the name of Jesus." The Lord ascends to the Father, he enters "into the sanctuary of heaven," he opens the doors and leaves them open because "he himself is the door" and "intercedes for us, until the end of the world," as a priest.

"He is praying for us before the Father. I have always liked this. Jesus, in his Resurrection, had a beautiful body: the wounds of the scourging, of the thorns, have disappeared, all of them. The bruises have disappeared. But he wanted to keep the wounds [of the nails], and these are precisely his prayer of intercession before the Father: 'But . . . look . . . I am asking you for this in my name, look!' This is the newness that Jesus is asking of us. He is telling us this news: have trust in his Passion, have trust in his victory over death, have trust in his wounds. He is the priest, and this is the sacrifice: his wounds. And this gives us confidence, it gives us the courage to pray."

So often we get bored in prayer. Prayer is not asking for this or that but is "the intercession of Jesus, who before the Father shows him his wounds.

"Prayer to the Father in the name of Jesus brings us out of ourselves; the prayer that bores us is always inside of ourselves, like a thought that comes and goes. But true prayer is getting out of ourselves to the Father in the name of Jesus; it is an exodus from ourselves."

But how "can we recognize the wounds of Jesus in heaven? Where is the school where we learn to know the wounds of Jesus, these priestly wounds, of intercession? There is another exodus from ourselves toward the wounds of our brothers: of our brothers and sisters in need.

"If we do not succeed in coming out of ourselves to our needy brothers, to the sick, the ignorant, the poor, the exploited, if we are not able to make this exit from ourselves toward those wounds, we will never learn the freedom that leads us to the other exit from ourselves, to the wounds of Jesus. There are two exits from ourselves: one toward the wounds of Jesus, the other toward the wounds of our brothers and sisters. And this is the path that Jesus wants our prayer to take.

"This is the new way to pray: with the trust, the courage that we get from knowing that Jesus is before the Father showing him his wounds, but also with the humility of those who go to know, to find the wounds of Jesus in his needy brothers" who "still carry the Cross and have not yet overcome, as Jesus overcame."

May 11, 2013   *Acts 18:23–28 ✤ John 16:23b–28*

37

The Holy Spirit is the unknown quantity of our faith

It is the Holy Spirit who permits the Christian to have the "memory" of the history and gifts received from God. Without this grace, there is the risk of slipping into idolatry.

The response that Saint Paul receives from a group of disciples of Ephesus, presented in the Acts of the Apostles, is surprising: "We have never even heard that there is a Holy Spirit." These words astonish Paul, but one can observe with realism that the lack of awareness manifested by Christians two thousand years ago is not only "something from early on; the Holy Spirit is always to some extent the unknown of our faith.

"Now so many Christians do not know who the Holy Spirit is, what the Holy Spirit is like. And sometimes we hear: 'But I'm doing just fine with the Father and the Son, because I pray the Our Father to the Father, I receive communion with the Son, but with the Holy Spirit I don't know what to do . . .' Or they say: 'The Holy Spirit is the dove, the one who gives us the seven gifts.' But this way the poor Holy Spirit is always last, and does not find a good place in our lives."

Instead the Holy Spirit is "God active in us, God who reminds us," who "awakens our memory." Jesus himself explains this to the apostles before Pentecost: he will send the Spirit of God to them in his name, he pledges, and "he will remind you of everything I have said." For a Christian, when the Holy Spirit is ignored, a dangerous slope appears.

"A Christian without memory is not a true Christian; he is a man or woman who is a prisoner of the circumstances, of the moment, with no history. He has it, but he doesn't know how to take hold of history. It is precisely the Spirit who teaches him how to take hold of history. The memory of history . . . When in the letter to the Hebrews the author says: 'Remember your fathers in the faith'—memory—'remember the first days of your faith, how courageous you were'—memory. The memory of our lives, of our history, the memory of the moment when we had the grace of encountering Jesus, the memory of all that Jesus has told us.

"That memory which comes from the heart, that is a grace of the Holy Spirit." And having memory also means remembering our miseries, which make us slaves, together with the grace of God, which redeems us from those miseries.

"And when a little vanity comes in, and we think we've won some sort of Nobel Prize for holiness, memory is good for us then too. 'But . . . remember where I took you from: from the back of the flock. You were in the back, in the flock.' Memory is a great grace, and when a Christian does not have memory—this is tough, but it's the truth—he is not a Christian; he is an idolater. Because he is before a god without a path, a god who can't go anywhere, and our God journeys with us, mingles with us, walks with us. He makes history with us. When we remember all of this, life becomes more fruitful, with this grace of memory."

The invitation is to ask for the grace of memory in order to be persons who do not forget the road we have traveled, "do not forget the graces in our lives, do not forget the forgiveness of our sins, do not forget that we were slaves and the Lord saved us."

May 13, 2013   *Acts 19:1–8 ✤ John 16:29–33*

38

He who gives his life for love is never alone

What we need is a "big heart" that is capable of love. The way of love is contrasted with that of selfishness, which we have to guard ourselves against because, as happened with Judas, it leads to the isolation of conscience and finally to the betrayal of Jesus.

If we truly want to follow Jesus, we must "live life as a gift" to be given to others, "not as a treasure to be kept." Jesus has strong words for us: "No one has a love stronger than this: to give one's life." But today's liturgy also shows us another person: Judas, "who had the exact opposite attitude." And this because Judas "never understood what a gift is.

"Let's think of that moment when a woman washed the feet of Jesus with the nard, so expensive: it is a religious moment, a moment of gratitude, a moment of love. And Judas stands apart with bitter criticism: 'But this could have been used for the poor!' This is the first reference that I have found, in the Gospel, to poverty as an ideology. The ideologue does not know what love is, because he does not know how to give himself."

Judas "stood apart, in his solitude" and this attitude of selfishness grew "to the point of betraying Jesus." He who loves "gives life as a gift"; the egotist, instead, "looks out for himself, grows in selfishness, and becomes a betrayer, but always alone." But he who "gives his life for love is never alone: he is always in community, in family." Moreover, the one who "isolates his conscience and selfishness" ultimately "loses [his life]." This is how Judas ended up, being "an idolater, attached to money.

"And this idolatry led him to isolate himself from the community of the others. This is the drama of the isolated conscience: when a Christian begins to isolate himself, he also isolates his conscience from the mind-set of the community, from the mind-set of the Church, from that love which Jesus gives to us. But the Christian who gives his life, who 'loses it,' as Jesus says, finds it, finds it again, in fullness. And the one, like Judas, who wants to keep it for himself, loses it in the end. John tells us that at that moment Satan entered into the heart of Judas. And we have to say this: Satan is a terrible paymaster. He always cheats us: always!"

Jesus, however, always loves and always gives himself. And this gift of his love drives us to love in order "to bear fruit. And the fruit remains."

"In these days of waiting for the feast of the Holy Spirit, let us ask: come, Holy Spirit, come and give me this big heart, this heart that is capable of loving with humility, with meekness, but always this big heart that is capable of love. And let's ask for this grace, from the Holy Spirit. And may he always free us from the other way, that of selfishness, which ultimately comes to a bad end. Let's ask for this grace."

May 14, 2013   *Acts 1:15–17, 20–26 ✢ John 15:9–17*

39

Pray for priests and bishops that they may be shepherds and not wolves

Pray for priests and bishops, that they may not give in to the temptations of money and vanity, but may be at the service of the People of God. Our reflection begins with the passage from the Acts of the Apostles in which Paul urges the "elders" of the Church of Ephesus to watch over themselves and over the whole flock, to be shepherds on the lookout for the "savage wolves." This is one of the "most beautiful pages of the New Testament, full of tenderness, of pastoral love," in which emerges the "beautiful relationship of the bishop with his people." Bishops and priests are at the service of others, to protect, edify, and defend the people. It is "a relationship of protection, of love between God and the pastor and the pastor and the people.

"In the end a bishop is not a bishop for himself, he is for the people; and a priest is not a priest for himself, he is for the people: at the service of the people, to build them up, to feed the people, his flock, right? To defend it from the wolves. This is such a beautiful thought! When the bishop does this he has a wonderful relationship with the people, as the bishop Paul did with his people, right? And when a priest has this wonderful relationship with the people, it brings us love: there is a love between them, a true love, and the Church becomes united."

The relationship of the bishop and of the priest with the people is an "existential, sacramental" relationship. "We need your prayers," because "the bishop and the priest can be tempted too." Bishops and priests must pray a great deal, proclaim Jesus Christ risen, and "preach that message of salvation with courage. But we too are men, and we are sinners," and "we are tempted." And what are the temptations of the bishop and the priest?

"Saint Augustine, commenting on the prophet Ezekiel, speaks of two of these: wealth, which can become avarice, and vanity. And he says: 'When the bishop or priest profits by the sheep for himself, the direction changes: it is not the priest or bishop for the people, but the priest or bishop takes from the people.' Saint Augustine says: 'He takes the food from the lambs and eats it, he profits for himself; he does deals and is attached to money; he becomes greedy and so many times even simoniac. Or he profits from the wool for the sake of vanity, to gloat over it.' "

So "when a priest, a bishop follows after money, the people do not love him, and that is a sign. But he himself will come to a bad end." Saint Paul recalls having worked with his hands; "he didn't have a bank account, he worked. And when a bishop, a priest follows the way of vanity, enters into the spirit of careerism—and this does so much harm to the Church—he becomes ridiculous in the end, bragging, showing off, such a big shot . . . and the people don't love him!" Pray for us, "that we may be poor, that we may be humble, meek, at the service of the people." The suggestion is what we read in chapter 20, verses 28–30 of the Acts of the Apostles, where Paul says: "Keep watch over yourselves and over the whole flock of which the Holy Spirit has appointed you overseers, in which you tend the Church of God that he acquired with his own blood. I know that after my departure savage wolves will come among you, and they will not spare the flock. And from your own group, men will come forward perverting the truth to draw the disciples away after them."

"Read this beautiful page and in reading it pray, pray for us bishops and for priests. We have so great a need to remain faithful, to be men who watch over the flock and also over ourselves, who stand our own watch, whose hearts are always turned to our flock. And also that the Lord may defend us from temptations, because if we go down the way of wealth, if we go down the way of vanity, we become wolves and not shepherds. Pray for this, read this and pray."

May 15, 2013   *Acts 20:28–38 ✣ John 17:11b–19*

40

The Church needs apostolic fervor

The Church has such need of the apostolic fervor that drives us forward in proclaiming Jesus. We have to take care not to become "armchair Christians" without the courage to "mix things up when they are too sedate."

Paul's whole life was a "battle," a "life with so many trials." The Apostle of the Gentiles spent his life going "from persecution to persecution," but he did not get discouraged. Paul's destiny "is a destiny with so many Crosses, but he moves forward; he looks to the Lord and moves forward.

"Paul is a nuisance: he is a man who with his preaching, his work, his attitude, is a nuisance, because he proclaims Jesus Christ, and the proclamation of Jesus Christ amid our comforts, so often amid our comfortable structures—even Christian ones, right?—is a nuisance. The Lord always wants us to go forward, forward, forward . . . Not for us to take refuge in a tranquil life or in fleeting structures, these things, right? Paul, preaching the Lord, was a nuisance. But he moved forward, because he had within himself that attitude which is so Christian it becomes apostolic zeal. He really had apostolic fervor. He was not a man of compromise. No! The truth: forward! The proclamation of Jesus Christ: forward!"

Saint Paul was certainly a "fiery man." But this is not only a matter of his temperament. It is the Lord who "gets involved in this," in this battle. More than that, it is the Lord himself who pushes Paul to "go forward," to bear witness even in Rome.

"As an aside, I like the fact that the Lord has been concerned about this diocese, even from that time . . . We are privileged! And apostolic zeal is not enthusiasm for power, to have something. It is something that comes from inside, that the Lord himself wants from us: Christians with apostolic zeal. And where does this apostolic zeal come from? It comes from knowing Jesus Christ. Paul found Jesus Christ, he encountered Jesus Christ, but not within intellectual, scientific knowledge—that is important, because it helps us—but with that first knowledge, that of the heart, of the personal encounter."

This is what pushes Paul to go forward, "to proclaim Jesus always. He is always in trouble, but in trouble not for the sake of trouble but for Jesus," in proclaiming Jesus "the consequences are these." Apostolic fervor can be understood only "in an atmosphere of love." Apostolic zeal "has something crazy about it, but a spiritual craziness, a sane craziness." And Paul "had this sane craziness." The exhortation to all of the faithful is that of asking the Holy Spirit to make this apostolic zeal grow in us, because it should not belong only to missionaries. On the other hand, also within the Church there are "lukewarm Christians," who "do not feel like moving forward."

"There are also armchair Christians, right? Educated, everything great, but they don't know how to bear children for the Church with proclamation and apostolic fervor. Today may we ask the Holy Spirit to give this apostolic fervor to all of us, even to give us the grace of mixing up things that are too sedate in the Church, the grace of going forward to the existential peripheries. The Church has such need of this! Not only in faraway lands, in young churches, in peoples that do not yet know Jesus Christ, but here in the city, right in the city, they need this proclamation of Jesus Christ. So let's ask the Holy Spirit for this grace of apostolic zeal, Christians with apostolic zeal. And if we are a nuisance, blessed be the Lord. Forward, as the Lord says to Paul: 'Courage!'"

May 16, 2013   *Acts 22:30; 23:6–11 ✢ John 17:20–26*

41

The problem is not in being sinners

The problem is not in being sinners, the problem is when we don't let ourselves be transformed in love by the encounter with Christ. In today's Gospel the Risen Jesus asks Peter three times if he loves him. "It is a dialogue of love, between the Lord and his disciple": from that first "follow me" to the new name—"You will be called Cephas, Rock"—which is also his mission, and even if "Peter didn't understand any of this . . . The mission was there." Then, when Peter recognizes him as the Christ and immediately afterward says no to the way of the Cross, Jesus responds: "Get away from me, Satan!" and "he accepts this humiliation." Peter often "thought he was special"; in Gethsemane he is "fiery" and "takes up the sword" to defend Jesus, but then he denies him three times. And when Jesus looks at him with that gaze that is "so beautiful," Peter weeps. "In these encounters it is as if Jesus is ripening the soul of Peter, the heart of Peter," he is ripening him in love. So when Peter hears Jesus ask him three times: "Simon, son of John, do you love me?" he is ashamed, because he remembers when he said three times that he did not know him.

"Peter was saddened when he asked him for the third time 'Do you love me?' This sadness, this shame . . . A great man, this Peter . . . sinner, sinner. But the Lord helps him to understand, and us as well, that we are all sinners. The problem is not in being sinners; the problem is when we do not repent of our sins, when we are not ashamed of what we have done. That is the problem. And Peter has this shame, this humility, doesn't he? The sin, the sin of Peter, is something that with the great heart that Peter had, led him to a new encounter with Jesus, to the joy of forgiveness."

The Lord does not give up on his promise, when he said to him "you are rock," and now he says to him "feed my flock" and "hands over his flock to a sinner.

"Peter was a sinner, but he was not corrupt. Sinners, yes, everyone; corrupt, no. I once knew a priest, a good pastor who worked hard; he was appointed bishop, and he was ashamed because he did not feel worthy, he was in spiritual turmoil. And he went to his confessor. The confessor listened to him and said: 'Don't be afraid. If Peter made that huge mistake, and he was made pope, you go ahead!' That's the way the Lord is. The Lord is like that. The Lord helps us to mature with so many encounters with him, even with our weaknesses, when we recognize them, with our sins . . ."

Peter "truly allowed himself to be molded" by his "many encounters with Jesus," and this "is necessary for all of us, because we are on the same path. Peter is a great man" not "because he is talented" but because "he is noble, he has a noble heart, and this nobility brings him to tears; it brings him to this pain, to this shame and also to take up his work of feeding the flock.

"Let's ask the Lord, today, that this example of the life of a man who continually comes into encounter with the Lord and is purified by the Lord, becoming more mature with these encounters, may help us to move forward, seeking the Lord and encountering him, having an encounter with him. But more important than this is allowing the Lord to encounter us. He is always seeking us, he is always close to us. So many times we are looking somewhere else because we don't want to talk with the Lord or to allow ourselves to encounter the Lord. But it is more important to allow the Lord to encounter us: this is a grace. This is the grace that Peter teaches us. Let's ask for this grace today."

May 17, 2013   *Acts 25:13b–21* ✢ *John 21:15–19*

42

Gossip in the Church is harmful

The Christian must overcome the temptation of "meddling in the lives of others." Gossip and envy do so much harm to the Christian community, and we cannot only "present the half that is convenient for us."

"What concern is it of yours?" This is the question that Jesus addressed to Peter, who had meddled in the life of another, in the life of the disciple John, the one "whom Jesus loved." Peter had "a dialogue of love" with the Lord, but then the dialogue "got onto the wrong track" and he too suffered a temptation: "to meddle in the lives of others." In other words, Peter was "nosy." There are two forms of this meddling in others' lives. The first is "comparison, comparing oneself with others." When there is this comparison, "we end up in bitterness and also in envy, but envy tarnishes the Christian community," it "does so much harm" to it, and "that's what the devil wants." The second form of this temptation is gossip. This is polite at first, but then we end up "bad-mouthing our neighbor.

"How much gossip there is in the Church! How much we Christians gossip! Gossip is nothing other than bad-mouthing. Hurting each other. As if we wanted to make the other smaller, right? Instead of growing myself, I make the other lower and then I feel big. That's no good! It feels good to gossip . . . I don't know why, but it feels good. Like eating candy, right? You take a piece—oh, that's good!—and then another, another, another, until you get a stomachache. And why? That's what gossip is like; it is sweet at the beginning, and then it ruins you, it ruins your soul! Gossip is destructive in the Church, it's destructive . . . It's a little like the spirit of Cain: to murder your brother, with your tongue; to murder your brother!"

If we go down this road, "we become Christians with good manners and terrible habits!" But what does gossip look like? Normally when we gossip, "we do three things.

"We give misinformation: we talk about the half that suits us, and not the other half; the other half we don't talk about because it doesn't interest us. Some of you are smiling . . . But is it true or not? Haven't you seen it? That's what happens. The second is defamation: when a person has a defect, when someone has really messed up, we tell all about it, 'give a full report' . . . And this person's reputation is ruined! And the third is calumny: saying things that are not true. This is really killing our brother! All three—misinformation, defamation, and calumny—are a sin! This is sin! Doing this is a slap in the face to Jesus in the person of his children, of his brothers."

This is why Jesus says to us just what he said to Peter: "What concern is it of yours? You follow me!" The Lord truly "shows us the way.

" 'Gossip will do you no good, because it will lead you right to this spirit of destruction in the Church. Follow me!' They are beautiful, these words of Jesus, so clear, so loving for us. It is as if he were saying: 'Quit fooling yourself, thinking that there's salvation in comparison with others or in gossip. Salvation is in following after me.' Follow Jesus! Let's ask the Lord Jesus today for this grace of never meddling in the lives of others, of not becoming Christians with good manners and terrible habits, of following Jesus, of walking behind Jesus, on his path. And this is all we need!"

When Saint Thérèse asked why Jesus gave so much to one and so little to another, her older sister took a thimble and a glass and filled them with water. Then she asked Thérèse which of the two was more full. "But they're both full," replied the future saint. That's what Jesus does with us, "he doesn't care if you're big, if you're small." He cares "if you are filled with the love of Jesus."

May 18, 2013   *Acts 28:16–20, 30–31* ✤ *John 21:20–25*

43

Humble, strong, courageous prayer

Prayer that is courageous, humble, and strong works miracles. Today's liturgy presents the passage from the Gospel in which the disciples are not able to heal a little boy; Jesus himself must intervene, and he laments the lack of faith among those present; and to the father of that boy who is asking for help, he responds that "everything is possible for those who believe." Often even those who love Jesus do not risk very much in their faith and do not entrust themselves completely to him.

"But why this incredulity? I believe it is precisely the heart that is not open, the closed heart, that heart which wants to have everything under control."

This is a heart, then, that "does not open" and does not "give control of things to Jesus," and when the disciples ask why they were not able to heal the boy, the Lord replies that "this kind of demon cannot be cast out except by prayer. We all have a little bit of disbelief on the inside." We need "strong prayer, and this strong and humble prayer allows Jesus to work the miracle. Prayer to ask for a miracle, to ask for an extraordinary action, must be an all-consuming prayer." This brings up something that happened in Argentina. A six-year-old girl was sick and the doctors gave her a few hours to live. Her father, an electrician and a "man of faith," seemed to lose his wits and took a bus to the Marian shrine of Luján, forty miles away.

"He arrived after nine in the evening, and everything was closed. And he began to pray to the Blessed Mother, with his hands on the iron bars of the gates. And he prayed, and wept, and prayed . . . And he stayed like this all night. Now this man fought: he fought with God, he actually fought with God for the healing of his little girl. Then, after six in the morning, he went to the station and took the bus home, and was at the hospital at around nine. And he found his wife crying. He thought the worst. 'But what's going on? I don't understand, I don't understand! What happened?' 'Well, the doctors came and told me that the fever is gone, she's breathing fine, there's nothing! They're keeping her for two more days, but they don't know what happened!' This still happens, miracles happen!"

But we must pray with our hearts.

"A courageous prayer that fights to get that miracle; not those courtesy prayers, 'Sure, I'll pray for you': I say an Our Father, a Hail Mary, and forget about it. No: courageous prayer, like that of Abraham, who fought with the Lord to save the city; like that of Moses, who lifted his hands up and became weary, praying to the Lord; like that of so many people who have faith and with faith they pray, they pray. Prayer works miracles, but we have to believe! I think we could say a wonderful prayer . . . and say to him all day long: 'I believe, Lord, help my unbelief' . . . And when they ask us to pray for so many people who are suffering in wars, all refugees, all these dramas there are now, pray, but with the heart of the Lord: Do it! But say to him: 'I believe, Lord. Help my unbelief.'

"Let's do this, today."

May 20, 2013   *Sirach 1:1–10 ✦ Mark 9:14–29*

44

In the Church the only path is service, not power

For a Christian, making progress means lowering oneself as Jesus did. True power is service, and there must be no power struggles in the Church.

Jesus speaks of his Passion, but the disciples are caught up in a discussion of who is the greatest among them. This is the bitter episode narrated by today's Gospel, which offers an occasion for a meditation on power and service. "Power struggles in the Church are nothing new," they "began right there with Jesus. In the evangelical vein of Jesus, power struggles should not exist in the Church," because true power, that which the Lord "taught us by his example," is "the power of service.

"True power is service. As he himself did, who came not to be served but to serve, and his service was precisely a service of the Cross. He lowered himself to the point of death, to death on the Cross, for us, to serve us, to save us. And there is no other way forward in the Church. For a Christian, moving forward, making progress, means lowering oneself. If we do not learn this Christian rule, we will never, ever be able to understand the true message of Jesus on power."

Making progress "means lowering oneself, always being of service." And in the Church "the greatest is the one who serves the most, who is most at the service of the others." This "is the rule." And nonetheless from the beginning until now there have been "power struggles in the Church," even "in our manner of speaking.

"When a person is given a position that in the eyes of the world is a high position, people say, 'Oh, that woman has been made president of that association, and this man has been promoted . . .' This verb, 'to promote': yes, it is a beautiful word, it must be used in the Church. Yes, this one has been promoted to the Cross, this one has been promoted to humiliation. That is the true promotion, the one that 'makes us look more' like Jesus!"

In his *Spiritual Exercises,* Saint Ignatius of Loyola asked the Lord "for the grace of humiliations." This is "the true power of the service of the Church." This is the true way of Jesus, true promotion, and not that of the world.

"The way of the Lord is his service. As he performed his service, we must follow after him, in the path of service. This is true power in the Church. I would like to pray today for all of us, that the Lord may give us the grace to understand this: the true power in the Church is service. And also to understand that golden rule which he has taught us by his example: for Christians, making progress, moving forward means lowering ourselves, lowering ourselves. Let's ask for this grace."

May 21, 2013   *Sirach 2:1–11 ✛ Mark 9:30–37*

45

The culture of encounter is the foundation of peace

"Doing good" is a principle that unites all of humanity, beyond the diversity of ideologies and religions, and creates that culture of encounter which is at the foundation of peace.

The Gospel speaks to us of the disciples of Jesus who are preventing a person outside of their group from doing good. "They complain" because they say: "If he is not one of ours, he cannot do good. If he is not of our party, he cannot do good." And Jesus corrects them: "'Do not prevent him. Let him do good.' The disciples were a bit intolerant," closed off in the idea of possessing the truth, in the conviction that "all those who do not have the truth cannot do good." And "this was wrong," and Jesus "widens the horizon." "The root of this possibility of doing good, which we all have," is "in creation.

"The Lord has created us in his image and likeness, and we are the image of the Lord, and he does good, and all of us have in our hearts this commandment: do good and do not do evil. All of us. 'But, Father, he's not Catholic! He can't do good!' Yes, he can. He must. It's not that he can; he must! Because he has this commandment inside. 'But, Father, he's not Christian, he can't do it!' Yes, he can. He must. Instead, this closed-mindedness of thinking that no good can be done on the outside, by everyone, is a wall that leads us to war and killing in the name of God. We cannot kill in the name of God. This is simply blasphemy. Saying that we can kill in the name of God, that is blasphemy.

"Instead, the Lord has created us in his image and likeness, and has given us this commandment inside of our hearts: do good and do not do evil.

"The Lord has redeemed, all of us with the blood of Christ; all, not only Catholics. All! 'Father, what about atheists?' Them too. All! And this blood makes us children of God first class! We have been created children in the likeness of God, and the blood of Christ has redeemed us all! And all of us have the duty to do good. And this commandment to all of us to do good, I believe this is an excellent way to peace. If we, each one of us for his part, does good for others, we will meet there, doing good, and slowly, gently, little by little, we will make up that culture of encounter. We have such need of this. Encountering each other by doing good. 'But I don't believe, Father. I am an atheist!' Well, do good: we'll meet there!

"Doing good" is not a question of faith, "it is a duty, it is an identity card that our Father has given to everyone, because he has made us in his image and likeness. And he does good, always.

"Today is the feast of Saint Rita, patroness of impossible causes, and this seems impossible. Let's ask her for this grace, this grace that all, all, all persons may do good and that we may encounter each other in this work, which is a work of creation; it resembles the creation of the Father. A work of family, because we are all children of God, all, all! And God loves us, all of us! May Saint Rita grant us this grace, which seems almost impossible."

May 22, 2013   *Sirach 4:11–19 ✤ Mark 9:38–40*

46

Without the salt of Jesus we are insipid

What is salt in the life of a Christian, that salt which Jesus has given us? The salt that the Lord gives us is the salt of faith, of hope, and of charity. But we must take care that this salt, which is given to us by the certainty that Jesus died and rose to save us, "may not become insipid, may not lose its strength." This salt "is not meant to be preserved, because if salt is kept in a shaker it doesn't do anything, it's no good.

"Salt makes sense when it is used to flavor things. I also think that when salt is kept in a shaker the humidity ruins its strength and it's no good. We must ask the Lord that we not become Christians with insipid salt, with salt closed up in the shaker. But salt has another characteristic: when salt is used well, you don't get the taste of the salt, the flavor of the salt . . . You don't taste it! You taste the flavor of each dish. Salt helps the flavor of that dish to be better, to be better preserved but also more flavorful. This is Christian originality!

"When we proclaim the faith, with this salt," those who "receive the proclamation, receive it according to their own uniqueness, like food that is salted." And so "each one with his own uniqueness receives the salt and becomes better.

"Christian originality is not uniformity! It takes each one as he is, with his personality, with his characteristics, with his culture, and leaves him with that, because it is precious. But it gives him something more: it gives him savor! This Christian originality is so beautiful, because when we want to make uniformity—everyone salted in the same way—it will be like when the cook puts in too much salt and you taste only the salt and not the flavor of the food seasoned with salt. Christian originality is precisely this: each one as he is, with the gifts that the Lord has given him."

This "is the salt that we must give." A salt that "is not to be kept, it is to be given." This is "part of the meaning of transcendence: going out with the message, going out with this wealth of salt that we have and giving it to others." On the other hand, there are two "openings" to keep the salt from being ruined. First: giving the salt "in the service of meals, in the service of others, in the service of persons." Second: "transcendence toward the author of the salt, the Creator." Salt "does not preserve only by being given in preaching" but "also needs the other transcendence, that of prayer, of adoration.

"And thus salt is preserved; it does not lose its savor. With the adoration of the Lord I transcend from myself to the Lord, and with the proclamation of the Gospel I go out of myself to give the message. But if we do not do this—these two things, these two forms of transcendence—the salt will remain in the shaker and we will become museum Christians. We can show the salt: this is my salt. Look how pretty it is! This is the salt I received in Baptism, this is the one I received in Confirmation, this is the one I received in catechesis . . . But look: museum Christians! A salt without savor, a salt that does nothing!"

May 23, 2013   *Sirach 5:1–8 ✤ Mark 9:41–50*

47

Bearing difficulties with patience and
overcoming hardship with love

E nduring with patience and overcoming with love": these are the
"graces characteristic of a Christian. Enduring with patience is
not easy! It is not easy, when difficulties come from outside, or when
problems arise in our hearts, in our souls, inner problems." But enduring is not "carrying a difficulty on our backs.

"Enduring is taking the difficulty and lifting it up, with strength,
so that the difficulty does not get us down. Lift it up with strength:
this is a Christian virtue. Saint Paul speaks of this a number of times.
Enduring. This means not allowing ourselves to be overcome by
the difficulty. This means that the Christian has the strength not to
put his arms down, to hold them up. And this is not easy, because
discouragement comes, and sometimes we want to lower our arms
and say: 'Oh, come on, let's do what we can but nothing more,'
something like that . . . But no, enduring is a grace. We must ask for
it when difficulties come."

The other grace we must ask for is "to overcome with love.

"We must overcome by so many means, but the grace that we are
asking for today is the grace of victory with love, by means of love.
And this is not easy. When we have enemies outside to make us suffer so much, it is not easy to overcome with love. The urge comes to
avenge ourselves, to get back at our enemies . . . Love: that meekness
which Jesus has taught us. And that is the victory! The apostle John
tells us: 'This is the victory: our faith.' Our faith is precisely this belief in Jesus, who has taught us love and has taught us to love everyone. And the proof that we love is when we pray for our enemies."

Praying for our enemies, for those who make us suffer, "this is
not easy." But we are "defeated Christians" if we do not forgive
our enemies and if we do not pray for them. And "how many sad,
discouraged Christians do we find" because "they have not had this
grace of enduring with patience and overcoming with love.

"For this, let's ask the Blessed Mother to give us this grace of enduring with patience and overcoming with love. How many people—so many elderly men and women—have made this journey! And it is wonderful to look at them; they have that beautiful expression, that serene happiness. They don't talk very much, but they have a heart that is patient and full of love. They know what it is to forgive their enemies, they know what it is to pray for their enemies. So many Christians are like this."

May 24, 2013 *Sirach 6:5–17 ✤ Mark 10:1–12*

48

Those who approach the Church should find the doors open

Those who approach the Church should find the doors open, and not inspectors of the faith. The Gospel speaks to us of Jesus, who rebukes the disciples who want to send away the children whom the people bring to the Lord so he will bless them. "Jesus embraced them, he kissed them, he touched them, all of them. But Jesus got so tired, and the disciples" wanted to stop him. And Jesus became indignant; "Jesus became angry sometimes." And he says: "Let them come to me, do not hinder them. To those who are like them, in fact, belongs the kingdom of heaven." "The faith of the People of God is a simple faith, it is perhaps a faith without much theology, but with a theology inside of it that does not go wrong, because it has the Spirit behind it." The documents of Vatican Council I and Vatican II say that "the holy people of God . . . cannot be mistaken in matters of belief" (*Lumen Gentium*). "If you want to know who Mary is, go to a theologian and he will explain to you who Mary is. But if you want to know how to love Mary, go to the People of God and they will teach you better." The People of God "always draw near to ask something of Jesus; sometimes they are a bit insistent in this. But it is the insistence of those who believe.

"I remember one time, going out in the city of Salta on the feast day of their patron saint. There was a humble lady who was asking a priest for a blessing. The priest said to her: 'Well, but you've already been to Mass!' And he explained to her the whole theology of the blessing at Mass. He did it so well . . . 'Oh, thank you, Father, yes, Father,' the lady said. When the priest walked away, she turned to another priest: 'Give me a blessing!' None of those words got through to her, because what she needed was something else: she needed to be touched by the Lord. This is the faith that we always find, and this faith is brought forth by the Holy Spirit. We must assist it, make it grow, help it to grow."

Let's think of the episode of the blind man of Jericho, rebuked by the disciples because he was crying out to the Lord: "Jesus, son of David, have pity on me!"

"The Gospel says that they didn't want him to cry out, they didn't want him to cry out and he was crying out even louder, and why? Because he had faith in Jesus! The Holy Spirit had put faith into his heart. And they were saying: 'No, you can't! There's no yelling out at the Lord. Protocol does not allow it. He is the second Person of the Trinity! Watch what you're doing . . .' It's as if that's what they were saying, isn't it?"

And think of the attitude of so many Christians.

"Let's think about good Christians, with goodwill; let's think about the secretary of the parish, a secretary of the parish . . . 'Hello, we want to get married.' And instead of saying, 'How wonderful!' the secretary says: 'Oh, very good, make yourselves comfortable. If you want a Mass, it's going to cost a lot . . .' These two, instead of receiving a good welcome—'It is a good thing to get married!'— receive this: 'You have your certificate of Baptism, everything's in order . . .' And they find a closed door. So many times we are inspectors of the faith, instead of becoming facilitators of faith among the people."

And the temptation that has always been there is that of "taking ownership, appropriating the Lord a bit.

"Think of a young mother who goes to church and says to the secretary of the parish: 'I want to baptize the child.' And this Christian says to her: 'No, you can't, because you are not married!' This young woman who had the courage to continue her pregnancy and not return the child to sender, what does she find? A closed door! This is not good zeal! It drives people away from the Lord! It doesn't open doors! So when we are on this path, in this attitude, we are not doing any good for persons, for the People of God. But Jesus instituted seven sacraments, and with this attitude we institute the eighth, the sacrament of the pastoral border checkpoint!

"Jesus becomes indignant when he sees these things" because those who suffer are "his faithful people, the people he loves so much.

"Today let's think about Jesus, who always wants everyone to approach him; let's think about the Holy People of God, simple people who want to approach Jesus; and let's think about the many Christians of goodwill who make mistakes, and instead of opening a door they close it. Let's ask the Lord that all those who approach the Church may find the doors open, open to encounter this love of Jesus. Let's ask for this grace."

May 25, 2013   *Sirach 17:1–15 ✤ Mark 10:13–16*

49

The culture of prosperity and the lure of the transitory

Jesus asks a young man to give all his wealth to the poor and follow him, but the man goes away saddened. "Wealth is an impediment" that "does not make the path to the Kingdom of God an easy one." Moreover, "everyone has his form of wealth, everyone." There is always some kind of wealth that "prevents us from getting close to Jesus." And this is what we have to try to do. Everyone "must make an examination of conscience on what our forms of wealth are, because these prevent us from approaching Jesus on the road of life." There are two kinds of "cultural wealth": first of all, "the culture of prosperity, which makes us lose our courage, makes us lazy, even makes us selfish." Prosperity "anesthetizes us, it is anesthesia.

" 'No, no, not more than one child, because then we can't go on vacation, we can't go here, we can't buy a house.' Following the Lord is fine, but up to a certain point. This is what prosperity does: we all know very well what prosperity is like, but it knocks us down, it takes away that courage, that strong courage to get close to Jesus. This is the first form of wealth in our culture today, the culture of prosperity."

Then there is "another form of wealth in our culture," a form of wealth that "prevents us from getting close to Jesus: it is the fascination of the temporary." We are "in love with the temporary." The "definitive proposals" that Jesus makes to us "are not to our liking." But we like the temporary, because "we are afraid of God's time," which is definitive.

"God is the Lord of time, we are the lords of the moment. Why? Because in the moment we are the boss: I'll follow the Lord up to here, then I'll see . . . I heard about one man who wanted to become a priest, but for ten years, no more . . . How many couples, how many couples get married without saying this, but in their hearts they are thinking: As long as love lasts, and then we'll see . . . The fascination of the temporary: this is a form of wealth. We have to become masters of time, to cut time down to the moment. These two forms of wealth are those that are preventing us from moving forward now. I think of the many, many men and women who have left their own countries to go out as missionaries their whole lives: that is definitive!"

But there are also many men and women who "have left their homes to make a marriage for their whole lives." That is "following Jesus up close! It is definitive!" The temporary "is not following Jesus," it is "our territory.

"Before the invitation of Jesus, before these two forms of cultural wealth, let's think about the disciples. They were bewildered. We too can be perplexed at these words of Jesus. When Jesus explained something they were still a bit astonished. Let's ask the Lord to give us the courage to move forward, stripping ourselves of this culture of prosperity, with hope in the one who is waiting for us at the end of the journey in time. Not with the little hope of the moment that's no good anymore."

May 27, 2013   *Sirach 17:20–24 ✤ Mark 10:17–27*

50

Following Jesus is not a career

The proclamation of Jesus is not a varnish, a coat of paint, but enters the heart and changes us. Following Jesus does not mean having more power, because his way is that of the Cross. Let's think of the question that Peter addresses to Jesus and that, at bottom, concerns the life of every Christian: What will be the reward that we will receive for following you? Jesus responds that those who follow him will have "many good things" but "with persecutions." The way of the Lord "is a way of 'abasement,' a way that ends in the Cross." This is why "there will always be difficulties, persecutions." These will always be there, "because he went this way before" us. And "when a Christian does not have difficulties in life—everything's fine, everything's wonderful—something is wrong." One can imagine that he is "a great friend of the spirit of the world, of worldliness." And this is "the characteristic temptation of a Christian.

"To follow Jesus, yes, but up to a certain point; to follow Jesus as a cultural form: I am Christian, I have this culture . . . But without the demands of really following Jesus, the demands of walking his path. If we follow Jesus as a cultural proposal, we use this as a way to get ahead, to have more power. And the history of the Church is full of this, beginning with some of the emperors and then continuing with so many other rulers and people, right? And even some—I don't want to say many, but some—priests, some bishops, right? Some say there are many . . . but some think that following Jesus is a career.

"In the literature a few centuries ago," it was customary to say that someone "wanted to have an ecclesiastical career since he was a child." And that "many Christians, tempted by the spirit of the world, think that following Jesus is good because you can make it a career, you can get ahead." But this "is not the spirit," it is instead the attitude of Peter when he talks about a career and Jesus responds to him: " 'Yes, I will give you everything with persecutions.' You cannot remove the Cross from the way of Jesus; it is always there."

And nonetheless this does not mean that the Christian must hurt himself. The Christian "follows Jesus out of love, and when one follows Jesus out of love, the envy of the devil does many things." The "spirit of the world does not tolerate this, it does not tolerate witness.

"Think about Mother Teresa: What does the spirit of the world say about Mother Teresa? 'Ah, Blessed Teresa is a wonderful woman, she did so many things for others . . .' The spirit of the world never says that Blessed Teresa, every day, for so many hours, was in adoration . . . Never! It reduces Christian activity to social work. As if Christian existence were a varnish, a gloss of Christianity. The proclamation of Jesus is not a gloss; the proclamation of Jesus goes to the core, to the heart, it gets inside and changes us. And the spirit of the world does not tolerate this, it does not tolerate it, and that is why persecutions come."

He who leaves home and family to follow Jesus receives a hundred times as much "now in this present age." A hundred times, with persecutions.

"Following Jesus is exactly this: going with him, behind him, out of love: the same journey, the same path. And the spirit of the world will be that which does not tolerate us and makes us suffer, but it is suffering like that of Jesus. Let's ask for this grace: to follow Jesus on the path that he showed us and taught to us. This is wonderful, because he never leaves us alone. Never! He is always with us."

May 28, 2013   *Sirach 35:1–12 ✛ Mark 10:28–31*

51

Triumphalism brings the Church to a standstill

Going out toward Jerusalem with the disciples, Jesus proclaims his Passion, death, and Resurrection. It is the journey of faith. The disciples have other plans; they are thinking of going on only half the journey, that it would be better to stop, and they are "discussing among themselves how to set up the Church, how to set up salvation." So John and James ask him if they can sit, when he is in his glory, one on his right and one on his left, raising a discussion among the others about who is the most important in the Church. "The temptation of the disciples is the same as that of Jesus in the desert, when the devil went to suggest another way to him: do everything fast, work a miracle, something so that everyone will see you. Let's go to the Temple and make you a skydiver without a parachute, so everyone will see the miracle and redemption is a done deal." It is the same temptation as that of Peter, when at first he does not accept the Passion of Christ. "It is the temptation of Christianity without the Cross, a Christianity stuck in the middle," which does not want to arrive at the place where the Father wants us. "It is the temptation of triumphalism. We want the triumph now, without going to the Cross, a worldly triumph, a reasonable triumph.

"Triumphalism in the Church brings the Church to a standstill. Triumphalism in Christians brings Christians to a standstill. It is a triumphalist Church, it is a Church stuck in the middle, a Church that is happy the way it is, well organized—well organized!—with all the offices, everything in place, everything great. Efficient. But a Church that renounces the martyrs, because it does not know that the martyrs are necessary to the Church for the journey of the Cross. A Church that thinks only of triumphs, of successes, that does not know that rule of Jesus: the rule of triumph through failure, human failure, the failure of the Cross. And this is a temptation that we all have . . .

"I remember one time, it was a dark moment in my spiritual life and I was asking for a grace from the Lord. Then I went to preach the *Spiritual Exercises* to the sisters, and on the last day they went to confession. One elderly sister came to confession, she was over the age of eighty, but with bright eyes, really sparkling: she was a woman of God. Finally I saw her as such a woman of God that I said to her: 'But, Sister, as a penance pray for me, because I need grace. I know that if you ask the Lord, he will certainly give it to me.' She paused for a moment, as if she were praying, and she said this to me: 'Be assured that the Lord will give you this grace, but make no mistake: in his divine way.' This did me so much good. Hearing that the Lord always gives us what we ask for, but in his divine way. And the divine way is this 'all the way to the end.' The divine way involves the Cross, not out of masochism; no, no! Out of love. Out of love, all the way to the end."

This, then, is the concluding prayer:

"Let's ask the Lord for the grace not to be a Church stuck in the middle, a triumphalist Church, with great successes, but to be a humble Church that walks with decisiveness, like Jesus. Onward, onward, onward. Heart open to the will of the Father, like Jesus. Let's ask for this grace."

May 29, 2013   *Sirach 36:1, 4–5a, 10–17 ✤ Mark 10:32–45*

52

The Gospel does not move forward with discouraged Christians

We can't proclaim Jesus with funeral faces, so we have to trace a line of demarcation with respect to a certain way of understanding the Christian life, marked by sadness. The two readings suggest this reflection to us. The first, from the prophet Zephaniah, presents the exclamation "Rejoice! Shout for joy, the Lord is in your midst!" The second, taken from the Gospel, recounts the episode of Elizabeth and the child who "exults with joy" in her womb at hearing the words of Mary, who had gone in "haste" to help her cousin. So "it is all joy, the joy that is celebration." Well then, "we Christians are not much accustomed to speaking of joy, of gladness. I believe that we often prefer complaining." And yet the one "who gives us joy is the Holy Spirit.

"It is the Spirit himself who guides us; he is the author of joy, the creator of joy. And this joy in the Spirit gives us true Christian freedom. Without joy, we Christians cannot become free; we become slaves of our sadness. The great Paul VI said that we cannot carry the Gospel forward with Christians who are sad, disheartened, discouraged. We cannot do it. This attitude like we're at a funeral. So many Christians have expressions like they're going to a funeral procession rather than going to praise God, right? They don't realize that from joy comes praise, this praise of Mary, this praise that Zephaniah speaks of, this praise of Simeon, of Anna: the praise of God!"

And how do we praise God? We praise him by getting out of ourselves, "gratuitously, just as the grace that he gives us is gratuitous." In order to conduct an examination of conscience on the ways of praying to God, we can ask someone who goes to Mass.

" 'You who are here at Mass, are you praising God or only asking God for something and thanking him? But do you praise God?' This is something new, something new in our spiritual life. Praising God, getting out of ourselves to praise, wasting time praising him. 'This Mass, it's getting long!' If you do not praise God, you do not know that gratuitousness of wasting time praising God, and the

Mass is long. But if you go with this attitude of joy, of praising God, how wonderful it is! Eternity will be that: praising God! And that will not be boring: it will be wonderful! This joy makes us free."

The model of this praise, and of this joy, is once again the Mother of Jesus. "The Church calls her 'cause of our joy,' *Causa Nostrae Laetitiae*. Why? Because she is the bearer of the greatest joy, which is Jesus.

"We must pray to the Blessed Mother, that in bearing Jesus she may give us the grace of joy, the freedom of joy. May she give us the grace of praising, of praising with a prayer of gratuitous praise, because he is always worthy of praise. Praying to the Blessed Mother and saying to her as the Church says: *Veni, Precelsa Domina, Maria, tu nos visita.* Our Lady, you who are so great, visit us and give us joy!"

May 31, 2013   Zephaniah 3:14–18a or Romans 12:9–16 ✢ Luke 1:39–56

53

It is the scandal of the Cross that makes the Church

With what authority do you do these things? This is the question addressed to Jesus by the scribes and high priests. Once again, they want to lay a "trap" for the Lord, trying to get him "in a corner," to trip him up. But what was the problem that these people had with Jesus? Was it the miracles he would perform? No, it wasn't that. In reality, "the problem that scandalized these people was that the demons were crying out to Jesus: 'You are the Son of God, you are the Holy One!'" This "is at the center," this scandal of Jesus: "he is God incarnate." With us as well "they lay traps for us in life," but what "is scandalous about the Church is the mystery of the Incarnation of the Word." And "he does not tolerate this, the devil does not tolerate this.

"How many times do we hear: 'Come on, you Christians, be a little bit more normal, like other people, be reasonable!' This is real snake charmer's talk: 'Come on, just be like this, okay? A little bit more normal, don't be so rigid . . . ' But behind it is this: 'Don't come here with your stories that God became man!' The Incarnation of the Word, that is the scandal behind all of this! We can do all the social work we want, and they will say: 'How great the Church is, it does such good social work.' But if we say that we are doing this because those people are the flesh of Christ, then comes the scandal. And that is the truth, that is the revelation of Jesus: that presence of Jesus incarnate."

And "this is the point: there will always be the seduction of doing good things without the scandal of the Word Incarnate, without the scandal of the Cross." We must instead "be consistent with this scandal, with this reality that scandalizes." It is "better this way: the consistency of the faith." The apostle John affirms: "Those who deny that the word came in the flesh are of the antichrist, they are the antichrist." On the other hand, "only those who say that the word came in the flesh are of the Holy Spirit." So "it is good for all of us to think about this: the Church is not an organization of culture, or even of religion, of social work.

"The Church is the family of Jesus. The Church confesses that Jesus is the Son of God come in the flesh. That is the scandal, and this is why they persecuted Jesus. And in the end, what Jesus did not want to say to the others—'With what authority do you do this?'—he says to the high priest. 'Are you the Son of God?' 'Yes!' He was sentenced to death for this. This is the center of the persecution. If we become reasonable Christians, activist Christians, do-gooder Christians, what will be the result? We will never have martyrs: that will be the result."

But when we Christians speak this truth, that "the Son of God came and became flesh," when we "preach the scandal of the Cross, persecutions will come, the Cross will come," and that "will be good. This is the way our life is.

"Let's ask the Lord not to be ashamed of living with this scandal of the Cross. And also for wisdom: let's ask for the wisdom not to let ourselves be trapped by the spirit of the world, which always makes us educated proposals, civil proposals, good proposals, but behind these is the denial of the fact that the Word came in the flesh, the denial of the Incarnation of the Word. Which in the end is what scandalizes those who persecute Jesus; it is what destroys the work of the devil."

June 1, 2013   *Sirach 51:12cd–20 ✣ Mark 11:27–33*

54

God weeps for the madness of war

"The Lord hears the prayers of all!" That of Solomon on the day of the consecration of the Temple, but also the prayer of each one of us. This is what the Gospel episode of the centurion who asks Jesus to heal his servant tells us. "This is the way our God is: he hears the prayers of all," not of all as if they were "anonymous," but the prayer "of all and of each one. Our God is the God of the great and the God of the small; our God is personal." He listens to all with his heart and "loves with his heart.

"We have come today to pray for our dead, for our wounded, for the victims of that madness which is war! It is the suicide of humanity, because it kills the heart, it kills precisely where the message of the Lord is: it kills love! Because war comes from hatred, from envy, from the desire for power, and also—we see this so many times—from the longing for more power."

And also in history, "so many times we have seen that local problems, economic problems, economic crises, the greats of the earth want to resolve them with war.

"Why? Because money is more important than people for them! And war is precisely this: it is an act of faith in money, in idols, in the idols of hatred, in the idol that leads you to kill your brother, that leads to killing love. I am reminded of those words of our Father God to Cain, who, out of envy, had killed his brother: 'Cain, where is your brother?' We can hear that voice today: it is our Father God who weeps, who weeps for this madness, who says to all of us, 'Where is your brother?'; who says to all the powerful of the earth, 'Where is your brother? What have you done?'"

From this comes the exhortation to pray to the Lord that "he may remove all evil from us," repeating that prayer "even with tears, with those tears of the heart.

"'Turn to us, O Lord, and have mercy on us, because we are sad, we are in anguish. See our misery and our pain and forgive all our sins,' because behind a war there are always sins: there is the sin of idolatry, the sin of exploiting men on the altar of power, sacrificing them. 'Turn to us, O Lord, and have mercy, because we are sad and in anguish. See our misery and our pain.' We are sure that the Lord will hear us and do something to give us the spirit of consolation."

June 2, 2013   Genesis 14:18–20 ✤ 1 Corinthians 11:23–26 ✤ Luke 9:11b–17

55

The corrupt do so much harm to the Church

What happens when we want to become the masters of the vineyard ourselves? The Gospel parable of the wicked tenants allows us to examine the "three models of Christians in the Church: the sinners, the corrupted, and the saints." About the sinners, "I don't have to talk very much, because we are all sinners." We know ourselves "from the inside, and we know what a sinner is. And if one of us does not feel that way, he should go visit the spiritual doctor," because "something is wrong." The parable, however, speaks to us of another group of people, those who want to "take over the vineyard, and have lost their relationship with the Master of the vineyard." A Master who "has called us with love, protects us, but then gives us freedom." These people "felt they were powerful, felt they were autonomous from God.

"Little by little they slid into this autonomy, an autonomy in their relationship with God: 'We don't need that Master, he'd better not come disturb us!' And they go forward like this. These are the corrupt! Those who were sinners like all of us, but then took it a step further, entrenching themselves in their sin: they don't need God! But that's just an act, because this relationship with God is in their DNA. And since they can't deny this, they make a special god, they themselves are god. They are the corrupt."

This "is also a danger for us." In "Christian communities" the corrupted think only of their own group: "Good, good. He's one of us," they think, but in reality, "it's every man for himself.

"It started with Judas: from a greedy sinner he ended up in corruption. It is a dangerous road, the road of autonomy. The corrupt are great amnesiacs, they have forgotten this love, with which the Lord made the vineyard—he made them! They have cut off their relationship with this love! And they become worshipers of themselves. How much harm the corrupted do in the Christian communities! May the Lord keep us from slipping down this path of corruption."

In today's Gospel, on the fiftieth anniversary of the death of Pope John XXIII, "a model of holiness," the saints are those who "go as servants. They know what is waiting for them, but they have to do it and they do their duty.

"The saints, those who obey the Lord, those who worship the Lord, those who have not lost the memory of love, with whom the Lord has made the vineyard. The saints in the Church. And just as the corrupted do so much harm to the Church, the saints do so much good. The apostle John says of the corrupted that they are the antichrist, that they are in the midst of us, but they are not of us. The Word of God speaks to us of the saints in terms of light, 'they who will be before the throne of God, in adoration.' Let's ask the Lord today for the grace of feeling that we are sinners, but truly sinners, not just sinners in some vague sense, but sinners for this, this, this, concretely, with the concreteness of sin. The grace of not becoming corrupted: sinners yes, corrupted no! And the grace of walking in the path of holiness."

June 3, 2013   *Tobit 1:3; 2:1b–8* ✠ *Mark 12:1–12*

Hypocrisy is the language of the corrupt

From the corrupt to their favorite language: hypocrisy. The Gospel scene of the tribute to Caesar, and the subtle question of the Pharisees and Herodians to Christ whether it is legitimate to pay the census tax offers the opportunity for a reflection in close continuity with the homily on the parable of the wicked tenants. Their intention in coming to Jesus is to make him "fall into the trap." Their question on whether or not it is permissible to pay taxes to Caesar is presented "in smooth words, with beautiful words, with too much sweet talk. They are seeking to show that they are friends," but it's all false. Because "they do not love the truth" but only themselves, "so they are seeking to deceive, to draw the other into their deception, into their lie. They have a lying heart, they cannot tell the truth.

"This is precisely the language of corruption, hypocrisy. And when Jesus speaks to his disciples, he says: 'Let your "Yes" mean "Yes," and your "No" mean "No."' Anything beyond that comes from the evil one.' Hypocrisy is not a language of truth, because the truth never goes off on its own. Never! It always goes with love! There is no truth without love. Love is the first truth. If there is no love, there is no truth. The hypocrites want a truth that is a slave of their own interests. There is a sort of love, we could say, but it is the love of themselves, love for themselves. That narcissistic idolatry which leads them to betray others, leads them to the abuse of trust."

What seems to be a "persuasive language" instead leads "to error, to falsehood." And those who approach Jesus today and "seem so amiable in their language are the same ones who will go on Thursday evening to arrest him in the Garden of Gethsemane, and on Friday will take him to Pilate." Jesus, instead, asks exactly the opposite of those who follow him, a language that is "yes, yes, no, no," a "word of truth and with love.

"And the meekness that Jesus wants for us has nothing of this adulation, with this sugary way of getting ahead. Nothing! Meekness is simple, it is like that of a child. And the child is not a hypocrite, because he is not corrupt. When Jesus tells us: 'Let your "Yes" mean "Yes," and your "No" mean "No"' with the soul of a child, he is speaking the opposite of the way these others speak."

A final consideration concerns that "certain inner weakness" stimulated by "vanity," according to which "we like it when they say good things about us. The corrupt know this," and "with this language they try to weaken us.

"Let's really think about this today: How do we talk? Do we speak in truth, with love, or do we speak a little with that social language of being sophisticated, even saying things that are beautiful but that we don't feel? Our speech should be evangelical! There are these hypocrites who begin with flattery, adulation, and all of that, and then end up seeking false witnesses to accuse the one they had flattered. Let's ask the Lord today that our speech may be the speech of the simple, the speech of a child, the speech of children of God, speaking in truth and from love."

June 4, 2013   *Tobit 2:9–14 ✧ Mark 12:13–17*

57

The cry of suffering before God is a prayer of the heart

The story of Tobit and Sarah presented in the first reading is at the center of our reflection: two righteous persons who are living through dramatic situations. The first becomes blind in spite of the fact that he does good works, even risking his life; the second marries seven men who die before their wedding night. Both of them, in their immense suffering, pray to God to let them die. "They are persons in straitened circumstances, living lives in the underbelly of existence, and they are looking for a way out. They complain, but they do not blaspheme.

"And complaining before God is not a sin. A priest I know once said to a woman who was complaining before God for her calamities: 'But, ma'am, that's a form of prayer. Go ahead.' The Lord hears, he listens to her complaints. Let's think of the greats, of Job, when in the third chapter he says: 'Cursed be the day on which I came into the world.' And also Jeremiah, in the twentieth chapter: 'Cursed be the day . . .' They even complain with a curse, not against the Lord but about that situation, don't they? This is human."

There are so many people living in borderline situations: malnourished children, refugees, the terminally ill. There are the Sadducees who present Jesus with the borderline case of a woman, the widow of seven men. They were not speaking of this situation with their hearts.

"The Sadducees were speaking of this woman as if she were in a laboratory, everything aseptic, everything . . . It was a case of morality. When we think of these people who suffer so much, do we think of them as if they were moral hypotheses, pure ideas—'But in this case . . . This case . . .'—or do we think with our hearts, with our flesh too? I don't like it when these situations are spoken of in such an academic and inhuman way, sometimes with statistics . . . but only there. In the Church there are so many people in these situations."

In these cases we have to do what Jesus says, pray.

"Pray for them. They have to enter into my heart, they have to be a disturbance for me: my brother is suffering, my sister is suffering. That's it . . . the mystery of the communion of the saints: to pray to the Lord: 'But, Lord, look at him: he's weeping, he's suffering.' To pray, allow me to say this, with our flesh; our flesh should pray too. Not with ideas. But with the heart."

And the prayers of Tobit and Sarah, who in spite of asking for death turn to the Lord, give us hope, because in their own way they are accepted by God, who does not let them die but heals Tobit and finally gives a husband to Sarah. "Prayer always arrives at the glory of God, always, when it is a prayer of the heart." But "when it is a case of morality, like this one the Sadducees were talking about, it never gets there, because it doesn't really come from us; it doesn't interest us. It's a mind game." The invitation is to pray for those who are living through dramatic situations and suffering so much, and like Jesus on the Cross are crying out: "Father, Father, why have you abandoned me?" "Let's pray that our prayer may arrive and be a bit of hope for all of us."

June 5, 2013   *Tobit 3:1–11a, 16–17a ✣ Mark 12:18–27*

58

Let's unmask the idols that keep us from loving God

When the scribe approaches Jesus to ask him which is, according to him, "the first of all the commandments," it is likely that his intention is not so innocent. The man comes to Christ giving the impression of "putting him to the test," if not in fact of trying to "make him fall into the trap." And when—to the biblical citation of Jesus: "Hear, O Israel! The Lord our God is Lord alone!"—the scribe replies with approval, Christ comments: "You are not far from the Kingdom of God." Jesus was telling the scribe: "You know the theory well," but "there is still some distance to the Kingdom of God," meaning that you must make a journey to transform "this commandment into reality," since "the confession of God" is made in the "journey of life.

"It is not enough to say: 'But I believe in God; God is the only God.' That's all fine, but how do you live this on the road of life? Because we can say: 'The Lord is the only God, alone, there is no other,' but live as if he were not the only God and have other divinities at our disposal . . . There is the danger of idolatry: the idolatry that is brought to us with the spirit of the world. And Jesus was clear about this: the spirit of the world, no. And he asks the Father to defend us from the spirit of the world, Jesus does at the Last Supper, because the spirit of the world leads us to idolatry.

"Idolatry is subtle"; we all "have our hidden idols," and "the way to have life, to be not far from the Kingdom of God," involves "discovering the hidden idols." Something that can be traced back to the Bible, to the episode in which Rachel, Jacob's wife, pretends that she does not have with her the idols that she had brought from her father's house and hidden under her saddle. We too "have hidden them in our saddle . . . But we have to seek them out and destroy them," because in order to follow God the only way is that of a love founded on fidelity.

"And fidelity requires that we throw away our idols, discover them. They are hidden in our personality, in our way of life. But these hidden idols prevent us from being faithful in love. The apostle James, when he says, 'He who is a friend of the world is an enemy of God,' begins by saying: 'Adulterers!' He reproves us, but with that adjective 'adulterers.' Why? Because he who is a 'friend' of the world is an idolater, he is not faithful to the love of God! The way to keep from being far away, to advance, to move forward to the King-dom of God is a way of fidelity that resembles that of marital love."

Given "the small or not so small idolatries that we have," how is it possible to be faithful "to a love that is so great"? In order to do this, we have to trust in Christ, who is "complete fidelity" and "loves us so much.

"We can ask Jesus today: 'Lord, you are so good, teach me this way to be every day less far from the Kingdom of God, this way to cast out all idols.' It is difficult, but we have to begin . . . The idols hidden in so many saddles, which we have in our personality, in our way of life. Casting out the idol of worldliness, which leads us to become enemies of God. Let's ask Jesus for this grace today."

June 6, 2013   Tobit 6:10–11; 7:1bcde, 9–17; 8:4–9a ✠ Mark 12:28–34

59

Let's allow ourselves to be loved by the tenderness of God

Jesus loved us so much, not with words but with works and with his life. How can we not remember this episode at the solemnity of the Most Sacred Heart of Jesus, which is "the celebration of love," of a "heart that loves so much." A love that, as Saint Ignatius repeated, "is manifested more in works than in words" and that above all is "more giving than receiving. These two criteria are like the pillars of true love," and it is the Good Shepherd who fully represents the love of God. He knows every one of his lambs, "because love is not an abstract or general love: it is love for each one.

"A God who draws near out of love journeys with his people, and this journey arrives at a point that is unimaginable. The Lord himself becomes one of us and journeys with us, remains with us, remains in his Church, remains in the Eucharist, remains in his word, remains in the poor, remains with us journeying. And this is closeness: the shepherd close to his flock, close to his lambs, whom he knows one by one."

The book of the prophet Ezekiel highlights another aspect of the love of God: care for the lost sheep and for the sick and wounded.

"Tenderness! The Lord loves us with tenderness. The Lord knows that wonderful science of caresses, that tenderness of God. He does not love us with words. He draws near—nearness—and gives us that love with tenderness. Nearness and tenderness! These are two aspects of the love of the Lord who draws near and gives all his love even with the smallest things: with tenderness. And this is a strong love, because nearness and tenderness show us the strength of God's love.

"But do you love the way I have loved you?" This is the question that we have to ask ourselves. Our love must "draw near to our neighbor," it must be "like that of the good Samaritan," and in particular in the sign of "nearness and tenderness." But how can we repay all of this love to the Lord? Certainly "by loving him," becoming "near to him, tender with him," but this is not enough.

"This may seem like heresy, but it is the greatest truth! Harder than loving God is allowing ourselves to be loved by him! The way to give back so much love is to open our hearts and let ourselves be loved. To let him get close to us and feel him near. To let him be tender and caress us. That is so difficult, letting him love us. And this is perhaps what we should ask for today in the Mass: 'Lord, I want to love you, but teach me the difficult science, the difficult habit of allowing myself to be loved by you, to feel you close and to feel your tenderness!' May the Lord give us this grace!"

June 7, 2013   *Ezekiel 34:11–16* ❧ *Romans 5:5b–11* ❧ *Luke 15:3–7*

60

Let's learn from Mary to interpret life with the Word of God

The Gospel tells of the amazement of the scholars in the Temple at hearing Jesus and of how Mary treasured the Word of God in her heart. Astonishment "is more than joy, it is a moment in which the Word of God comes and is sown in our hearts." But "we cannot always live in amazement," we must bring that amazement "into our life by keeping it." And this is precisely what Mary does, she of whom it is said that she "marvels" and keeps the "Word of God.

"To keep the Word of God: What does this mean? I receive the word and then I get a bottle, put the word in the bottle and keep it? No. Keeping the Word of God means that our heart opens, it is open to that word like the earth that opens up to receive the seed. The Word of God is a seed and is sown. And Jesus told us what happens to the seed: some of it falls along the path and the birds come and eat it; this word is not kept, these hearts do not know how to receive it."

Other seeds fall onto rocky ground and die. And Jesus says that these "are unable to keep the Word of God because they are not constant; when tribulation comes they forget." The Word of God falls onto ground that is not prepared, that is not cared for, where there are thorns. And what are the thorns? Jesus speaks of "attachment to wealth, vices." So "keeping the Word of God means always meditating on what this word is saying to us with the things that happen in our lives." And this "is what Mary did; she meditated and made the comparison." This "is a great spiritual labor.

"John Paul II said that Mary had, with this labor, a particular fatigue in her heart; she had a weary heart. But this is not an anxiety, it is an effort, a labor. Keeping the Word of God is done through this labor: the labor of seeking what this means at this moment, what the Lord is trying to tell me in this moment, this situation in comparison with the Word of God as I understand it. It means interpreting life with the Word of God, and this is what it means to keep the Word of God."

But also remembering. "Memory is a keeping of the Word of

God. It helps us to keep it, to remember all that the Lord has done in my life." It reminds us "of all the wonders of salvation in his people and in my heart. Memory keeps the Word of God." The invitation is therefore to think "about how we keep the Word of God, how we preserve this amazement, so that the birds do not eat it and the vices do not suffocate it.

"It's good for us to ask ourselves: 'With the things that happen in my life, what is the Lord saying with his word, in this moment?' This is called keeping the Word of God, because the Word of God is precisely the message that the Lord is giving us at every moment. Keeping it with this: keeping it with our memory. And also keeping it with our hope. Let's ask the Lord for the grace to receive the Word of God and to keep it, and also the grace to have a heart that is wearied in this keeping."

June 8, 2013   *Tobit 12:1, 5–15, 20* ✤ *Luke 2:41–51*

61

To understand the Beatitudes we must open our hearts

What is consolation for a Christian? At the beginning of the second letter to the Corinthians, Saint Paul repeatedly uses the word "encouragement." The Apostle of the Gentiles is speaking to Christians who are "young in the faith," persons "who have just begun on the way of Jesus." And he insists precisely on this, even if "they were not all persecuted." They were ordinary people, "but they had found Jesus." This is why "it is such a change of life that they needed special strength from God," and this strength is consolation. Consolation "is the presence of God in our hearts," but in order for the Lord "to be in our hearts, we need to open the door," we need "conversion.

"This is salvation: living in the consolation of the Holy Spirit, not living in the consolation of the spirit of the world. No, that is not salvation, that is sin. Salvation is moving forward and opening our hearts, so that this consolation of the Holy Spirit, which is salvation, may come to us. But can't we negotiate a bit here and there? Make a bit of a salad, let's say, why not? A little Holy Spirit, a little spirit of the world . . . No! One thing or the other."

The Lord says this clearly: "We cannot serve two masters: either we will serve the Lord or we will serve the spirit of the world." We cannot "mix" them. So when we are open to the Spirit of the Lord, we can understand "the new law that the Lord brings to us": the Beatitudes. The Beatitudes "can be understood only if our hearts are open; they are understood by the consolation of the Holy Spirit," while "they cannot be understood with human intelligence alone.

"They are the new commandments. But if our hearts are not open to the Holy Spirit, they will seem like foolishness. But look, being poor, being meek, being merciful does not seem like something that would lead us to success. If our hearts are not open and we have not tasted that consolation of the Holy Spirit, which is salvation, we cannot understand this. This is the law for those who have been saved and have opened their hearts to salvation. This is the law of the free, with that freedom of the Holy Spirit."

We can "organize our lives, set up a list of commandments or procedures," a "merely human" list. But "in the end this does not lead us to salvation"; only the open heart leads us to salvation. So many people were interested in "examining" the "new doctrine and then arguing with Jesus." And this happened because "they had their hearts closed up in their own things, things that God wanted to change." Why, then, are there people who "have their hearts closed to salvation"? Because "we are afraid of salvation. We need it, but we are afraid," because when the Lord comes "to save us we must give him everything. And he's in charge! And we are afraid of this" because "we want to be in charge." In order to understand "these new commandments," we need the freedom that "comes from the Holy Spirit, who saves us, who consoles us" and "gives us life.

"We can ask the Lord today for the grace of following him, but with this freedom. Because if we want to follow him with just our own human freedom, in the end we will become hypocrites like those Pharisees and Sadducees, the ones who argued with him. Hypocrisy is this: not allowing the Spirit to change our hearts with his salvation. The freedom of the Spirit, which the Spirit gives us, is also a sort of slavery, a 'slavery' to the Lord, who makes us free; it is another freedom. But our freedom is only a form of slavery, not to the Lord but to the spirit of the world. Let's ask for the grace of opening our hearts to the consolation of the Holy Spirit, so that this consolation, which is salvation, may help us really understand these commandments."

June 10, 2013   *2 Corinthians 1:1–7* ✠ *Matthew 5:1–12*

62

A wealthy Church is a Church that's getting old

D o not procure for yourselves gold nor silver nor money for your belts": this is the exhortation that Jesus addressed to the apostles who were sent out to proclaim the Kingdom of God. A proclamation that the Lord "wants to be made in simplicity." That simplicity "which leaves room for the power of the Word of God," because if the apostles had not had "trust in the Word of God, perhaps they would have done something else." The "key word" of the commission given by Jesus is therefore: "Freely have you received, freely give." Everything is grace, and "when we want to do things so that grace" is "somewhat left aside, the Gospel has no efficacy.

"The preaching of the Gospel emerges from gratuitousness, from the astonishment of the salvation that comes and that which I have received gratuitously, I must give gratuitously. And this is the way things were in the beginning. Saint Peter didn't have a bank account, and when he had to pay the taxes, the Lord sent him to the sea to catch a fish and find the coin inside the fish to pay. When Philip met the finance minister of Queen Candace, he didn't think: Okay, great, let's make an organization to support the Gospel. No! He didn't make a 'deal' with him: he proclaimed, baptized, and went his way."

The Kingdom of God "is a gratuitous gift." From the beginning of the Christian community, this attitude has been subject to temptation. There is "the temptation of seeking strength" elsewhere than in gratuitousness, while "our strength is in the gratuitousness of the Gospel. Always, in the Church, there has been this temptation" and this creates "a bit of confusion," since in this way "the proclamation seems like proselytism, and this is not the way to go." The Lord "has invited us to proclaim, not to make proselytes." Citing Benedict XVI, it can therefore be emphasized that "the Church grows not by proselytism, but by attraction." And this attraction comes from the witness of "those who gratuitously proclaim the gratuitousness of salvation.

"All is grace. All. And what are the signs when an apostle is living this gratuitousness? There are many, but I will emphasize two of them: first, poverty. The proclamation of the Gospel must go by the way of poverty. The witness of this poverty: I have no riches; my wealth is only the gift that I have received, God. This gratuitousness: this is our wealth! And this poverty saves us from becoming organizations, entrepreneurs . . . We have to carry the works of the Church forward, and some of these are a bit complex; but with the spirit of poverty, not with the heart of an investor or entrepreneur, right?

"The Church is not an NGO; it is something else, more important, and it emerges from this gratuitousness. Received and proclaimed."

The other sign "is the capacity for praise. When an apostle does not live this gratuitousness, he loses the capacity to praise the Lord." Praising the Lord, in fact, "is essentially gratuitous, it is a gratuitous prayer; we are not asking for anything, only praising.

"These are the two signs that an apostle is living this gratuitousness: poverty and the capacity to praise the Lord. And when we find apostles who want to make a rich Church and a Church without the gratuitousness of praise, the Church gets old, the Church becomes an NGO, the Church has no life. Let's ask the Lord today for the grace of recognizing this gratuitousness: 'Freely have you received, freely give.' To recognize this gratuity, that gift of God. And also for us to move forward in the preaching of the Gospel with this gratuitousness."

June 11, 2013   *Acts 11:21b–26; 13:1–3 ✦ Matthew 10:7–13*

63

Christians must overcome the temptation to "go backward"

"Do not think that I have come to abolish the law." Jesus addresses these words to the disciples in the Gospel passage that follows that of the Beatitudes, "an expression of the new law" more demanding than that of Moses. This law is "the fruit of the covenant" and cannot be understood without it. "This Covenant, this law is sacred because it led the people to God," and the "maturity of this law" is like the "bud that opens and lets the flower come out." Jesus "is the expression of the maturity of the law," and Paul in fact speaks to us of two eras "without cutting the continuity" between the law of history and the law of the Spirit.

"The hour of the fulfillment of the law, the hour in which the law comes to its maturity: this is the law of the Spirit. The journey along this way is a bit risky, but it is the only way to maturity, to move away from the time in which we are not mature. On this road toward the maturity of the law, which comes with the preaching of Jesus, there was always fear, fear of the freedom that the Spirit gives us. The law of the Spirit makes us free! This freedom scares us a little, because we are afraid of confusing the freedom of the Spirit with another human freedom."

The law of the Spirit "leads us on a path of continual discernment to do the will of God, and this" scares us. A fear that "has two temptations." The first is that of "going back," saying that "up to this point is fine, but no farther," and so in the end "let's stay here." This "is to some extent the temptation of the fear of freedom, the fear of the Holy Spirit." A fear according to which "it is best to play it safe." During the 1930s, a superior general had "collected all of the anticharism prescriptions" for his religious, "a labor of years." When he went to Rome he met a Benedictine abbot who, upon hearing what he had done, told him that he had "killed the charism among his congregation, he had killed its freedom," because "this charism bears fruit in freedom and he had stopped the charism.

"This temptation of going back, because we are 'safer' back there.

But complete safety is in the Holy Spirit, who carries you forward, who gives you this trust—as Paul says—and the Spirit is more demanding because Jesus tells us: 'Amen, I say to you, until heaven and earth pass away, not the smallest letter or the smallest part of a letter will pass from the law.' He is more demanding! But he does not give us that human safety. We cannot control the Holy Spirit. That is the problem! This is a temptation."

And then there is another temptation, that of "adolescent progressivism," which leads us "off the road." Seeing a culture and "not being very detached" from it.

"Let's take a little bit from here, a little bit from there, the values of this culture . . . Do they want this law? Let's go forward with this law. Do they want to go forward with that? Let's widen the road a bit. In the end, as I say, it is not true progressivism. It is adolescent progressivism, like teenagers who want to have it all with enthusiasm, and in the end? It's a tailspin . . . It's like when the road is frozen and the car skids and goes off the road . . . This is the other temptation at this moment! No, in this moment of the Church's history, we can neither go backward nor go off the road!"

The road "is that of freedom in the Holy Spirit, who makes us free in the continual discernment of the will of God to move forward on this road, without going backward and without sliding off the road." Let's ask the Lord "for the grace that the Holy Spirit gives us to move forward."

June 12, 2013   *2 Corinthians 3:4–11 ✦ Matthew 5:17–19*

64

Let's follow the law of meekness

Your righteousness should be greater than that of the Pharisees": Jesus speaks these words to the disciples after the Beatitudes, and after emphasizing that he has not come to dissolve the law but to bring it to completion. His "is a reform without rupture, a reform in continuity: from the seed all the way to the fruit." The one who "enters into Christian life has demands greater than those of the others, he does not have greater advantages." And Jesus mentions some of these demands and touches in particular "on the theme of negative relationships with our brothers." He who curses, Jesus says, "deserves hell." If there is "something negative" toward your brother in your heart, "there is something that is not working and you must convert, you must change. Anger is an insult against our brother, it is something that already stands in the shadow of death, it kills him." Especially in the Latin tradition, there is a sort of "marvelous creativity" in inventing epithets. "When this epithet is friendly it's fine, the problem is when there is the other epithet," when there is "the mechanism of the insult, a form of denigration of the other.

"And there is no need to go to the psychologist to know that when someone denigrates another it is because he himself cannot grow, and he needs the other to be brought down so he can feel like somebody." And this is "an ugly mechanism." Jesus "says in all simplicity that we should not speak evil of each other. Do not denigrate each other. Do not discredit each other." And this "because at bottom we are all walking the same path, we are all going on the way that will lead us to the end." So "if things do not go by the fraternal route, we will all end up in trouble: the one who insults and the one who is insulted. If someone is not capable of controlling his tongue, he is lost," and "the natural aggression that Cain showed toward Abel is repeated over the span of history." It's not that we are bad; "we are weak and sinners." This is why "it is much easier to take care of a situation with an insult, with a calumny, with a defamation, rather than taking care of it with good words.

"I would like to ask the Lord to give all of us the grace of paying more attention to our language, to what we say to others." This is "a small penance, but it bears good fruit. At times one may feel hungry" and may think: "What a shame that I have not tasted the sweetness of a delicious comment against the other." But "in the long run that hunger is fruitful and does us good." This is why we must ask the Lord for this grace: to bring our life into line "with this new Law, which is the Law of meekness, the Law of love, the Law of peace, and at least 'prune' our tongues a little, 'prune' the comments that we make toward others or the explosions that lead to insult or easy anger. May the Lord grant all of us this grace!"

June 13, 2013   *2 Corinthians 3:15–4:1, 3–6* ✤ *Matthew 5:20–26*

65

If the Christian flees from superficial humility,
the power of God is within him

Aware of being a weak vessel of clay, and yet containing a great treasure that has been given to him in a completely gratuitous way: this is the follower of Christ in front of his Lord. The prompting for this reflection is given by the letter in which Paul explains to the Christians of Corinth that, in order to make it clear that the "surpassing power" of faith is the work of God, this has been poured into sinful men, into "vessels of clay." But precisely from the relationship "between the grace and power of Jesus Christ" and us poor sinners comes "the dialogue of salvation." And yet in this dialogue we must shun any sort of "self-justification," instead "we must speak as we are.

"Paul spoke so many times—it's like a refrain, isn't it?—about his sins. 'But, I tell you this: I who was an enemy of the Church, I persecuted . . .' He always returns to his memory of sin. He feels like a sinner. But even in that moment he does not say: 'I was, but now I am holy,' no. Even now, a thorn of Satan is in his flesh. He shows us his weakness. His sin. He is a sinner who accepts Jesus Christ. He dialogues with Jesus Christ."

The key is therefore humility. Paul himself demonstrates this. He publicly recognizes "his service record," all that he has done as an apostle sent by Jesus. But he doesn't hide what could be called his "rap sheet," meaning his sins.

"This is the model of humility for us priests. If we just brag about our résumé and nothing more, we are mistaken. We cannot proclaim Jesus Christ as Savior because at bottom we do not feel him. But we must be humble, but with a real humility, with first and last name: 'I am a sinner for this, for this, for this.' Like Paul does: 'I persecuted the Church,' like he does: concrete sins. Not sinners with that humility which looks more like the face on a holy card, right? No, strong humility.

"The humility of the priest, the humility of the Christian is concrete," and if a Christian is not able "to make this confession to himself and to the Church, something is not right." And the first thing that is not right is the inability "to understand the beauty of the salvation that Jesus brings us.

"Brothers, we have a treasure: it is Jesus Christ the Savior. The Cross of Jesus Christ, this treasure of which we boast. But we have it in a vessel of clay. Let's also brag about our rap sheet, about our sins. And this is Christian and Catholic dialogue: concrete, because the salvation of Jesus Christ is concrete. Jesus Christ did not save us with an idea, with an intellectual program, no. He saved us with his flesh, with the concreteness of the flesh. He lowered himself, became man, became flesh to the end. But this can only be understood, can only be received, in vessels of clay."

The Samaritan woman who encounters Jesus and after speaking with him tells her countrymen first about her sin and then about having encountered the Lord also behaves in a way similar to that of Paul. "I believe that this woman is in heaven, sure," because, as Alessandro Manzoni says, "'I have never found that the Lord has begun a miracle without finishing it,' and this miracle that he began he surely finished in heaven." Let's ask her "to help us to be vessels of clay in order to be able to carry and understand the glorious mystery of Jesus Christ."

June 14, 2013   *2 Corinthians 4:7–15* ✣ *Matthew 5:27–32*

66

The Christian takes to the streets to proclaim the peace of Christ

Christian life does not mean sitting on a corner carving out a path that leads comfortably to heaven, but it is a dynamism that drives us to be "on the street" to proclaim that Christ has reconciled us with God, becoming sin for our sake. In the passage from the letter to the Corinthians, in a few lines an insistent Paul, almost "in a hurry," uses a form of the verb "reconcile" five times. And he does it in alternation with "strength" and "tenderness," first urging and then almost on his knees: 'I beseech you in the name of Christ: allow yourselves to be reconciled with God.'

"But what is reconciliation? Taking one on this side, one on another, and uniting them? No, this is part of it, but it's not it . . . True reconciliation is that God, in Christ, took our sins and made himself sin for us. And when we go to confession, for example, it is not that we tell our sins and God forgives us. No, that's not it! We find Jesus Christ and we say to him: 'This is yours, and I am making you become sin yet again.' And he likes this, because it was his mission: becoming sin for us, to set us free."

This is the beauty and the "scandal" of the redemption worked by Jesus. And it is also the "mystery" from which Paul draws the "zeal" that spurs him to "go forward" and to repeat to all "such a wonderful thing," the love of a God "who gave his Son over to die for me." And yet there is the risk of "never arriving at this truth" whenever we "undervalue Christian life a little bit," reducing it to a list of things to observe, obscuring the ardor, the power of the "love that is inside" of it.

"But the philosophers say that peace is a certain tranquillity in order: everything ordered and tranquil . . . That is not Christian peace! Christian peace is an unquiet peace; it is not a tranquil peace. It is an unquiet peace, that goes forward to advance this message of reconciliation. Christian peace drives us to go forward. This is the beginning, the root of apostolic zeal. Apostolic zeal is not going forward to make proselytes and make statistics: this year Christians grew in that country, in these movements . . . Statistics are good, they are helpful, but that is not what God wants from us, making proselytes . . . What the Lord wants from us is precisely the proclamation of this reconciliation, which is the heart of his message."

Precisely this is the "pillar" of Christian life, that "Christ became sin for me! And my sins are there, in his Body, in his Soul. This is crazy, but it's beautiful, it's the truth! This is the scandal of the Cross!

"Let's ask the Lord to give us this urgency in proclaiming Christ, to give us a bit of that Christian wisdom which comes precisely from his side pierced out of love. Even that he will convince us a little that Christian life is not some sort of end-of-life therapy: being at peace until we get to heaven . . . No, Christian life is on the road, in life, with this urgency of Paul. The love of Christ possesses us, but it drives us, it pushes us, with this emotion that we feel when we see that God loves us. Let's ask for this grace."

June 15, 2013   *2 Corinthians 5:14–21 ✧ Matthew 5:33–37*

67

Jesus is the secret of Christian magnanimity

"When someone strikes you on your right cheek, turn the other one to him as well." These are the unsettling words that Jesus addresses to his disciples. This image of the slap "has become a classic for making fun of Christians." In life the "normal logic" teaches us that "we have to fight, we have to defend our position," and if they give us a slap, "we will give two back, that's how we defend ourselves." Besides, "whenever I talk to parents about spanking I always say, 'Never on the cheek,' because 'the cheek is the dignity.'" Jesus, instead, after the slap on his cheek, goes further and also says to give our cloaks, stripping ourselves of everything.

"The justice that he brings is a justice completely different from that of an eye for an eye, a tooth for a tooth. It is another kind of justice." And we can understand this when Saint Paul speaks of Christians as "people who have nothing" and "yet possess everything." So the security of a Christian is precisely in this "everything" that is Jesus. "The 'all' is Jesus Christ. Other things are 'nothing' for the Christian. For the spirit of the world, however, 'everything' means things: wealth, vanities, getting ahead," and "the 'nothing' is Jesus." So if a Christian can walk a hundred miles when someone asks him to go ten, "it is because for him this is 'nothing,'" and with tranquillity "he can give his cloak when someone asks for his tunic." This is "the secret of Christian magnanimity, which always goes hand in hand with meekness"; it is the "all," it is Jesus Christ.

"The Christian is a person who opens his heart, with this magnanimity, because he has the 'all' that is Jesus Christ. Other things are 'nothing.' They are good, they are useful, but at the moment of comparison he always chooses the 'all,' with that meekness, that Christian meekness which is the sign of the disciples of Jesus: meekness and magnanimity. And to live this way is not easy, because they really slap you, they really do! And on both cheeks. But the Christian is meek, the Christian is magnanimous; he opens his heart. But when we find these Christians with closed hearts, with shriveled hearts, that don't work . . . This is not Christianity. This is egoism masquerading as Christianity."

The true Christian is able to resolve this polar opposition, this tension between the "all" and the "nothing," as Jesus advised us to do: "Seek first the Kingdom of God and his justice, and the rest will come.

"The Kingdom of God is the 'all'; the rest is secondary, it is not the main thing. And all of the mistakes of Christians, all the mistakes of the Church, all of our mistakes arise from this, when we say to the 'nothing' that it is the 'all' and to the 'all' that, well, it seems you don't matter . . . Following Jesus is not easy, it is not easy. But it is not difficult either, because on the way of love the Lord arranges things so that we can move forward; the Lord himself expands our hearts."

And this is the prayer that we must make "in the face of these remarks about the slap, the cloak, the hundred miles." We must pray to the Lord, that he may expand "our hearts," so that "we may be magnanimous, we may be meek," and not fight "over little things, over the 'nothing' of every day.

"When someone opts for the 'nothing,' that option gives rise to clashes within a family, with friends, in society even; the clashes that end up in war: over 'nothing'! The 'nothing' is a seed of war, always. Because it is a seed of egoism. The 'all' is great, it is Jesus. Let's ask the Lord to expand our hearts, to make us humble, meek, and magnanimous, so that we may have the 'all' in him, and to defend us from building everyday problems around the 'nothing.'"

June 17, 2013   *2 Corinthians 6:1–10 ✤ Matthew 5:38–42*

68

Forgiving our enemies makes us like Jesus

How can we love our enemies? How can we love those "who make the decision to bomb and kill so many people"? And again, how can we "love those who out of love of money do not allow medicine to get to elderly people and allow them to die"? Or those who are seeking only "their own interests, their own power, and do so much harm? It seems a difficult thing to love our enemies," but this is what Jesus asks of us. The liturgy of these days is proposing precisely this "attitude of the law that Jesus gives," from the law of Mount Sinai to the law of the Mount of the Beatitudes. We all have enemies, but at bottom we ourselves can become enemies of others.

"So many times we too become enemies of others; we do not care about them. And Jesus tells us that we must love our enemies! And this is not easy! It is not easy . . . We even think that Jesus is asking too much of us! Let's leave this to the cloistered sisters, they're holy; let's leave it to a few holy souls, but for ordinary life it doesn't work. And it has to work! Jesus says: 'No, we've got to do this! Because if you don't, you will be like the tax collectors, like the pagans. You are not Christians.'"

So how can we love our enemies? Jesus "tells us two things": first of all, look at the Father, who "makes the sun rise on the good and on the bad" and "makes it rain on the just and the unjust." God "has love for all." And then Jesus tells us to "be 'perfect as your heavenly Father is perfect,' to imitate the Father with that perfection of love." Jesus "forgives his enemies; he does everything to forgive them." Getting revenge is not Christian. But how can we succeed in loving our enemies? By praying. "When someone prays for what is making him suffer, it is as if the Lord comes with the oil and prepares our hearts for peace.

"Pray! This is what Jesus tells us: 'Pray for your enemies! Pray for those who persecute you! Pray!' And say to God: 'Change his heart. He has a heart of stone, but change it, give him a heart of flesh, that can feel and love.' I'll just put this question out there, and each of us can respond in his heart: Do I pray for my enemies? Do I pray for those who don't care about me? If we say yes, I will say: Keep going, pray more, that's the right way. If the response is no, the Lord says: 'Poor thing. You too are the enemy of others!' Pray that the Lord may change their hearts. We can even say: But this guy really pulled a nasty one on me, or these people have done terrible things, and this one impoverishes persons, impoverishes humanity. And with this argument we want to go forward with our revenge or with that eye for an eye, tooth for a tooth."

It is true, love for our enemies "impoverishes us." But "it makes us poor" like Jesus "when he came to us, lowered himself and became poor" for our sake. Some could say that this is not a good deal "if my enemy makes me poor," and of course, "according to the criteria of the world, it's not a good deal." But this is "the path that Jesus took"; from being rich he made himself poor for our sake. In that poverty, "in that abasement of Jesus is the grace that has justified all of us, has made us rich." It is the "mystery of salvation.

"With forgiveness, with love for our enemies, we become poor: love impoverishes us, but that poverty is a seed of fecundity and of love for others. We who are at Mass today, let's think about our enemies, about those who don't care about us. It would be wonderful to offer up the Mass for them: Jesus, the sacrifice of Jesus, for them, for those who do not love us. And also for us, that the Lord may teach us this wisdom that is so difficult, but so beautiful because it makes us resemble the Father, our Father, and brings the sun out for everyone, good and bad. And it makes us resemble the Son, Jesus, who in his abasement became poor in order to enrich us with his poverty."

June 18, 2013   *2 Corinthians 8:1–9 ✣ Matthew 5:43–48*

69

Do not be hypocrites and moralists

The hypocrites who "lead the People of God to a road with no way out," these are the main characters in the passage from the Gospel of Matthew. We see the contrast between the behavior of the scribes and Pharisees—who show off in public, giving alms, praying, and fasting—and that which Jesus tells his disciples is the right attitude to take in the same circumstances, namely "secrecy," the discretion that is pleasing to God and rewarded by him. In particular, in addition to the vanity of the scribes and Pharisees, what he criticizes most is their "imposing so many precepts on the faithful." These "hypocrites of casuistry, intellectuals without talent, do not have the intelligence to find God, to explain God with intelligence," so they prevent themselves and others from entering into the Kingdom of God.

"Jesus tells them: 'You do not enter, and you do not allow others to enter.' They are ethicists without goodness, they do not know what goodness is. But sure, they are ethicists: 'You have to do this, and this, and this . . .' They load you up with precepts, but without goodness. And those others with the philacteries who put on so many vestments, so many things, to look majestic, perfect, they have no sense of beauty. They have no sense of beauty. The closest they get is the beauty of the museum. Intellectuals without talent, ethicists without goodness, bearers of museum beauties. These are the hypocrites whom Jesus chastises so severely.

"But it doesn't end here"; in this page of the Gospel "the Lord speaks of another class of hypocrites, those who trample upon the sacred.

"The Lord speaks of fasting, prayer, of almsgiving: the three pillars of Christian piety, of inner conversion, which the Church proposes to all of us during Lent. Even on this road there are the hypocrites, who make a show of their fasting, their almsgiving, their prayer. I think that when we reach that point in our relationship with God, when we become hypocrites we are fairly close to the sin against the

Holy Spirit. These know nothing about beauty, these know nothing about love, these know nothing about truth; they are petty, vile.

"Let's think about hypocrisy in the Church, how much harm it does to everyone." The "icon" to be imitated is instead a figure described in another passage of the Gospel. This is the tax collector who with humble simplicity prays saying: "Have mercy on me, Lord, who am a sinner." "This is the prayer that we should make every day, in the awareness that we are sinners," but "with concrete sins, not theoretical." This is the prayer that will help us to travel "the road opposite" to hypocrisy, a temptation that "we all have.

"But we all have grace too, the grace that comes from Jesus Christ: the grace of joy; the grace of magnanimity, of generosity. The hypocrite does not know what joy is, does not know what generosity is, does not know what magnanimity is."

June 19, 2013   *2 Corinthians 9:6–11 ⚜ Matthew 6:1–6, 16–18*

70

We cannot pray to the Father if we have enemies in our heart

Prayer is not a kind of magic, but rather entrusting ourselves to the Father's embrace. Jesus immediately gives us advice for our prayer: "Don't waste words, don't make noise, the noise of worldliness, the noise of vanity. Prayer is not a magic trick; we're not making magic with prayer." Someone "tells me that when a person goes to a 'sorcerer,' he has to say many words to heal him." But that "is pagan." Jesus teaches us that we "do not have to go to him with many words," because "he knows everything." The first word is "Father," this "is the key to prayer. Without saying, without feeling this word we cannot pray.

"To whom do I pray? To God Almighty? Too far away. No, I'm not feeling it. Jesus didn't feel it either. To whom do I pray? To the cosmic God? That's just more of the same these days, isn't it? . . . Praying to the cosmic God, right? This polytheistic style that comes to us with 'culture lite' . . . You have to pray to the Father! Now that's a strong word, 'Father.' You have to pray to the one who has begotten you, who has given you life, has given life to you. Not to all: 'to all' is too anonymous. To you. To me. And also the one who accompanies you on your journey; he knows your whole life. All of it: the good and the not so good. He knows it all. If we don't begin our prayer with these words, not spoken with the lips but spoken by the heart, we cannot pray as Christians.

" 'Father' is a strong word," but "it opens the doors." At the moment of his sacrifice, Isaac realized that "something was wrong," because "the lamb was missing," but he trusted his father and "he cast his worry into the heart of his father." And again, "Father" is the word that came to the mind of "that son" who had gone away with his inheritance "and then wanted to return home." And that father "saw him coming and ran" to him; "he threw himself upon his neck, to fall on him in love." "Father, I have sinned": this is "the key to every prayer, feeling ourselves loved by a father.

"We have a Father. He is so close that he embraces us . . . All of these worries, all of these cares that we may have, let's leave them to the Father; he knows what we need. But Father, who? My Father? No: our Father! Because I am not an only child, none of us is, and if I can't be a brother, it's going to be hard for me to be a son of this Father, because he is a Father of all. Mine, sure, but also of the rest, of my brothers. And if I am not at peace with my brothers, I cannot say 'Father' to him."

After Jesus taught us the Our Father, he emphasized that if we do not forgive others, the Father will not forgive our sins. "It is so difficult to forgive others, it is really difficult, because we always have that resentment inside." We think: "'He did that to me, you just wait . . . until I get back at him.'

"No, we cannot pray with enemies in our hearts, with brothers and enemies in our hearts, we cannot pray. This is difficult; yes, it is difficult. 'Father, I can't say "Father," it doesn't work for me.' It's true, I understand this. 'I can't say "our," because this guy did this to me, and that . . . it's too much! These guys should go to hell, right? They're not my brothers!' It's true, it's not easy. But Jesus promised us the Holy Spirit; he is the one who teaches us, from the inside, from the heart, how to say 'Father' and how to say 'our.' Let's ask the Holy Spirit today to teach us to say 'Father' and to say 'our,' making peace with all our enemies."

June 20, 2013   *2 Corinthians 11:1–11* ✢ *Matthew 6:7–15*

71

The treasures that save our hearts

The hunt for the only treasure that we can take with us into the life after life is a Christian's reason for being. It is the reason for being that Jesus explains to the disciples in the passage from the Gospel of Matthew: "Where your treasure is, there also will your heart be." The problem lies in not mixing up the forms of wealth. There are "dangerous treasures" that seduce us, "but we have to let them be," those accumulated during life but that prove to be empty when we die. "I have never seen a moving van behind a funeral procession, never." But there is also a treasure that "we can take with us," a treasure that no one can steal, which is not "that which you have saved for yourself" but "that which you have given to others."

"That treasure which we have given to others, that is what we take with us. And that will be our 'merit,' but it is the merit of Jesus Christ in us. And we have to take that with us. It is what the Lord lets us take. Love, charity, service, patience, goodness, tenderness are beautiful treasures, those we take with us. The others, no."

So as the Gospel says, the treasure that matters in the eyes of God is that which already on earth is being stored up in heaven. But Jesus goes a step further: he connects the treasure with the "heart"; he creates a "relationship" between the two terms. This is because ours "is a restless heart," which the Lord "has made this way so that it will seek him."

"The Lord has made us restless so that we will seek him, find him, grow. But if our treasure is a treasure that is not near the Lord, that is not of the Lord, our heart becomes restless for things that are no good, for these other treasures . . . So many people, we ourselves are restless . . . To have this, to get that, and in the end our heart becomes tired; it is never satisfied; it becomes tired, lazy, a heart without love. The weariness of the heart. Let's think about that. What do I have: a tired heart, that just wants to make itself comfortable, three or four things, a nice bank account, this, the other? Or a restless heart that is always seeking the things that it cannot possess, the things of the Lord? We have to look after this restlessness of the heart, always."

At this point, Christ also warns us about the "eye," which is a symbol "of the intention of the heart" and reflects upon the body. A "heart that loves" makes the body "luminous"; an "evil heart" makes it dark. The contrast between light and darkness influences "our judgment on things," as is also demonstrated by the fact that from a "heart of stone, attached to a treasure of the earth"—to a "selfish treasure" that can even become a treasure "of hatred—come wars . . . Let's ask instead for the grace of a new heart," a "heart of flesh.

"All of these pieces of the heart that are made of stone, may the Lord make them human, with that restlessness, with that good anxiety of moving forward, seeking him and letting ourselves be sought by him. May the Lord change our hearts! And this is how he will save us. He will save us from the treasures that cannot help us in the encounter with him, in the service of others, and he will also give us the light to know and judge according to the real treasure: his truth. May the Lord change our hearts to seek out the real treasure and thus become luminous persons, and not persons of darkness."

June 21, 2013   *2 Corinthians 11:18, 21–30* ✤ *Matthew 6:19–23*

72

Let's serve the Word of God, not the idolatry of wealth

No one can serve two masters." Jesus has "a clear idea about this": it is "wealth and the worries of the world" that suffocate the Word of God; these are the thorns that suffocate the seed that falls onto the ground, as in the parable of the Sower.

"Wealth and the worries of the world suffocate the Word of God and do not allow it to grow. And the word dies, because it is not cared for; it is suffocated. In that case we are serving wealth or serving our worries, but not serving the Word of God. And this too has a temporal meaning, because the parable is sort of built—the words of Jesus in the parable—on time, isn't it? Do not worry about tomorrow, about what you will do tomorrow . . . And the parable of the sower is also built upon time: he sows, then the rain comes and the seed grows. What does this do in us, what do wealth and worries do? They just take up our time."

Our whole life is founded on three pillars: one in the past, one in the present, and another in the future. The pillar of the past "is that of the election of the Lord." Each one of us, in fact, can say that the Lord "has chosen me, has loved me," he has said to me "come," and with Baptism "he has chosen me to walk on a path, the Christian path." The future, however, is about "walking toward a promise"; the Lord "has made a promise to us." The present, finally, "is our response to this God who is so good that he has chosen me. He makes a promise, he proposes a covenant, and I make a covenant with him." So these are the three pillars: "election, covenant, and promise.

"The three pillars of all salvation history. But when our hearts get caught up in what Jesus is talking about, in serving wealth and the worries of the world, we mutilate time: we cut off the past, cut off the future, and get caught up in the present. When someone is attached to wealth he doesn't care about the past or the future, he has everything right there. It's an idol, wealth is. I don't need a past, a promise, an election: nothing. Someone who worries about what is going to happen cuts off his relationship with the future—'But could this be?'—and the future has prospects but doesn't offer any promise; it remains confused and cut off."

This is why Jesus tells us we must follow either the Kingdom of God or the wealth and worries of the world. With Baptism, "we are chosen in love" by him; we have a "Father who has set us on the journey." And so "the future too is joyful," because "we are walking toward a promise." The Lord "is faithful, he does not deceive us," so we too are called to do "what we can" without disappointment, "without forgetting that we have a Father in the past who has chosen us." Wealth and worries are the two things that "make us forget our past," that make us live as if we did not have a Father. And our present also "is a present that doesn't work.

"Forgetting the past, not accepting the present, disfiguring the future: this is what wealth and worries do. The Lord tells us: 'Calm down! Seek the Kingdom of God and his justice, and all the rest will come.' Let's ask the Lord for the grace not to go wrong with worries, with the idolatry of wealth, and always to remember that we have a Father who has chosen us; to remember that this Father promises us something good, which is walking toward that promise and having the courage to take the present as it comes. Let's ask this grace from the Lord!"

June 22, 2013   *2 Corinthians 12:1–10* ✦ *Matthew 6:24–34*

73

Jesus asks us what he means to us; let's answer with our hearts

"Who do you say that I am?" A question to which Peter responds: "You are the Christ of God, the Anointed of the Lord," which even two thousand years later brings us to a crisis point, a test of our journey of faith. A question that is directed to the heart, to which we must respond with the humility of a sinner, beyond the ready-made or convenient answers. It almost contains another question, the mirror image and just as decisive: "Who do we think we are for Jesus?

"We, we too, who are apostles and servants, must answer, because the Lord is asking us: 'What do you think of me?' He really does this, he does it so many times! 'What do you think of me?' says the Lord. And we can't be like those who don't really understand. 'But, you are the Anointed One! Yes, I've read about it.' We can't talk about Jesus like a historical personage, a figure from history, right? Jesus is alive in front of us. It's a living person who is asking us this question. And we have to respond, but from the heart."

Today Jesus is still calling us to make that radical decision which the apostles made, a total decision, according to the logic of "all or nothing," a journey we cannot make without being illuminated by a "special grace," to live always on the solid foundation of veneration and love for Jesus.

"Veneration and love for his Holy Name. The certainty that he has established us upon a rock, the rock of his love. And based on this love we respond, we give the response. And when Jesus asks this question—'Who am I for you?'—we have to think about this: I have been established upon the rock of his love. He is guiding me. I have to respond standing firmly upon that rock and under his own guidance.

"Who am I for you?" Jesus asks us. Sometimes we are ashamed of responding to this question because we know that there's something wrong with us, we are sinners. But this is precisely the moment to trust in his love and respond with that sense of truth, as Peter did on the Sea of Tiberias: "Lord, you know everything." And precisely in the moment in which we feel like sinners, the Lord loves us so much, and just as he made the fisherman Peter the head of his Church, so also he will do something good with us.

"He is greater, he is greater! And when we say, from veneration and love, sure, sure on the rock of love and through his guidance, 'You are the Anointed One,' this will do us so much good and will carry us forward with surety and help us every day to take up the Cross, which is heavy sometimes. Let's go forward like this, with joy, and asking for this grace: Give your people, Father, the grace to live always in veneration and love for your Holy Name! And with the certainty that you never deprive of your guidance those you have established on the rock of your love!"

June 23, 2013   *Zechariah 12:10–11; 13:1* ✤
                                             Galatians 3:26–29 ✤ *Luke 9:18–24*

74

May the Church speak of the word and not of its own ideas

The figure of John the Baptist is not always easy to understand. "When we think about his life he is 'a prophet,' " a "man who was great and then ended up as a poor wretch." So who is John? He himself explains this: "I am a voice, a voice in the desert," but "he is a voice without a word, because the word is not him, it is Another." So this is the mystery of John: "he never lords it over the Word"; John "is the one who points, the one who gestures." The "meaning of John's life is to point out another." It is striking that "the Church would choose as the feast day for John" a period during which the days are the longest of the year, "they have more light." And John truly "was the man of light, he brought light, but he was not the light himself, he was a reflected light." John was "like a moon," and when Jesus began to preach, John's light "began to diminish, to go down. Voice, not Word, light, but not the source.

"John seems to be nothing. That is John's vocation: to make himself nothing. And when we contemplate the life of this man, so great, so powerful—everyone thought he was the Messiah—when we contemplate his life, how he lowers himself to the darkness of a prison cell, we are contemplating a great mystery. We don't know what John's last days were like. We don't know. We know only that he was killed, his head put upon a platter, a big present from a dancer to an adulteress. I don't think you can get any lower than this. This was how John ended up."

In prison, John experienced doubts; he was in anguish and called for his disciples to go to Jesus to ask him: "Are you the one, or are we to wait for another?" There is "real darkness and pain over his life. John wasn't even spared this. The figure of John reminds me very much of the Church.

"The Church exists to proclaim, to be the voice of the Word, of her Bridegroom, who is the Word. And the Church exists to proclaim this Word to the point of martyrdom. Martyrdom precisely at the hands of the most arrogant powers of the earth. John could have made himself important, he could have said something about himself. But I think he never did, only this: he pointed, he felt like a voice, not the Word. The secret of John. Why is John holy and not sinful? Because he never, never took a truth as his own. He didn't want to become an ideologue. The man who denied himself, so that the Word could increase. And we, as a Church, can ask today for the grace not to become an ideological Church."

The Church must listen to the Word of God and become a voice, proclaim the Word with courage. "This is the Church without ideologies, without a life of its own: the Church that is the *mysterium lunae,* that receives light from its Bridegroom and must diminish so that he may increase.

"This is the model that John offers us today, for us and for the Church. A Church that is always at the service of the Word. A Church that never takes anything for itself. Let's ask, in prayer, for the grace of joy; let's ask the Lord to gladden this Church in its service of the Word, to be the voice of this Word, to preach this word. Let's ask for the grace to imitate John, without ideas of our own, without a Gospel taken as property, only a Church-as-voice that calls attention to the Word, and this to the point of martyrdom."

June 24, 2013   *Isaiah 49:1–6* ✣ *Acts 13:22–26* ✣ *Luke 1:57–66, 80*

75

Being Christian is a call of love

In the first reading, taken from the book of Genesis, Abram and Lot are discussing the division of the land. "When I read this, I think about the Middle East, and I beg the Lord to give us all the wisdom, this wisdom—let's not fight, I'll go here and you go there—for peace." Abraham "continues to walk. He had left his land to go he didn't know where, but wherever the Lord would tell him." So he continues to walk, because he believes in the Word of God that "had called him to leave his land." This man, perhaps in his nineties, looks at the land that the Lord shows him and believes.

"Abraham leaves his land with a promise; his whole journey is going toward this promise. And his path is also a model for our path. God calls Abraham, a person, and from this person he makes a people. If we go to the book of Genesis, to the beginning, to the Creation, we can find that God creates the stars, creates the plants, creates the animals, plural, plural, plural. But he creates man: in the singular, one. God always speaks to us in the singular, because he has created us in his image and likeness. And God speaks to us in the singular. He spoke to Abraham and gave him a promise, and asked him to leave his land. We Christians have been called in the singular; none of us is Christian by pure coincidence! No one!"

There is a call "with a name, with a promise: Go forward, I am with you! I am walking by your side." And Jesus knew this; even "in the most difficult moments he turned to the Father.

"God accompanies us, God calls us by name, God promises us descendants. And this is what the assurance of the Christian is like. It's not a coincidence, it's a call! A call that helps us go forward. Being Christian is a call of love, of friendship; a call to become a child of God, a brother of Jesus, to become fruitful in the transmission of this call to others, to become instruments of this call. There are so many problems, so many problems; there are difficult moments. Jesus went through so many of them! But always with this assurance: 'The Lord has called me. The Lord is like me. The Lord has promised me.'"

The Lord "is faithful, because he can never betray himself; he is faithfulness." And thinking of that passage in which Abraham "is anointed father for the first time, father of peoples, let's think that we too have been anointed in Baptism, and let's think about our Christian life.

"Someone may say, 'Father, I am a sinner' . . . But we all are. Everybody knows that. The problem is, sinners, go forward with the Lord, go forward with that promise he has made to us, with that promise of fruitfulness. And say to others, tell others that the Lord is with us, that the Lord has chosen us and that he doesn't leave us alone, ever! May the Lord give us, all of us, this desire to go forward that Abraham had, in the midst of problems; but to go forward, with that assurance that he who has called me, who has promised me so many wonderful things, is with me!"

June 25, 2013   *Genesis 13:2, 5–18 ✣ Matthew 7:6, 12–14*

76

May priests have the grace of spiritual paternity

The "desire for fatherhood" is implanted in the deepest fibers of a man, and a priest is no exception, although his desire is directed and lived in a particular way.

"When a man does not have this desire, something is missing in this man. Something is wrong. All of us, in order to be, in order to become fulfilled, in order to be mature, have to feel the joy of fatherhood, even we celibates. Fatherhood is giving life to others, giving life, giving life . . . For us it may be pastoral fatherhood, spiritual fatherhood, but it is giving life, becoming fathers."

In the passage from Genesis, God promises the elderly Abraham the joy of a son, together with descendants as numerous as the stars in the sky. To seal this pact, Abraham follows God's instructions and prepares a sacrifice of animals that he then defends from birds of prey. "It's touching for me to look at this man in his nineties with his staff in his hand," defending his sacrifice. "It reminds me of a father defending his family, his children.

"A father who knows what it means to defend his children. And this is a grace that we priests must ask for: to be fathers, to be fathers. The grace of fatherhood, of pastoral fatherhood, of spiritual fatherhood. We may have many sins, but this is of the *commune sanctorum;* we all have sins. But not having children, not becoming a father, it's as if life has not reached its end; we stop halfway there. So we must be fathers. But this is a grace that the Lord gives. People talk this way: 'Father, Father, Father . . .' He wants us to be like this, fathers, with the grace of pastoral fatherhood."

Our thoughts go out with affection to Cardinal De Giorgi, who has reached the sixtieth anniversary of his priesthood. "I don't know what dear Salvatore has done," but "I am sure he has been a father." "And this is a sign." Every tree "bears fruit, and if he is good the fruit has to be good, right?"

"Let's thank the Lord for this grace of fatherhood in the Church, which goes from father to son, and so on . . . And finally I think of these two icons, and of one more: the icon of Abraham asking for a son, the icon of Abraham with his staff in his hand, defending his family, and the icon of the elderly Simeon in the Temple, when he receives the new life. He conducts a spontaneous liturgy, a liturgy of joy. And as for you, may the Lord give you great joy today."

June 26, 2013   *Genesis 15:1–12, 17–18 ✛ Matthew 7:15–20*

77

Joyfully build your lives on Jesus the rock

Rigid and sad. Or cheerful but with no idea about Christian joy. These are two "houses," in a certain way opposite, inhabited by two categories of believers, and in both cases they have a serious defect: they are founded on a Christianity made of words and not based on the "rock" of the word of Christ. This twofold group is the subject of the famous passage of the houses on the sand and on the rock in the Gospel of Matthew.

"In the history of the Church there have been two classes of Christians: Christians in word—who say 'Lord, Lord, Lord'—and Christians of action, in truth. There has always been the temptation of living our Christianity outside of the rock that is Christ. The only one who gives us the freedom to say 'Father' to God is Christ, the rock. He is the only one who supports us in difficult moments, isn't he? As Jesus says: the rain falls, the rivers overflow, the winds blow, but on the rock there is safety; when it's just words, the words fly away, they are no use. But there is the temptation of these Christians in word, a Christianity without Jesus, a Christianity without Christ. And this has happened and happens today in the Church: being Christians without Christ."

These "Christians in word" have specific characteristics. There is a first type—who can be called "Gnostic—who instead of loving the rock love beautiful words" and therefore just bob around on the surface of Christian life. And then there is the other, who can be called "Pelagians," who have a serious and buttoned-up way of life. Christians who "look at their own shoes.

"And this temptation is there today. Superficial Christians who believe in God, in Christ, but vaguely; they believe it is not Jesus Christ who gives you a foundation. They are the modern Gnostics. The temptation of Gnosticism. A 'liquid' Christianity. On the other hand, there are those who believe that Christian life must be taken so seriously that they end up confusing solidity, firmness, with rigidity. They are the rigid ones! They think that being Christian means moping around all the time."

The fact is that "there are many" of these Christians. But "they are not Christians, they masquerade as Christians. They don't know what the Lord is, they don't know what the rock is, they don't have the freedom of Christians. And to say it a bit more simply, they have no joy.

"The first have a certain superficial 'cheerfulness.' The others live in a constant funeral vigil, but they don't know what Christian joy is. They don't know how to enjoy the life that Jesus gives us, because they don't know how to talk with Jesus. They do not feel that they are founded on Jesus, with the firmness that the presence of Jesus gives us. And not only do they have no joy but they have no freedom. In the one group they are slaves of superficiality, of this vague life; and in the other they are slaves of rigidity, they are not free. There is no room for the Holy Spirit in their lives. It is the Spirit who makes us free! The Lord invites us today to build our Christian life on him, the rock, who gives us freedom, sends the Spirit to us, helps us go forward with joy on his way, according to his plan."

June 27, 2013   *Genesis 16:1–12, 15–16 ✤ Matthew 7:21–29*

78

May the Christian be patient and blameless

The Lord enters slowly into Abraham's life: he is ninety-nine years old when God promises him a son. But he enters immediately into the life of the leper: Jesus hears his prayer, touches him, and works the miracle. The Lord chooses to get involved "in our lives, in the life of his people." Abraham and the leper. "When the Lord comes he does not always act the same way. There is no protocol for the action of God in our lives; it doesn't exist." One time "he acts one way, another time he acts another way," but he always acts. "There is always this encounter between us and the Lord.

"The Lord always chooses his way to enter our lives. Many times he does this so slowly that we are at risk of losing our patience: 'But Lord, when?' And we pray, we pray . . . And he doesn't intervene in our lives. Other times, when we think about what the Lord has promised us, it is so great that we are a bit incredulous, a bit skeptical, and like Abraham—on the sly—we smile . . . It says in the first reading that Abraham hid his face and laughed . . . He was skeptical: 'But how can I, at almost one hundred years old, have a son, and how can my wife have a son at ninety?'"

This is the same skepticism that Sarah has at the oak of Mamre, when the three angels say the same thing to Abraham. "How many times do we, when the Lord does not come, does not work the miracle, does not do what we want him to do, become either impatient or skeptical?

"But he doesn't do it, he can't do it for skeptics. The Lord takes his time. But in this relationship with us he has so much patience. We are not the only ones who have to be patient; he is too! He waits for us! And he waits for us until the end of our lives! Let's think about the good thief: right at the end, at the end, he acknowledged God. The Lord walks with us, but often he doesn't show himself, like with the disciples at Emmaus. The Lord is involved in our lives— this is sure!—but many times we don't see him. This requires patience from us. But the Lord who walks with us, he too has so much patience with us."

Let's think "of the mystery of God's patience, because in walking with us, he walks at our pace." Sometimes in life "things become so gloomy, there is so much darkness, that we want—if we are in difficulty—to get down off the Cross." This "is the exact moment; it's always darkest before the dawn. And whenever we get down from the Cross, we always do this five minutes before liberation comes, in the moment of the greatest impatience.

"Jesus, on the Cross, heard that they were challenging him: 'Get down, get down! Come on!' Patience to the end, because he has patience with us. He always enters, he is involved with us, but in his own way and when he thinks it is best. He says to us just what he said to Abraham: 'Walk in my presence and be perfect,' be blameless, that's the right word. Walk in my presence and try to be blameless. This is the way with the Lord, and he intervenes, but we have to wait, wait for the moment, always walking in his presence and trying to be blameless. Let's ask for this grace from the Lord: always to walk in his presence, seeking to be blameless."

June 28, 2013   *Genesis 17:1, 9–10, 15–22 ✛ Matthew 8:1–4*

79

To touch the heart of God, pray

Abraham speaks to the Lord with courage and insistence to defend Sodom from destruction. "Abraham is a courageous man, and he prays with courage"; Abraham "feels the power to speak face-to-face with the Lord and tries to defend the city." And he does this with insistence. So in the Bible, we see that "prayer must be courageous.

"When we talk about courage, we always think about apostolic courage, going to preach the Gospel, these things . . . But there is also courage before the Lord. That frankness before the Lord: going to the Lord courageously to ask for things. It may be funny, and that's fine, but it's funny because Abraham is talking with the Lord in a special way, with this courage, and we can't quite tell if we're looking at a man who is praying or a 'Phoenician trader,' because he keeps lowering the price, down, down . . . And he insists; from fifty he succeeds in lowering the price to ten. He knew it wasn't possible. There was only one just man: his nephew, his cousin . . . But with that courage, with that insistence, he went forward."

Sometimes we go to the Lord to "ask for something for a person"; we ask for this and that and then go our way. "But that is not prayer," because "if you want the Lord to give you a grace, you have to go with courage and do what Abraham did, with that insistence." It is Jesus himself who tells us that we must pray like the widow who pesters the dishonest judge, like the man who knocks at his friend's door in the middle of the night. With insistence: "that's what Jesus teaches us." And in fact Jesus praises the Syro-Phoenician woman who asks with insistence for the healing of her daughter. Insistence, even though she is tired, and "she is really tired." But this "is an attitude of prayer." Saint Teresa of Avila "speaks of prayer as a negotiation with the Lord," and this "is possible only when there is familiarity with the Lord. It is tiring, that's true, but this is prayer, this is getting a grace from God." Abraham, in his prayer, "takes his arguments and reasoning from the very heart of Jesus.

"Convincing the Lord with the virtues of the Lord himself! That's beautiful! Abraham's argument goes to the Lord's heart, and Jesus teaches us the same thing: 'The Father knows how things are. The Father—don't worry—sends rain on the just and the sinners, sunshine for the just and for the sinners.' Abraham continues along this line of reasoning. I will stop here: praying is negotiating with the Lord, even becoming a nuisance with the Lord. Praying is praising the Lord for the wonderful things that he has and saying to him that these wonderful things, he should send them to us. And that if he is so merciful, so good, he should help us!

"Today I would like all of us, for five minutes, no more, at some point in the day to take out the Bible and slowly read Psalm 103: Bless the Lord all my soul, and all that is in me bless his Holy Name! Forget not all his benefits. He pardons all our offenses, heals all our infirmities, saves your life from the pit, surrounds you with goodness and mercy . . . And with this we will learn the things that we must say to the Lord when we are asking him for grace. 'You who are merciful, you who forgive, grant me this grace.' Like Abraham did in prayer, and like Moses did. Let's go forward in prayer, courageously, and with these arguments that come right from the heart of God."

July 1, 2013   *Genesis 18:16–33* ✤ *Matthew 8:18–22*

80

Let's flee from sin with no looking back

Acting slowly, looking back, being afraid, and turning to the Lord, to the grace of the Holy Spirit. There are four "possible attitudes in situations of conflict, in difficult situations." The first attitude is that of the "slowness" of Lot. He had decided to leave the city before it was destroyed, but he does so slowly. The angel tells him to run away, but "he can't let go of evil, of sin. We want to get out, we are determined," but "there is something that pulls us back," and so Lot even tries to negotiate with the angel.

"It is so difficult to break with a sinful situation. It's difficult! Even in a temptation, it's difficult! But the voice of God speaks this word to us: 'Flee! you cannot fight there, because the fire, the brimstone will kill you. Flee!' Saint Thérèse of the Child Jesus taught us that sometimes, in some temptations, the only solution is to run away and not be ashamed of running away; to recognize that we are weak and we have to run away. And our people in their simple wisdom say it with a touch of humor: 'He who fights and runs away may live to fight another day.' Running away in order to continue forward on the path of Jesus."

The angel then says, "Do not look back," run away and look forward. This is a piece of advice for overcoming the nostalgia for sin. Let's think of the People of God in the desert: "They had everything, the promises, everything." And yet "there was the nostalgia for the onions of Egypt," and this "nostalgia made them forget that they ate those onions at the table of slavery." There was "the nostalgia to go back, to go back." And the advice of the angel "is wise: don't look back! Go forward." We must not be like Lot's wife; we have to "cut off all nostalgia, because there is also the temptation of curiosity for the past.

"When faced with sin, run away without nostalgia. Curiosity is no good, it's harmful! 'But in such a sinful world, what can we do? What could this sin be like? I'd like to know . . .' No, leave it alone!

Curiosity will hurt you! Run and don't look back! We are weak, all of us, and we have to protect ourselves.

"The third situation is on the boat: it is fear. When a great tempest came on the sea, the boat was swamped by the waves. 'Save us, Lord, we are lost!' they say. Fear! This too is a temptation of the devil: fear of going forward on the path of the Lord."

There is the temptation that says that "it is better to remain here," where I am safe. "But this is the Egypt of slavery!" I am "afraid of going forward, I am afraid of where the Lord is taking me." Fear, however, "is not a good adviser." Jesus "said it many times: 'Do not be afraid!' Fear doesn't help us."

The fourth attitude "is the grace of the Holy Spirit." When Jesus lulls the stormy sea, the disciples on the boat are amazed. "Always, in the face of sin, in the face of nostalgia, in the face of fear," we have to turn to the Lord.

"Look to the Lord, contemplate the Lord. This will give us that amazement, so beautiful, of a new encounter with the Lord. 'Lord, I have this temptation: I want to remain in this situation of sin; Lord, I am curious to know what these things are like; Lord, I am afraid.' And they looked to the Lord and said: 'Save us, Lord, we are lost!' And then came the amazement of the new encounter with Jesus. Let's not be simpletons or lukewarm Christians; let's be valorous, courageous. We are weak, but we have to be courageous in our weakness. And so many times our courage has to be expressed in running away and not looking back, so that we don't fall into harmful nostalgia. Don't be afraid, and always look to the Lord!"

July 2, 2013   *Genesis 19:15–29 ✤ Matthew 8:23–27*

81

We meet God in kissing the feet of Jesus in the weakest of our brothers

After the Resurrection, Jesus appeared to the apostles, but Thomas wasn't there. "He wanted him to wait a week. The Lord knows why he does what he does. And he gives each one of us the time that he believes is best for us. He gave Thomas a week." Jesus shows himself with his wounds: "His whole body was clean, beautiful, full of light, but the wounds were there, and they are still there," and when the Lord comes, at the end of the world, "he will show us his wounds." In order to believe, Thomas wanted to put his fingers into those wounds:

"He was stubborn. But the Lord wanted a stubborn man to help us understand something greater. Thomas saw the Lord; he was invited to put his finger in the nail marks, to put his hand in his side, and he did not say: 'It is true, the Lord is risen!' No! He went further. He said: 'My Lord and my God!' The first of the disciples who makes the confession of the divinity of Christ, after the Resurrection. And he worshiped him.

"And in this way we understand the Lord's intention in making him wait: to use even his incredulity to bring him not to the affirmation of the Resurrection but to the affirmation of his divinity." The "way to the encounter with Jesus-God is his wounds. There is no other.

"In the history of the Church there have been some mistakes in the way toward God. Some have believed that the living God, the God of the Christians can be found by the way of meditation, and going higher in meditation. That is dangerous. How many get lost on that way and do not arrive. Perhaps they do arrive at the knowledge of God, but not of Jesus Christ, Son of God, second Person of the Trinity. They don't get there. It is the way of the Gnostics, isn't it? They are good, they work, but it's not the right way. It is very complicated, and it does not bring you to a good harbor.

"Others have thought that in order to get to God we have to be mortified, austere, and have chosen the way of penance: just penance and fasting. And these too have not arrived at the living God, at the living God Jesus Christ. They are the Pelagians, who believe they can get there by their own efforts." But Jesus tells us that the way to encounter him is by finding his wounds.

"And you find the wounds of Jesus by doing the works of mercy, giving to the body—to the body—and also to the soul, but to the body—I emphasize this—of your stricken brother, because he is hungry, because he is thirsty, because he is naked, because he is humiliated, because he is a slave, because he is in prison, because he is in the hospital. These are the wounds of Jesus today. And Jesus is asking us to make an act of faith, to him, but through these wounds. 'Okay, great! Let's set up a foundation to help all of these, and we'll do so many good things to help them.' That is important, but if we remain on this level we will be only philanthropists. We have to touch the wounds of Jesus, we have to caress the wounds of Jesus, we have to care for the wounds of Jesus with tenderness, we have to kiss the wounds of Jesus, and this literally. Think about what happened to Saint Francis, when he embraced the leper. The same as with Thomas: it changed his life!"

In order to touch the living God, what is needed is not "to take a refresher course" but to enter into the wounds of Jesus, and for this "it is enough to go out into the street." "Let's ask Saint Thomas for the grace to have the courage to enter into the wounds of Jesus with our tenderness, and we will surely have the grace to worship the living God."

July 3, 2013   *Ephesians 2:19–22* ✤ *John 20:24–29*

82

We are children of God; no one can steal this identity card

In the Gospel passage on the healing of the paralytic, Jesus says at the beginning: "Courage, son, your sins are forgiven." Perhaps this man was a little "shaken up," because he wanted physical healing. Then, in the face of the criticisms of the scribes who were accusing him of blasphemy—"because only God can forgive sins"—Jesus also heals him in body. In reality the healings, the teaching, the strong words against hypocrisy were "only a sign, a sign of something greater that Jesus was doing," the forgiveness of sins. In Jesus the world is reconciled with God; this is the "more profound miracle.

"This reconciliation is the re-creation of the world: this is the most profound mission of Jesus. The redemption of all of us sinners, and Jesus does this not with words, not with gestures, not walking on the path, no! He does it with his flesh! It is precisely he, God, who becomes one of us, man, to heal us from within, us sinners."

Jesus frees us from sin by making himself "sin," taking upon himself "all sin," and "this is the new creation." Jesus "descends from glory and lowers himself to the point of death, to death on the Cross" to the point of crying out: "Father, why have you abandoned me!" This "is his glory and this is our salvation.

"This is the greatest miracle, and what does Jesus do with this? He makes us children, with the freedom of children. Because of what Jesus has done we are able to say: 'Father.' Without him, we never would have been able to say this: 'Father!' And to say 'Father' with an attitude that is so good and so beautiful, with freedom! This is the great miracle of Jesus. We, slaves of sin, he has made all of us free, he has healed us right at the core of our existence. It will do us good to think about this and to think that it is so wonderful to be children, it is so wonderful to have this freedom as children, because the child is at home, and Jesus has opened the doors of home . . . We are at home now!"

Now we can understand why Jesus says: "Courage, son, your sins are forgiven!

"This is the root of our courage. I am free, I am a child . . . The Father loves me and I love the Father! Let's ask the Lord for the grace to really understand this work of his, what God has done in him. God has reconciled the world with himself in Christ, entrusting to us the word of reconciliation and the grace to carry forward with strength, with the freedom of children, this word of reconciliation. We are saved in Jesus Christ! And no one can steal this identity card from us. That's my name: child of God! What a beautiful identity card! Legal status: free!"

July 4, 2013   *Genesis 22:1b–19 ✤ Matthew 9:1–8*

83

Mercy: the heart of God's message

I desire mercy, not sacrifice": these are the words of Jesus to the Pharisees who are criticizing the Lord because he eats with sinners. And the tax collectors "were sinners twice over, because they were attached to money and also traitors to their country," because they collected taxes from their people on behalf of the Romans. Jesus, then, sees Matthew, the tax collector, and looks at him with mercy.

"And that man, seated at the tax collector's booth, at first Jesus looks at him, and that man feels something new, something he didn't know—with that gaze of Jesus upon him—he feels an astonishment inside, he feels the invitation of Jesus: 'Follow me! Follow me!' At that moment this man is full of joy, but he's also a bit doubtful, because he is so attached to money. It just took a moment—which we know as Caravaggio succeeded in expressing it: that man who is looking but also, with his hands, grasping at the money—just one moment in which Matthew says yes, leaves everything, and goes with the Lord. It is the moment of mercy received and accepted: 'Yes, I'm coming with you!' It is the first moment of the encounter, a profound spiritual experience.

"Then comes the second moment: the celebration. The Lord celebrates with sinners"; they are celebrating the mercy of God that "changes their lives." After these two moments, the amazement of the encounter and the celebration, comes "the daily labor," proclaiming the Gospel.

"This labor has to be nourished with the memory of that first encounter, of that celebration. And this is not a moment, this is a season, until the end of life. Memory. Memory of what? Of those events! Of that encounter with Jesus, who has changed my life! Who has had mercy on me! Who has been so good with me and has even said: 'Invite your sinful friends, so that we can celebrate!' That memory gives strength to Matthew and to all of us for going forward. 'The Lord has changed my life! I have encountered the

Lord!' This is something to remember always. It is like blowing on the coals of that memory, isn't it? Blowing to keep the flame alive, always."

The Gospel parables speak of the many who rejected the invitation to the feast of the Lord. And Jesus went to "seek out the poor, the sick, and he celebrated with them.

"And Jesus, continuing with this habit, celebrates with sinners and offers sinners his grace. 'It is mercy that I desire, and not sacrifices. I have not come, in fact, to call the just, but sinners.' He who believes himself to be just, let him stew in his own juices! He came for us sinners, and this is beautiful. Let's look into the merciful eyes of Jesus, celebrate, and keep the memory of this salvation!"

July 5, 2013   *Genesis 23:1–4, 19; 24:1–8, 62–67 ✦ Matthew 9:9–13*

84

Let's renew the structures of the Church

New wine in new wineskins." Jesus is the bearer of renewal. "The teaching of the law is enriched with Jesus, renewed," and "Jesus makes all things new." His is "a true renewal of the law, the same law but more mature, renewed. The demands of Jesus were stronger, greater than those of the law." The law permits hatred of one's enemy; Jesus instead says to pray for him. So this is "the Kingdom of God that Jesus preaches." A renewal that "is first of all within our hearts." We "think that being Christian means" doing this or that. But that's not true.

"Being Christian means allowing Jesus to renew us in this new life. I am a good Christian, every Sunday from eleven to noon I go to Mass, and I do this, I do that . . . As if it were a collection. But the Christian life is not a collage. It is a harmonic totality, harmonious, created by the Holy Spirit! He renews everything: renews our hearts, our lives, and makes us live in a different way, but in a way that takes in the totality of life. We cannot be Christian in pieces, part-time. Being a part-time Christian doesn't work! Everything, the totality, full-time. It is the Spirit who brings about this renewal. Being Christian ultimately does not mean doing things but allowing ourselves to be renewed by the Holy Spirit or, to use the words of Jesus, to become new wine."

The innovation of the Gospel is "an innovation, but in the same law that comes in salvation history." And this innovation "goes beyond us," it renews us "and it renews the structures." This is why Jesus tells us that new wine requires new wineskins.

"In Christian life, and also in the life of the Church, there are old structures, outdated structures; they have to be renewed! And the Church has always been attentive to this, in dialogue with culture . . . It always allows itself to be renewed according to places, times, and persons. The Church has always done this work! Right from the beginning, let's remember the first theological controversy: in order to become Christian: is it necessary to observe all Jewish practices or not? No! They said no! The Gentiles may enter as they are: Gentiles . . . Enter into the Church and receive Baptism. A first renewal of the structure . . . And this is how the Church has always gone forward, allowing the Holy Spirit to renew these structures, structures of the Church. Don't be afraid of this! Don't be afraid of the innovation of the Gospel. Don't be afraid of the innovation that the Holy Spirit works within us! Don't be afraid of the renewal of the structures!

"The Church is free; it is the Holy Spirit who leads it forward." The Gospel teaches this: "The freedom to find always the innovation of the Gospel among us, in our lives and also in the structures." The Christian is a man who is free "with that freedom" which Jesus gives us, "he is not a slave of habits, of structures . . . It is the Holy Spirit who leads him forward." On the day of Pentecost, the Blessed Mother was there with the disciples.

"And where the mother is, the children are safe! All of us! Let's ask for the grace not to be afraid of the innovation of the Gospel, not to be afraid of the renewal that the Holy Spirit brings, not to be afraid of letting the outdated structures that imprison us fall away. If we are afraid, we know that our Mother is with us and, like children who are a little bit afraid, let's go to her and she—as the most ancient antiphon says—'guards us with her mantle, with her protection as mother.'"

July 6, 2013   *Genesis 27:1–5, 15–29 ✢ Matthew 9:14–17*

85

We must never kill our neighbors with our tongues

The Gospel of Saint Luke recounts the encounter of Jesus with his countrymen, the inhabitants of Nazareth. They admire Jesus, but they expect something amazing from him. "They wanted a miracle, they wanted a spectacle" in order to believe in him. So Jesus says that they do not have faith, and "they became angry, furious. They got up and pushed Jesus to the side of the mountain to throw him down, to kill him.

"But look how things have changed. They started with beauty, with admiration, and ended with a crime: they wanted to kill Jesus. This was because of jealousy, envy, all of these things . . . This is not something that happened two thousand years ago; this happens every day in our hearts, in our communities. They may say in a community: 'He's really great, this newcomer!' They say good things about him the first day, the second not so much, by the third they start to gossip, and end up ripping him to shreds."

So the Nazarenes "wanted to kill Jesus.

"But those in a community who gossip about their brothers, about the members of the community, they want to kill. They really do! The apostle John tells us this in his first letter: 'He who hates his brother in his heart is a murderer.' We are used to chatter, to gossip. But how often our communities, even our families, are a hell where this crime goes on, of killing our brother and sister with our tongues!

"A community, a family is destroyed by this envy, which the devil sows in the heart and which makes a person speak evil of another, and so it is destroyed. In these days there is so much talk about peace." We see the victims of weapons, but we also have to think about our everyday weapons: "the tongue, chatter, gossip." Every community instead must live with the Lord and be "like heaven.

"In order for there to be peace in a community, in a family, in a country, in the world, we have to start here: being with the Lord.

And where the Lord is there is no hatred, there is no jealousy. There is brotherhood. Let's ask the Lord for this: never to kill our neighbor with our tongues, and to be with the Lord as we will all be in heaven."

September 2, 2013   *1 Thessalonians 4:13–18 ✢ Luke 4:16–30*

86

Jesus doesn't need armies; his power is humility

The Christian identity is "an identity of light, not of darkness." Saint Paul addresses these words to the first disciples of Jesus: "Brothers, you are not in darkness, you are all sons of the light." This light "was not welcomed by the world." But Jesus came to save us from sin; "his light saves us from the darkness." On the other hand, "one may think that it is possible" to have the light "with all sorts of scientific things and things of humanity.

"One may understand everything, have knowledge about everything and this light on things. But the light of Jesus is something else. It is not a light of ignorance, no! It is a light of wisdom and understanding, but it is something other than the light of the world. The light that the world offers us is an artificial light, which may be bright—that of Jesus is brighter—bright like fireworks, like a camera flash. But the light of Jesus is a meek light, it is a tranquil light, it is a light of peace, it is like the light of Christmas Eve: without conceit."

It is a light that "offers itself and gives peace." The light of Jesus "doesn't put on a show; it is a light that comes into the heart." Nonetheless "it is true that the devil often comes disguised as an angel of light. He likes to imitate Jesus and makes himself look good; he speaks softly to us, as he spoke to Jesus after he fasted in the desert." This is why we have to ask the Lord "for the wisdom of discernment in order to know when it is Jesus who is giving the light and when it is the devil, disguised as an angel of light.

"How many believe they are living in the light and are in the darkness, but they don't realize it. What is it like, the light that Jesus offers to us? We can know the light of Jesus, because it is a humble light. It is not a light that imposes itself; it is humble. It is a meek light, with the strength of meekness. It is a light that speaks to the heart, and it is also a light that offers you the Cross. If in our light on the inside we are meek, we hear the voice of Jesus in our hearts and look at the Cross without fear: that is the light of Jesus."

But if, instead, a light comes that "makes you prideful," a light that "leads you to look down your nose at others," to despise others, "to arrogance, that is not the light of Jesus; it is the light of the devil, disguised as Jesus, as an angel of light." And the way to distinguish the true light from the false is this: "Wherever Jesus is there is humility, meekness, love, and the Cross. We will never find a Jesus who is not humble, meek, without love, and without the Cross." So we have to follow after him, "without fear," follow his light because the light of Jesus "is beautiful and does so much good." In today's Gospel, Jesus drives out the devil, and the people are seized with fear at a word that can drive out the unclean spirits.

"Jesus doesn't need an army to drive out demons, he doesn't need arrogance, he doesn't need power, pride. 'What word can this be that commands the unclean spirits with authority and power and they go?' This is a humble word, meek, with so much love; it is a word that accompanies us in the moments of the Cross. Let's ask the Lord to give us today the grace of his light and to teach us to distinguish when the light is from him and when it is an artificial light, made by the enemy, to deceive us."

September 3, 2013   *1 Thessalonians 5:1–6, 9–11 ✢ Luke 4:31–37*

87

Jesus has a promise and a mission for every Christian

A promise that comforts, a request for generosity, a mission to fulfill. This is how Jesus makes himself present in the life of a Christian. There is no dispensing with any of these three facets. Christ shows himself to Peter, James, and John with the sign of the miraculous catch of fish. First of all, Jesus reassures Peter, who has been unsettled by this sign, promising to make him "a fisher of men." Then he invites him to leave everything to follow him, entrusting a mission to him. In the case of the apostles, "the Lord enters into their lives with a miracle. He does not always pass in front of or inside of us with a miracle," but "he always makes himself heard.

"Whenever the Lord comes into our lives, when he passes into our hearts, he speaks a word to us; he speaks a word and also this promise: 'Go forward . . . Courage, don't be afraid, you can do this!' It is an invitation to mission, an invitation to follow him. And when we feel that we are in this second moment, we see that there is something in our lives that isn't working, that we have to correct this, and we leave it behind, with generosity. Or sometimes in our lives there is something good, but the Lord inspires us to leave it behind, in order to follow him more closely, as happened here. These have left everything, says the Gospel. And after tethering their boats to the shore, they left everything: boats, nets, everything! And they followed him."

Nonetheless, Jesus does not ask us to leave everything for a purpose that remains obscure to the one who has chosen to follow him. On the contrary, the objective is declared immediately, and it is a dynamic objective.

"Jesus never says 'Follow me!' without explaining the mission. No! 'Follow me, and I will make you this.' 'Follow me, for this.' 'If you want to be perfect, leave what you have and follow me to be perfect.' Always the mission. We travel on the path of Jesus in order to do something. Going the way of Jesus is not for show. We follow after him to do something: it is the mission."

Promise, request, mission. These three moments are found not only in active life but also in prayer. First, "a prayer without a word about Jesus and without trust, without promise, is not a good prayer." Second, it is good to ask Jesus to help us be ready to leave something behind, and this gets us ready for the third moment, because there is no prayer in which Jesus does not inspire "something to do.

"It is a true Christian prayer to hear the Lord with his word of comfort, peace, and promise; to have the courage of depriving ourselves of something that prevents us from going in haste to follow him and take on the mission. This does not mean that there are not temptations. There will be so many! But, look, Peter sinned gravely, by denying Jesus, but then the Lord forgave him. James and John committed the sin of careerism, wanting to get ahead, but the Lord forgave them."

September 5, 2013   *Colossians 1:9–14 ✢ Luke 5:1–11*

88

Marriage, an image of the union between Christ and the Church

"Can you make the wedding guests fast while the bridegroom is with them?' As long as they have the bridegroom with them they cannot fast," Jesus responds to the scribes. The Lord often comes back to this image of the bridegroom. Jesus has us see the relationship between him and the Church as a wedding. "I think this is the most profound reason why the Church takes such care of the sacrament of marriage and calls it a great sacrament, because it is precisely the image of the union of Christ with the Church." The Christian must have two attitudes at this wedding: first of all, "joy, because it is a great celebration.

"The Christian is fundamentally joyful. And this is why when wine is mentioned, it reminds me of the wedding of Cana. And this is why Jesus worked that miracle; this is why the Blessed Mother, when she realized there was no more wine, knew if there is no wine, there is no celebration . . . Let's imagine concluding that wedding by drinking tea or juice; it doesn't work. It needs to be a celebration. The Blessed Mother asks for the miracle. This is what Christian life is like. Christian life has this joyful attitude, joyful at its heart."

Of course, "there are really moments of the Cross, moments of suffering, but there is always that profound peace of joy, because Christian life is lived as a celebration, as the wedding of Jesus with the Church." Some of the first martyrs went to martyrdom as if they were going to a wedding; even at that moment they had "a joyful heart." The Church unites herself with the Lord "like a bride with her bridegroom, and at the end of the world there will be the definitive celebration."

The second attitude that the Christian must have we find in the parable of the wedding of the king's son. Everyone is invited to the celebration, good and bad. But when the celebration begins, the king sees someone who does not have a wedding garment.

"The thought comes to us: 'But, Father, what are they supposed to do? If they're out on the road when they are invited, how are they supposed to come in a wedding garment? There's something wrong here. What does this mean?' It's very simple! God asks only one thing to enter into this celebration: totality. What is really important is the bridegroom; the bridegroom permeates everything! And this brings us to the first reading, which speaks so strongly about the totality of Jesus, the firstborn of all creation. In him all things were created, by him all things were created, and in view of him. Everything! He is the center, the all in all!"

Jesus "is also 'the head of the Body, the Church. He is the beginning.' And God has given to him the fullness, the totality, so that all things may be reconciled in him." So if the first attitude is celebration, "the second attitude is recognizing him as the One!" The Lord "asks only this of us: to recognize him as the One Bridegroom." He "is always faithful, and he asks faithfulness of us." This is why when we want "to have a little party of our own, which is not this grand celebration, it's no good." The Lord tells us that we cannot serve two masters: we either serve God or serve the world:

"This is the second Christian attitude: recognizing Jesus as the all, the center, the totality. But we will always have the temptation of tossing this innovation of the Gospel, this new wine, into old attitudes. This is sin; we are all sinners. But recognize it: 'This is a sin.' Don't say this goes with that. No! Old wineskins cannot hold the new wine. This is the innovation of the Gospel. Jesus is the Bridegroom, the bridegroom who marries the Church, the bridegroom who loves the Church, who gives his life for the Church. And Jesus gives this wedding banquet! Jesus asks us to have the joy of the celebration, the joy of being Christian. And he also asks us for the totality; it is all him. And if we have something that is not of him, to repent of this, ask for forgiveness, and go forward. May the Lord give all of us the grace of always having this joy, as if we were going to a wedding. And also of having this faithfulness that the sole Bridegroom is the Lord."

September 6, 2013   *Colossians 1:15–20* ✠ *Luke 5:33–39*

89

May the center be always Jesus

J esus is the center. Jesus is the Lord." But we don't always understand these words very well, "we don't understand them easily."
Jesus "is not this lord or that lord," but "the Lord, the one Lord."
And he is the center that "regenerates us and grounds us"; this is
the Lord: "the center." One passage of the Gospel speaks to us of
Pharisees who were putting "the center of their religious devotion in
many commandments." And even today, "if Jesus is not the center,
there will be other things." And so "we meet so many Christians
without Christ, without Jesus.

"For example, there are Christians who have the sickness of the
Pharisees, who put their faith, their religious devotion into many
commandments, into so many 'Ah, I have to do this, I have to do
this, I have to do this.' Christians who are holding a pose . . . 'But
why are you doing this?' 'That's just what you do!' 'But why?' 'Oh,
I don't know, that's just what you do.' And Jesus, where is he? A
commandment is valid if it comes from Jesus: I am doing this because the Lord wants me to do it. But since I am a Christian without
Christ, I do this and I don't know why."

There are "other Christians without Christ, those who are looking only for devotions, but Jesus is not there. If your devotions lead
you to Jesus, that's fine. But if that's all you're doing, something is
wrong."

Then there is "another group of Christians without Christ: those
who seek things that are a bit more rare, a bit more special, who
follow after private revelations," although revelation has concluded
with the New Testament. In these Christians there is the desire to
go "to the spectacle of revelation, to hear new things." It is difficult
to urge these people to "Take up the Gospel!"

"'But, Father, what is the rule for being Christian with Christ,
and not becoming Christians without Christ? And what is the sign
that a person is Christian with Christ?' The rule is simple: only what
leads you to Jesus is valid, and only what comes from Jesus is valid.

Jesus is the center, the Lord, as he himself says. Is this leading you to Jesus? Go ahead. But if it's not leading you to Jesus, and it doesn't come from Jesus . . . it's hard to say, but it's a bit dangerous."

And again: "What is the sign that I am a Christian with Jesus?" The sign is simple: it is that of the man born blind who prostrates himself before Jesus to worship him.

"But if you are not able to worship Jesus, you're missing something. A rule, a sign. The rule is: I am a good Christian, I am on the way of the good Christian if I do what comes from Jesus and I do what leads me to Jesus, because he is the center. The sign is I am capable of worshiping, adoration. This prayer of adoration before Jesus. May the Lord make us understand that only he is the Lord. And may he give us the grace of loving him so much, of following him, of going on the path that he taught us."

September 7, 2013   *Colossians 1:21–23 ✛ Luke 6:1–5*

90

Christian hope is not optimism, it is Jesus

Hope is "a gift" of Jesus, hope is Jesus himself, it has his "name." Hope does not mean "seeing the glass as half full." This is simply "optimism," and "optimism is a human attitude that depends upon many things." This reflection is prompted by the reading in which Paul writes to the Colossians, "Christ in you, the hope for glory." And yet, "hope is a 'second-class' virtue," the "humble virtue" if it is compared to the more frequently cited faith and charity. This is why it can sometimes be confused with a peaceful good mood.

"But hope is something else; it is not optimism. Hope is a gift, it is a gift of the Holy Spirit. And this is why Paul says: 'It never disappoints.' Hope never disappoints, why? Because it is a gift that the Holy Spirit has given us. But Paul says that hope has a name. Hope is Jesus. We cannot say: 'I have hope in life, I have hope in God,' no. If you do not say: 'I have hope in Jesus, in Jesus Christ, a living Person, who now comes in the Eucharist, who is present in his Word,' it is not hope. It is a good mood, optimism."

From the Gospel we then get the second point of the reflection. The episode is the one in which Jesus cures a man's paralyzed hand on the Sabbath, bringing down the reproof of the scribes and Pharisees. With his miracle, Jesus frees the hand from illness and demonstrates "to the rigid" that theirs "is not the way of freedom. Freedom and hope go together; where there is no hope there cannot be freedom. Jesus frees this man from illness, from rigor, and from his paralyzed hand; he gives him a new life.

"Jesus, who is hope, remakes everything. He is a constant miracle. Not only has he worked the miracles of healing, so many things. Those were only signs, signals of what he is doing now, in the Church. The miracle of remaking everything: what he does in my life, in your life, in our lives. Remakes. And what he remakes is precisely the reason for our hope. It is Christ who remakes all things more marvelously than creation, this is the reason for our hope. And this hope does not disappoint, because he is faithful. He cannot deny himself. This is the virtue of hope."

A virtue, hope, that should be of particular inspiration for priests. "It is a little bit sad when we see a priest without hope," while it is wonderful to find one who comes to the end of life "not with optimism, but with hope. This priest is attached to Jesus Christ, and the People of God need us priests to give this sign of hope. Let's live this hope in Jesus, who remakes everything.

"The Lord who is the hope of glory, who is the center, who is the totality, may he help us on this way: to give hope, to have passion for hope. And, as I have said, it is not optimism, but it is what the Blessed Mother, in her heart, had amid the greatest darkness: from the evening of [Good] Friday until the early morning of [Easter] Sunday. That hope: she had it. And that hope has remade everything. May the Lord give us this grace."

September 9, 2013   *Colossians 1:24–2:3 ❧ Luke 6:6–11*

91

Proclaiming Jesus without fear or shame

Jesus is the Victor, the one who has conquered death and sin. This is how Jesus is described in the letter of Saint Paul to the Colossians. Saint Paul advises all of us to walk with Jesus "because he has conquered, to walk in him, rooted in him and built upon this victory, firm in the faith." This is the key point: "Jesus is risen!" But it is not always easy to understand this. For example, when Saint Paul addressed the Greeks of Athens, they listened to him with interest until he started talking about the Resurrection. "This scares us, better leave it alone." An episode that still demands a response from us today.

"There are many Christians without the Resurrection, Christians without the Risen Christ. They accompany Jesus to the tomb, they weep, they love him so much, but only to that point. Thinking of this attitude of Christians without the Risen Christ, I have found three kinds, but there are many: timorous Christians; those who are ashamed; and the triumphalists. These three have not encountered the Risen Christ! The timorous: these are the ones of the morning of the Resurrection, those of Emmaus who go away, they are afraid."

The apostles shut themselves up in the Upper Room out of fear of the Jews; even the Magdalene is weeping because they have taken away the body of the Lord. "This is what the timorous are like: they are afraid of thinking about the Resurrection." It is as if they are stuck "in the first part of the story; they are afraid of the Risen One." Then there are the Christians who are ashamed. "Confessing that Christ is risen is a bit embarrassing in this world" that "is making such strides in science." Paul tells these Christians to take care that none of them become the prey of philosophy, with its empty gyrations inspired by human tradition. These "are ashamed" of saying that "Christ, with his flesh, with his wounds, is risen." Finally there is the group of Christians who "deep inside do not believe in the Risen One, and want to make theirs a more majestic resurrection than the real one." These are the "triumphalistic" Christians.

"They don't know the word 'triumph,' they say only 'triumphalism,' because they have something like an inferiority complex. When we look at these Christians, with all of their triumphalistic attitudes, in their lives, in their words, and in their pastoral practice, in the liturgy, so many things like this, it is because deep down they do not believe in the Risen One. And he is the Victor, the Risen One. So he has conquered. This is why, without fear, without shame, without triumphalism, we should simply look at the Risen Lord, at his beauty, even putting our fingers into the wounds and our hand into his side.

"This is the message that Paul gives us today": Christ "is everything"; he is the totality and the hope, "because he is the Bridegroom, the Victor." The Gospel shows us a crowd of people who are going to listen to Jesus, and there are also many sick people who are trying to touch him, because from him "went out a power that healed all."

"Our faith, faith in the Risen One: that conquers the world! Let's go to him and like these sick people allow ourselves to be touched by him, by his power, because he is there with his flesh and bones, not a spiritual idea . . . He is alive. He is truly risen. And this is how he has conquered the world. May the Lord give us the grace to understand and live these things."

September 10, 2013   *Colossians 2:6–15 ⚜ Luke 6:12–19*

92

If you want to love your enemy, contemplate the Passion of Jesus and the gentleness of Mary

The Gospel is demanding. It asks "strong things" of a Christian: the capacity to forgive, magnanimity, love for one's enemies . . . There is only one way to succeed in putting this into practice: "contemplating the Passion, the humanity of Jesus" and imitating his Mother. Our thoughts go first to the Blessed Mother, whose "Holy Name" the Church commemorates today. Today's feast used to be called "of the sweet Name of Mary." Afterward the definition changed, "but in prayer there remained this sweetness of her name.

"We need this today, this sweetness of the Blessed Mother, in order to understand these things that Jesus is asking of us, don't we? Because this is a list that is not easy to live. Love your enemies, do good, lend without expecting anything . . . To the one who strikes you on the cheek, offer the other as well, to the one who takes away your mantle, do not refuse your tunic . . . But these are strong things, right? But all of this, in its way, was lived by the Blessed Mother; it is the grace of gentleness, the grace of meekness."

Saint Paul as well, in the letter to the Colossians in today's liturgy, invites Christians to put on "sentiments of tenderness, of goodness, of humility, gentleness," of mutual forbearance and forgiveness. And here "the question arises immediately: But how can I do this? How can I prepare myself to do this? What do I have to study to do this?" The answer "is clear: we, with our efforts, cannot do it. We can't do this. Only a grace can do it in us." And this grace goes by a precise path.

"Think only of Jesus. If our heart, if our mind is with Jesus, the Victor, the one who conquered death, sin, the devil, everything, we can do this thing that Jesus himself is asking of us and that the apostle Paul is asking of us: meekness, humility, goodness, tenderness, gentleness, magnanimity. If we do not look to Jesus, if we are not with Jesus, we cannot do this. It is a grace; it is the grace that comes from the contemplation of Jesus."

In particular, there is one aspect of the life of Jesus on which Christian contemplation must focus: his Passion, his "suffering humanity. So it is from the contemplation of Jesus, from our life with Jesus and God, that we can carry forward these attitudes, these virtues that the Lord is asking of us. There is no other way.

"Think of his meek silence. This will be your effort. He will do the rest. He will do everything that's missing. But you have to do that: hide your life in God with Christ. This is done with the contemplation of the humanity of Jesus, of suffering humanity. There is no other way; there is none. It is the only one. To be good Christians, contemplate the humanity of Jesus and suffering humanity. To give testimony, in order to be able to give this testimony, that's what we need. To forgive, contemplate Jesus suffering. In order not to hate your neighbor, contemplate Jesus suffering, in order not to gossip against your neighbor, contemplate Jesus suffering. The only way. Hide your life with Christ in God: this is the advice that the apostle gives us. It is the advice to become humble, meek, and good, magnanimous, tender."

September 12, 2013   *Colossians 3:12–17 ❧ Luke 6:27–38*

93

Gossip kills God and neighbor

"Why do you notice the splinter in your brother's eye, but do not perceive the wooden beam in your own?" The question posed by Jesus shakes the conscience of every person, and every time. After speaking of humility, Jesus speaks to us of its opposite, "of that hateful attitude toward our neighbor, of becoming our brother's judge." And here Jesus "uses a strong word: 'hypocrite.'

"Those who live judging their neighbor, speaking evil of their neighbor, are hypocrites, because they do not have the strength, the courage to look at their own defects. The Lord doesn't say many words about this. Later he will say that the one who has hatred toward his brother in his heart is a murderer . . . The apostle John, in his first letter, also says this clearly: he who hates his brother is walking in darkness; he who judges his brother is walking in darkness."

Every time we "judge our brothers in our hearts and, worse, when we talk about this with others, we are murderous Christians.

"A murderous Christian . . . I'm not the one saying it, the Lord says it. And on this point, there is no place for subtleties. If you speak evil of your brother, you are killing your brother. And every time we do this, we imitate that action of Cain, the first murderer of history."

At this time when there is talk about wars and there are so many appeals for peace, "there is a need for an act of conversion on our part. Gossip always feeds into this dimension of criminality. There is no innocent gossip." The tongue is for praising God, "but when we use our tongue to speak evil of our brother or sister, we are using it to kill God, the image of God in our brother." Some may say that certain persons deserve the gossip that they get. But this cannot be.

"Well, go pray for him! Go and do penance for her! And then, if it is necessary, speak to the person who is able to remedy the problem. But don't talk about it to everyone! Paul was a serious sinner, and he says this about himself: 'Before, I was a blasphemer, a persecutor, and violent. But I was treated with mercy.' Perhaps none of us blasphemes—perhaps. But if any of us gossips, he is certainly a persecutor and violent. Let's ask for ourselves, for the whole Church, the grace of conversion from the criminality of gossip to the love, to the humility, to the meekness, to the gentleness, to the magnanimity of love for our neighbor."

September 13, 2013   *1 Timothy 1:1–2, 12–14 ❧ Luke 6:39–42*

94

Prayer and tears to glimpse the mystery of the Cross

The mystery of the Cross is a great mystery for man and can be approached only in prayer and in tears. In the mystery of the Cross we find the history of man and the history of God, summarized by the Fathers of the Church in the comparison between the tree of the knowledge of good and evil, in Paradise, and the tree of the Cross.

"That tree had done so much evil, and this tree leads us to salvation, to health. It forgives that evil. This is the journey of man: a journey to find Jesus Christ the Redeemer, who gives his life out of love. "God did not send his Son into the world to condemn the world, but that the world might be saved through him." This tree of the Cross saves us, all of us, from the consequences of that other tree, the origin of self-sufficiency, pride, the arrogance of wanting to know—ourselves—everything, according to our mentality, according to our criteria, and even according to that presumption of being and becoming the sole judges of the world. This is the history of man: from one tree to the other."

In the Cross there is also "the history of God, because we can say that God has a history." In fact, "he wanted to take on our history and walk with us." He abased himself by becoming man, whereas we wanted to raise ourselves up, and he took on the condition of a slave, becoming obedient to death on the Cross, in order to raise us up again.

"God makes this journey out of love! There is no other explanation: only love does these things. Today let's look at the Cross, the history of man and the history of God. Let's look at this Cross, where we can taste that honey of aloes, that bitter honey, that bitter sweetness of the sacrifice of Jesus. But this mystery is very great, and on our own we cannot really understand it.

"First of all, the mystery of the Cross. We can understand just a little bit of this on our knees, in prayer, but also through tears. It is tears that draw us nearer to this mystery. Without weeping, weeping in our hearts, we will never be able to understand this mystery." It is "the weeping of the penitent, the weeping of the brother and sister who look upon so much human misery" and see this misery in Jesus, but "on their knees and weeping" and "never alone, never alone!

"In order to enter into this mystery, which is not a labyrinth but resembles one a bit, we always need our Mother, our mom's hand. May she, Mary, help us to feel how great and how humble this mystery is; how sweet like honey it is and how bitter like aloes. May she accompany us on this journey, which no one but us can make. Each one has to do it! With mom, weeping and on our knees."

September 14, 2013   Numbers 21:4b–9 ✣ Philippians 2:6–11 ✣ John 3:13–17

95

Love for the people and humility, necessary virtues for leaders

The Gospel of the centurion who asks with humility and trust for the healing of his servant and the letter of Saint Paul to Timothy with the call to pray for rulers offer the occasion for a "reflection on how authorities provide service." The one who governs "must love his people," because "a governor who does not love cannot govern; at the most he can discipline, bring a bit of order, but not govern." This reminds us of David, "how he loved his people," so much that after the sin of conducting the census he tells the Lord to punish not the people but him. So "the two virtues of a governor" are love for the people and humility.

"One cannot govern without love for the people and without humility! And every man, every woman who must take possession of a government post, must ask himself these two questions: Do I love my people, to serve them better? Am I humble, and do I listen to all the others, the different opinions, to choose the best way? If he does not ask himself these questions, his government will not be good. The governor, man or woman, who loves his people is a humble man or woman."

On the other hand, Saint Paul urges us to lift up prayers "for kings and for all in authority, so that we may lead a calm and tranquil life." Politics cannot be ignored. "None of us can say: 'But I don't have anything to do with this, they're in charge.' No, no, I am responsible for their governance, and I must do the best I can so that they govern well, and I must do the best I can by participating in politics as I am able. Politics—as the social doctrine of the Church says—is one of the highest forms of charity, because it is serving the common good. I cannot wash my hands; we all have to give something!"

There is a habit of saying only bad things about politicians and chattering about "things that are not going well. And you listen to the television report and they hammer away, hammer away; you read the newspaper and they hammer away . . . Always the bad, always against! The governor may be a sinner, as David was, but I must collaborate by contributing my opinion, with my words, and even with my correction," because all of us "must participate in the common good"! And if "many times we have heard 'a good Catholic should not get mixed up in politics,' this is not true, this is not a good path.

"A good Catholic gets mixed up in politics, offering the best of himself, so that the governor can govern. But what is the best thing that we can offer to governors? Prayer! This is what Paul says: 'Pray for all men and for the king and for all those who are in power.' 'But, Father, he's a bad person, he should go to hell.' 'Pray for him, pray for her, that he may govern well, that he may love his people, that he may serve his people, that he may be humble!' A Christian who does not pray for the leaders is not a good Christian! 'But, Father, how can I pray for this one? This guy's no good.' 'Pray that he may convert!' But pray. And it's not me saying this, Saint Paul says it, the Word of God."

So "let's give the best of ourselves—ideas, suggestions—the best, but above all the best is prayer. Let's pray for our leaders, that they may govern us well, that they may lead our country, our nation forward and also the world, that there may be peace and the common good."

September 16, 2013   *1 Timothy 2:1–8* ✢ *Luke 7:1–10*

96

The Church is a courageous mother

Jesus has "the capacity to suffer with us, to be close to our sufferings and make them his own." In the encounter between Jesus and the widow of Nain, Jesus "was seized by great compassion" for this widowed woman who had also lost her only son. "He knew what this meant for a widowed woman at that time," and "the Lord has a special love for widows; he cares for them." Reading this passage of the Gospel, "I think that this widow is also an icon of the Church, because the Church too is in a certain sense a widow.

"Her Bridegroom is gone, and she walks through history, hoping to find him, to encounter him. And she will be the definitive bride. But in the meantime she—the Church—is alone! The Lord is not visible. She has a certain dimension of widowhood. This courageous Church, who defends her children, like that widow who went to the corrupt judge to defend, and won in the end. Our Mother Church is courageous! She has that courage of a woman who knows that her children are her own and must defend them and bring them to the encounter with her Bridegroom."

In the Bible there are various figures of widows, in particular the courageous Maccabean widow with her seven sons who are martyred for refusing to renounce God. The Bible says that this woman spoke to her sons "in dialect, in the first language"; our Mother Church also speaks to us in dialect, in "that language of true orthodoxy which we all understand, that language of the catechism" that "gives us the strength to go forward in the fight against evil.

"This dimension of widowhood of the Church, who walks in history, hoping to encounter, to find her Bridegroom . . . This is what our Mother Church is like! She is a Church who, when she is faithful, knows how to weep. When the Church is not weeping, something is wrong. She weeps for her children and prays! A Church who moves forward and raises her children, gives them strength, and accompanies them to the last good-bye in order to leave them in the hands of her Bridegroom, whom she too will find in the end. This is our Mother Church! I see her in this widow who is weeping. And what does the Lord say to the Church? 'Do not weep. I am with you, I accompany you, I am waiting for you there, at the wedding, the last wedding, that of the Lamb. Stop, this son of yours who was dead, he is alive now!'"

And this "is the dialogue of the Lord with the Church." She "defends her children, but when she sees that her children are dead, she weeps and the Lord says to her: 'I am with you, and your child is with me.'" As he told the young man of Nain to get up from his deathbed, many times Jesus also tells us to get up "when we are dead through sin, and we go to ask for forgiveness." So what does Jesus do "when he forgives us, when he gives us our life back? He restores us to our mother.

"Our reconciliation with the Lord does not end in the dialogue 'I, you, and the priest who gives me forgiveness'; it ends when he restores us to our mother. That is where reconciliation ends, because there is no journey of life, there is no forgiveness, there is no reconciliation outside of Mother Church. And so, seeing this widow, I am reminded of all these things, a bit randomly . . . But I see in this widow the icon of the widowhood of the Church, who is on the journey to find her Bridegroom. I would like to ask the Lord for the grace of always trusting this 'mom,' who defends us, teaches us, raises us, and speaks to us in dialect."

September 17, 2013   *1 Timothy 3:1–13 ♣ Luke 7:11–17*

97

No to the idolatry of money

"One cannot serve God and money." These are the words of Saint Paul on the relationship "between the way of Jesus Christ and money" that invite us to observe that there is something "in the attitude of the love of money that distances us from God." There are "so many illnesses, so many sins, but Jesus emphasizes this one so much: the love of money, in fact, is the root of all evil." Seized by "this desire, some have deviated from the faith and have acquired many torments for themselves. So great is the power of money that it makes you deviate from the faith," and even "takes your faith away. It weakens it, and you lose it!

"But money also sickens thought; it sickens faith and puts it on another path. These idle words, useless discussions . . . And it goes further. From this comes envy, quarreling, gossip, evil suspicions, the conflicts of men who are corrupted in their minds and devoid of truth, who consider religion a source of profit. 'I am Catholic. I go to Mass because this gives me a certain status. I am looked upon well. But underneath it's my business, right? I am a devotee of money.' And these are words that we find so often, so frequently in the newspapers: 'Men corrupted in their minds.' Money corrupts! There is no way out."

If you choose "the way of money, in the end you will be corrupted." Money "has this seduction of making you slide slowly into your perdition." This is why "Jesus is so tough" on this topic.

" 'You cannot serve God and money.' You can't: one or the other! And this is not communism. This is pure Gospel! These are the words of Jesus! What happens with money? Money offers you a certain well-being at the beginning. Well, okay. Then you start feeling important, and vanity comes in. We read this in the psalm, that this vanity comes in. This vanity that is no good, but you feel like an important person: that's vanity. And from vanity to arrogance, to pride. There are three steps: wealth, vanity, and pride.

"No one can save himself with money!" Nonetheless, "the devil always takes this way of temptation: wealth, in order to feel that you are self-sufficient; vanity, to feel that you are important; and in the end, pride, arrogance. This is his real language, arrogance.

"'But, Father, I've read the Ten Commandments, and none of them says anything bad about money. What commandment is someone sinning against when he does something for money?' 'Against the first! You are sinning by idolatry! Here's why: because money becomes an idol, and you are worshiping it!' This is why Jesus tells us: 'You cannot serve the idol money and the Living God: one or the other.' The early Church Fathers—I'm talking about the third century, more or less around the year 200, the year 300—had a tough way of putting it: 'Money is the devil's dung.' This is because it makes us idolaters and sickens our minds with pride, making us maniacs over pointless questions and distancing us from the faith. It corrupts."

Saint Paul tells us to avoid these things, but to hold on "to justice, to piety, to faith, to charity." And also to patience, "against vanity and pride," and "to meekness." This is "the way of God, not that of the idolatrous power that can give you money." Humility is "the path for serving God. May the Lord help all of us not to fall into the trap of the idolatry of money."

September 20, 2013   *1 Timothy 6:2c–12* ✣ *Luke 8:1–3*

98

The gaze of Jesus changes our lives

Jesus looks in the eyes of Matthew, a tax collector, a public sinner. Money is his life, his idol. But now he feels "in his heart the gaze of Jesus, who is looking at him.

"And that gaze completely captivated him, it changed his life. We say: he converted him. He changed his life. As soon as he felt that gaze within his heart, he got up and followed him. And this is true: the gaze of Jesus always raises us up. It is a gaze that lifts us up; it never leaves you there, never. It never lowers you, it never humiliates you. It invites you to get up. A gaze that leads you to grow, to go forward, that encourages you, because he loves you. He makes you feel that he loves you. And this gives you the courage to follow him: 'And he got up and followed him.'"

The gaze of Jesus is not something "magical: Jesus was not a hypnotist. Jesus looked at everyone, and everyone felt that he was looking at them, that Jesus was speaking their names. And this gaze changed their lives, for everyone." It changed Peter, who after denying him encounters his gaze and weeps bitterly. Then there is the last "gaze of Jesus on the Cross: he looked at his mom, he looked at his disciple and said to us, with that gaze, he said to us that his mom was ours and that the Church is mother. With a gaze." Then he looked at the good thief and once again at Peter, "who was fearful after the Resurrection, asking those three questions: 'Do you love me?' A gaze that made him ashamed. It would do us good to think, to pray about this gaze of Jesus, and also to let him look at us."

Jesus now goes to Matthew's house, and while he is sitting at the table many sinners arrive. "The word had gone out. And the whole society—but not the pure segment of society—felt invited to that meal," as happens in the parable of the king who orders his servants to go to the crossroads to invite to his son's wedding banquet those that they would encounter, good and bad.

"And the sinners, the tax collectors and sinners . . . Jesus had looked at them, and that gaze of Jesus upon them I believe was like a breath on the embers, and they felt that there was still fire inside, and that Jesus was lifting them up, restoring their dignity. The gaze of Jesus always makes us worthy; it gives us dignity. It is a generous gaze. 'But look at that Teacher; he eats with the filth of the city!' But under that filth were the embers of desire for God, the embers of God's image in us that needed someone to fan them into flame. And this is what the gaze of Jesus did.

"All of us in our lives have felt this gaze, and not just one time: many times! Perhaps in the person of a priest who taught us doctrine or forgave our sins . . . Perhaps in the help of friends . . . But we will all find ourselves before that gaze, that wonderful gaze. And let's go forward in life, in the certainty that he is looking at us. But also that he is waiting for us to look at us definitively. And that last gaze of Jesus on our life will be forever, it will be eternal. I ask all of these saints who have been looked at by Jesus that they may prepare us to allow ourselves to be looked at in our lives, and that they may also prepare us for that last—and first!—gaze of Jesus."

September 21, 2013   *Ephesians 4:1–7, 11–13* ✢ *Matthew 9:9–13*

99

A sacrament is not a magic ritual

L et us go with joy to the house of the Lord." The presence of the Lord in our lives is a presence that accompanies. In the history of the People of God there are "beautiful moments that give joy" and also ugly moments "of pain, of martyrdom, of sin.

"And in both the ugly moments and the beautiful moments one thing is always the same: the Lord is there, he never abandons his people! Because the Lord, on that day of sin, of the first sin, made a decision, he made a choice: to make history with his people. And God, who does not have a history, because he is eternal, wanted to make history, to walk close to his people. But more than that: to become one of us and like one of us, to walk with us, in Jesus. And this speaks to us, it tells us about the humility of God."

So the greatness of God is precisely his humility: "he wanted to walk with his people." And when his people "distanced themselves from him with sin, with idolatry, he was there" waiting for them. And Jesus too comes with "this attitude of humility." He wants "to walk with the People of God, to walk with sinners, even to walk with the arrogant." The Lord did so much "to help the arrogant hearts of the Pharisees.

"Humility. God is always waiting. God is next to us, God walks with us, he is humble; he is always waiting for us. Jesus is always waiting for us. This is the humility of God. And the Church sings with joy of this humility of God who accompanies us, as we have done with the psalm. 'Let us go with joy to the house of the Lord.' Let us go with joy because he accompanies us, he is with us. And the Lord Jesus also accompanies us in our personal lives, with the sacraments. A sacrament is not a magic ritual, it is an encounter with Jesus Christ; we are encountering the Lord. It is he who is beside us and accompanies us."

Jesus becomes "our traveling companion. The Holy Spirit also accompanies us and teaches us all that we do not know, in our hearts," and "he reminds us of all that Jesus has taught us." And in this way "he helps us feel how beautiful it is to be on the right path. God, Father, Son, and Holy Spirit are our traveling companions; they make history with us." And the Church celebrates this "with so much joy, also in the Eucharist" with the fourth Eucharistic prayer, where "we sing of that love of God that is so great that he wanted to be humble, that he wanted to be the traveling companion of all of us, that he even wanted to make history with us.

"And if he entered into history with us, let's also enter a little into history with him, or at least ask for the grace of allowing him to write our history. May he be the one who writes our history. It is reliable."

September 24, 2013   *Ezra 6:7–8, 12b, 14–20 ✤ Luke 8:19–21*

Pray incessantly for peace in Syria, Lebanon, and the Middle East

S hame before God, prayer to implore the divine mercy, and full trust in the Lord are the main points of today's reflection. The readings of the liturgy and, in particular, the passage taken from the book of Ezra come across as a reminder of the Maronite bishops and evoke three concepts. First of all, Ezra's attitude of shame and confusion before God, to the point of not being able to raise his eyes to him. The shame and confusion of all of us for the sins we have committed, which have led us into slavery because we have served idols that are not God.

Prayer is the second concept. Following the example of Ezra, who kneels down and lifts his hands to God imploring mercy, we should do the same thing for our countless sins. A prayer also has to be lifted up for peace in Syria, Lebanon, and the whole Middle East. Prayer is always and in every case the way that we must travel to confront difficult moments, like the most dramatic trials and the darkness that sometimes envelops us in unpredictable situations. In order to find the way out from all of this, we have to pray incessantly.

Finally, absolute trust in God, who never abandons us. This is the third concept. We are certain that the Lord is with us, and therefore our journey must be persevering, thanks to the hope that infuses us with strength. The word of pastors will become reassuring for the faithful: the Lord will never abandon us.

September 25, 2013   *Ezra 9:5–9 ✢ Luke 9:1–6*

We can't get to know Jesus in first class

Who is this man, where does he come from? The question that Herod poses about Jesus is a question that in reality is posed to all of those who encounter Jesus. It is a question "that can be asked out of curiosity" or "can be asked for the sake of safety." And reading the Gospel, we see that "some were beginning to be afraid of this man, because he might lead them into a political conflict with the Romans. But who is this man who is causing so many problems?" they ask themselves. Because truly "Jesus causes problems."

"We can't get to know Jesus without having problems. And I would dare to say: 'If you want to have a problem, go out into the street to get to know Jesus. You won't have just one, you'll have many!' But this is the way to get to know Jesus! We can't get to know Jesus in first class! Jesus is known in going out day after day. We can't get to know Jesus in tranquillity, not even in the library. Get to know Jesus!"

Of course, "we can get to know Jesus in the catechism," because "the catechism teaches us many things about Jesus. We have to study it, we have to learn it." In this way "we get to know the Son of God, who came to save us; we understand all the beauty of the history of salvation, of the Father's love, by studying the catechism." And yet, how many have read the *Catechism of the Catholic Church* since it was published more than twenty years ago?

"Yes, we have to get to know Jesus in the catechism. But it is not enough to know him with our minds. That is one step. We have to get to know Jesus in dialogue with him, speaking with him, in prayer, on our knees. If you don't pray, if you don't talk with Jesus, you don't know him. You know things about Jesus, but you do not have that knowledge which comes from your heart in prayer. Getting to know Jesus with the mind, the study of the catechism; getting to know Jesus with the heart, in prayer, in dialogue with him. This helps us quite a bit, but it's not enough. There is a third way for knowing Jesus: it is following him. Going with him, walking with him."

We have to "go, travel his paths, by walking." It is necessary "to get to know Jesus with the language of action." So this is how we can truly get to know Jesus, with these "three languages: of the mind, of the heart, and of action." So if "I know Jesus is like this, I am involved with him.

"We cannot get to know Jesus without involving ourselves with him, without staking our lives for him. When so many people—even we ourselves—ask this question—But who is this man?—the Word of God answers us: 'Do you want to know who he is? Read what the Church says about him, talk with him in prayer, and walk his path with him. This is how you will get to know who this man is.' This is the way! Everyone must make his choice!"

September 26, 2013   *Haggai 1:1–8 ✤ Luke 9:7–9*

102

A Christian must not avoid the Cross

Yes, "but up to a certain point." The danger of lukewarmness, of a faith made up of calculations and steps withheld, is always around the corner. In the passage from the Gospel of Luke, Jesus first asks the disciples what the people say about him, and then who they say he is, until Peter responds: "The Christ of God." "This question is also addressed to us," and there is a series of responses that reveals the essence of a faith that is only half grown-up. "Who am I for you? The boss of this company, a good prophet, a good teacher, someone who warms your heart?" This is "all true." But am I "someone who walks with you in life, who helps you to go forward, to be a little bit good?" Yes, it's true, but it doesn't end there either.

"It was the Holy Spirit who touched Peter's heart to say who Jesus is. If he is the Christ, the Son of the living God, this is a mystery. Who can explain this? . . . But he said it. And if each of us, in his prayer, looking at the Tabernacle, says to the Lord: 'You are the Christ, the Son of the living God,' at first he cannot say it on his own, it must be the Holy Spirit who says it in him. And, second, prepare yourself, because he will answer you: 'It is true.'"

At Peter's response, Jesus asks them not to reveal him to anyone, and then proclaims his Passion, his death, and his Resurrection. And this is the reaction of the head of the apostles described in the Gospel of Saint Matthew: "This will never happen to you." "Peter is frightened, he is scandalized," neither more nor less than so many Christians who say: "This will never happen to you! I will follow you to here." So this is a way of "following Jesus to get to know him up to a certain point.

"This is the temptation of spiritual prosperity. We have everything: we have the Church, we have Jesus Christ, the sacraments, the Blessed Mother, everything, a great job for the Kingdom of God; we are good, all of us. Because at least we have to think this, because if we think the opposite it is sin! But spiritual prosperity goes only so far. Like that young man who was rich; he wanted to go with

Jesus, but up to a certain point. He was missing that last anointing of the Christian, to be truly Christian: the anointing of the Cross, the anointing of humiliation. Jesus humiliated himself to the point of death, the death of everything. This is the touchstone, the test of our Christian reality: Am I a Christian of the culture of prosperity? Am I a Christian who accompanies the Lord all the way to the Cross? The sign is the capacity to bear humiliations."

The scandal of the Cross, however, remains an obstacle for many Christians. All want to rise again, but "not all" intend to do so by the way of the Cross. On the contrary, they complain of the wrongs or affronts that they have undergone, behaving opposite to what Jesus did and asked us to imitate.

"The test of whether a Christian is truly a Christian is his capacity to bear humiliations with joy and patience; and this is something we don't like. There are many Christians who, looking to the Lord, ask for humiliations in order to resemble him more. This is the choice: either a Christian of prosperity—that you will go to heaven, you will surely be saved—or a Christian close to Jesus, on the path of Jesus."

September 27, 2013 *Haggai 2:1–9 ✣ Luke 9:18–22*

103

Asking for the grace not to flee the Cross

"The Son of Man is about to be given over into the hands of men." These words of Jesus chill the disciples, who were thinking of a triumphant journey. Words that "remained so mysterious for them that they did not grasp their meaning" and "were afraid of questioning him on this topic." For them it was "better not to talk about it," it was "better not to understand than to understand the truth" that Jesus was telling them.

"They were afraid of the Cross, they were afraid of the Cross. Peter himself, after that solemn confession in the region of Caesarea Philippi, when Jesus says this again, reproves the Lord: 'No, never, Lord! Not this!' He was afraid of the Cross. But not only the disciples, not only Peter, Jesus himself was afraid of the Cross! He couldn't fool himself; he knew. Jesus was so afraid that on that Thursday evening he sweated blood. Jesus was so afraid that he almost said the same thing as Peter, almost . . . 'Father, take this cup away from me. Your will be done!' This was the difference!"

The Cross also scares us in the work of evangelization, but there is the "rule" that "the disciple is not greater than his Master. There is the rule that there is no redemption without the shedding of blood." There is no fruitful apostolic work without the Cross.

"Perhaps we think, each one of us might think: And to me, what's going to happen to me? What will my Cross be like? We don't know. We don't know, but it will come! We have to ask for the grace not to flee from the Cross when it comes. We may greet it with fear! That's true! It scares us. But that's where following Jesus ends up. I am reminded of the last words that Jesus spoke to Peter, at that pontifical coronation at the Sea of Tiberias: 'Do you love me? Feed my sheep! Do you love me? Feed my lambs!' . . . But his last words were these: 'They will take you where you do not want to go!' The promise of the Cross."

The homily closes with a prayer to Mary:

"So close to Jesus, at the Cross, was his mother, his mom. Perhaps it would be good to ask her for the grace not to take away the fear—that has to come, the fear of the Cross—but the grace not to become frightened and flee from the Cross. She was there, and she knows how to be close to the Cross."

September 28, 2013   *Zechariah 2:5–9, 14–15a ✢ Luke 9:43b–45*

104

Peace and joy, signs of the presence of God in the Church

The disciples were enthusiasts, they had plans, projects for the future of the organization of the burgeoning Church. They were discussing who was the greatest and preventing those who did not belong to their group from doing good in the name of Jesus. But Jesus surprises them, moving the center of the discussion from organization to the children. "He who is the least among all of you," he says, "he is great!" So the reading from the prophet Zechariah talks about the signs of the presence of God: not "a beautiful organization" or "a government that's moving forward, everything clean and everything perfect," but the elderly sitting in the streets and the children playing. The risk is that of discarding both the elderly and the children. And Jesus has harsh words for those who scandalize the smallest.

"The future of a people is right here and here, in the elderly and in the children. A people that does not take care of its elderly and its children has no future, because it cannot have memory and it cannot have promise! The elderly and the children are the future of a people! So often they are left aside, aren't they? The children, pacified with a piece of candy, with a game: 'Do it, do it, go, go.' And the elderly not allowed to speak, no attention paid to their advice: 'They're old, poor things . . .'"

The disciples didn't understand.

"I understand, the disciples wanted results, they wanted the Church to move forward without problems, and this can become a temptation for the Church: the Church of functionalism! The well-organized Church! Everything in its place, but without memory and without promise! This kind of Church would not work; it would be a Church of power struggles, a Church of jealousy among the baptized and so many other things that come about when there is no memory and no promise."

So the "vitality of the Church" does not come from documents and meetings "to plan and to do things well." These are necessary realities, but they are not "the sign of the presence of God.

"The sign of the presence of God is this, this is what the Lord said: 'Old men and old women will again sit in the streets of Jerusalem, each with staff in hand because of old age. The city will be filled with boys and girls playing in its streets.' Play makes us think of joy: it is the joy of the Lord. And these elderly seated with staff in hand, so tranquil, make us think of peace. Peace and joy: this is the atmosphere of the Church!"

September 30, 2013   *Zechariah 8:1–8 ✠ Luke 9:46–50*

105

Our work should make us more humble

Jesus reproves the two apostles who wanted to bring down fire from heaven on those who didn't welcome them. But the way of the Christian is not a "way of vengeance." The way of the Christian is that of humility, meekness. And today's commemoration of Saint Thérèse of the Child Jesus "should make us think hard about this spirit of humility, of tenderness, of goodness." A meek spirit that the Lord "wants to encounter in all of us." So where is the strength "that leads us to this spirit"? Precisely "in love, in charity, in the awareness that we are in the hands of the Father. When we feel this we lose interest in bringing down fire from heaven.

"The other spirit comes, that of the charity that suffers all, forgives all, that does not boast, that is humble, that does not seek itself. Some may say—and there have been some philosophers who have thought this way—that this is like the humiliation of the majesty of man, of the greatness of man. This is sterile! The wise Church has made this saint—humble, small, trusting in God, meek—it has made her the Patroness of the Missions."

The power of the Gospel is precisely there, "because the Gospel reaches its highest point in the humiliation of Jesus: humility that becomes humiliation!" And the power of the Gospel "is precisely in humility, the humility of the child who allows himself to be guided by the love and tenderness of the Father.

"The Church—as Benedict XVI told us—does not grow by proselytism, it grows by attraction, by testimony. And when the people see this testimony of humility, of meekness, gentleness, they feel the need that the prophet Zechariah talks about: 'We want to come with you!' The people feel this need in the face of this testimony of charity, of this humble charity, without pretension, not self-sufficient, but humble, that adores and serves.

"Charity is simple: worshiping God and serving others! And this testimony makes the Church grow." This is why a sister "who is so humble, so trusting in God," like Saint Thérèse of the Child Jesus, "has been named Patroness of the Missions, because her example makes people say, 'We want to come with you!'"

October 1, 2013   *Zechariah 8:20–23 ✤ Luke 9:51–56*

106

The Mass is not a social event

Ezra reads from on high the book of the law, which was thought to be lost, and the people weep for joy. The passage from the book of Nehemiah allows us to focus on the theme of memory. The People of God "had the memory of the Law, but it was a distant memory," but on that day "the memory drew near" and "this touched their hearts." They wept "for joy, not out of sorrow, because they had the experience of the nearness of salvation.

"And this is important not only in the great moments of history but in the moments of our lives. We all have the memory of salvation, all of us. But this is what I would like to know: Is this memory close to us, or is it a distant memory, a bit vague, a bit archaic, like something in a museum? It can drift away . . . And when the memory is not close, when we do not have this experience of the nearness of the memory, it enters into a process of transformation, and the memory becomes nothing more than a reminder."

When the memory drifts away, "it becomes a reminder; but when it draws near, it turns into joy, and this is the joy of the people." This constitutes "a principle of our Christian life." When the memory draws near, "it does two things: it warms the heart and it gives us joy.

"And this joy is our strength. The joy of having the memory close. But when memory is domesticated, when it drifts away and becomes a mere reminder, it doesn't warm the heart, it doesn't give us joy, and it doesn't give us strength. This encounter with the memory is an event of salvation; it is an encounter with the love of God, who has made history with us and has saved us; it is an encounter of salvation. And it is so wonderful to be saved that we have to celebrate.

"When God comes and draws near there is always a celebration." And "many times we Christians are afraid of celebrating, this simple and fraternal celebration that is a gift of the nearness of the Lord." Life "leads us to distance ourselves from this nearness, to keep only the reminder of salvation, not the memory that is alive." The Church has "its memory": the "memory of the Passion of the Lord." But he warned that it also happens to us that we "distance ourselves from this memory and turn it into a reminder, into a habitual event.

"Every week we go to Church, or someone has died, we go to the funeral . . . And this memory, so often, it bores us, because it is not close. It is sad, but many times the Mass is turned into a social event and we are not near the memory of the Church, which is the presence of the Lord in front of us. Let's imagine this beautiful scene in the book of Nehemiah: Ezra is carrying the book of the memory of Israel, and the people are drawing near to their memory and weeping; the heart is warmed, it is joyful, it feels that the joy of the Lord is its strength. And it celebrates, without fear, in simplicity.

"Let's ask the Lord for the grace of always having his memory near us, a close memory that is not domesticated by habit, by so many things, and pushed away into a simple reminder."

October 3, 2013   *Nehemiah 8:1–4a, 5–6, 7b–12 ✤ Luke 10:1–12*

107

Someone "far away" can hear God better than someone "near"

J onah serves the Lord, he prays a lot and does good, but when the Lord calls him, he starts to run away. Jonah "had his whole story written out" and "he didn't want to be disturbed." The Lord sends him to Nineveh, and he "takes a ship headed for Spain. He was running away from the Lord.

"The flight from God. We can run away from God, even if we are Christian, Catholic, a member of Catholic Action, priest, bishop, pope . . . All of us, all of us can run away from God! It is a daily temptation. Not to listen to God, not to listen to his voice, not to feel his proposal, his invitation, in our hearts. We can just plain run away. But there are other ways of fleeing from God, a bit more educated, a bit more sophisticated, right? In the Gospel there is this man who has been left for dead on the road, and a priest happens to walk down the same road—a respectable priest, with the cassock and everything, good, great! He saw and looked—'I'll be late for Mass'—and he kept going. He didn't listen to the voice of God there."

Then a Levite passed by, who may have thought, "If I take him with me or get too close, he may be dead, and tomorrow I will have to go to the judge to give testimony." And he kept going. He too flees "from this voice of God." The only one able to hear the voice of God is someone "who habitually fled from God, a sinner," a Samaritan. This man "is a sinner, far from God," and yet "he listened to the voice of God and drew near." The Samaritan "was not used to religious practices, to the moral life; even theologically he was mistaken," because the Samaritans "believed that God had to be worshiped in another place, and not where the Lord wanted." And nonetheless, the Samaritan "understood that God was calling him, and he did not run away. He drew near, he bound up the man's wounds, pouring on oil and wine, and then placed him on his animal" and "brought him to an inn and took care of him. He lost his whole evening.

"The priest arrived in time for Holy Mass, all of the faithful content; the Levite had, the following day, a peaceful day according to what he had planned to do, because he had not had this entanglement of having to go to the judge and all these things . . . And why did Jonah flee from God? Why did the priest flee from God? Why did the Levite flee from God? Because their hearts were closed, and when your heart is closed, you cannot hear the voice of God. But a Samaritan who was traveling 'saw and had compassion on him.' His heart was open, he was human. And his humanity drew him near.

"Jonah had a plan for his life; he wanted to write his story, and so did the priest and the Levite. He had an action plan." But this sinner, the Samaritan, "allowed God to write his life. Everything changed that evening, because the Lord brought to him the person of this poor man, wounded, badly wounded, left lying in the road.

"I ask myself, and I also ask you: Do we allow God to write life, our lives, or do we want to write it ourselves? And this speaks to us of docility. Are we docile to the Word of God? You may say 'Yes, I want to be docile!' But do you have the capacity to listen to it, to hear it? Do you have the capacity to find the Word of God in the story of every day, or do you rely on your own ideas, and do not allow the surprise of the Lord to speak to you?

"Three persons who are fleeing from God and another in an irregular situation," who is "capable of listening, opening his heart, and not running away. I am sure that we all see that the Samaritan, the sinner, did not run away from God. May the Lord grant us to listen to the voice of the Lord, his voice, which says to us: 'Go and do likewise!'"

October 7, 2013   *Jonah 1:1–2:2, 11* ✤ *Luke 10:25–37*

108

A prayer made with the heart can work miracles

Martha and the prophet Jonah. These evocative figures of the New and Old Testaments shared the same inability: they couldn't pray. When, in the Gospel, Martha tells Jesus almost in a tone of reproof that her sister should help her to serve, instead of sitting there listening to him, Jesus replies: "Mary has chosen the better part." And this "part" is "prayer, that of the contemplation of Jesus."

"In her sister's eyes this was a waste of time, and may even have seemed a bit scatterbrained: looking at the Lord as if she were an awestruck child. Who wants that? The Lord does: This is 'the better part,' because Mary listens to the Lord and prays with her heart. And the Lord is also saying this to us: 'The first task in life is this: prayer.' But not the prayer of words, like parrots; but prayer of the heart: looking at the Lord, listening to the Lord, asking questions of the Lord. We know that prayer works miracles."

And prayer also produces a miracle in the ancient city of Nineveh, to which the prophet Jonah proclaims, at the behest of God, its imminent destruction, and which is instead saved because the inhabitants believe in the prophecy and convert from the first to the last, begging for divine forgiveness with all their strength. Nonetheless, in this story of redemption as well there is a mistaken attitude, that of Jonah, who is more inclined to merciless justice in a way similar to that of Martha, inclined to service that excludes interiority.

"And this is what Martha did: What did she do? She didn't pray! There are others like this stubborn Jonah, who are the dispensers of justice. He went and prophesied, but in his heart he was saying: 'But they deserve this. They deserve it. They asked for it!' He prophesied, but he wasn't praying! He was not asking the Lord to forgive them. Only to punish them. They are the dispensers of justice, those who believe they are just! And in the end—the book of Jonah continues—it is clear that Jonah was a self-centered man, because when the Lord saved Nineveh because of the prayers of the people, Jonah became angry with the Lord, as if he were saying: 'You're always like that. You always forgive!'"

So the prayer that is just a formula without any heart, as well as pessimism or the desire for justice without forgiveness, is a temptation against which Christians must always protect themselves in order to be able to choose "the better part.

"We, too, when we do not pray, what we are doing is closing the door on the Lord. And not praying is this: closing the door on the Lord, so that he can't do anything. But praying before a problem, a difficult situation, a calamity is opening the door to the Lord so that he can come in. So that he can remake things. He knows how to arrange things, to reorganize things. Praying is this: opening the door for the Lord, so that he can do something. But if we close the door, the Lord can't do anything! Let's think of this Mary, who has chosen the better part and shows us the way, how to open the door for the Lord."

October 8, 2013   *Jonah 3:1–10 ✛ Luke 10:38–42*

109

The true gift is God himself

The parable of the annoying friend who gets what he wants through his insistence makes us reflect on the quality of our prayer.

"How do we pray? Do we pray out of habit, with devotion but also with tranquillity, or do we really place ourselves before the Lord with courage in order to ask for grace, in order to ask for the object of our prayer? Courage in prayer. Prayer that is not courageous is not real prayer. The courage of trusting that the Lord listens to us, the courage of knocking at the door . . . The Lord says this: 'For everyone who asks, receives; and the one who seeks, finds; and to the one who knocks, the door will be opened.' But we have to ask, seek, and knock.

"Do we really get involved in prayer? Do we know how to knock at God's heart?" In the Gospels, Jesus says: "If you then, who are wicked, know how to give good gifts to your children, how much more will the Father in heaven give the Holy Spirit to those who ask him?" This "is a tremendous thing.

"When we pray courageously, the Lord gives us the grace, but he also gives himself in the grace: the Holy Spirit, that is, himself! The Lord never sends us grace in the mail, never! He brings himself! It is him, the grace! What we are asking is a bit like . . . It is the wrapping paper of the grace. But the real grace is him, who comes to bring it to me. It is him. Our prayer, if it is courageous, receives what we are asking for but also what is more important: the Lord.

"In the Gospels, some receive the grace and go away." Of the ten lepers healed by Jesus, only one of them returns to thank him. The blind man of Jericho also finds the Lord in healing and praises God. But we have to pray with the "courage of faith," pushing ourselves to ask for what the prayer itself does not dare to hope for—God himself.

"We ask for a grace, but we do not dare to say: 'But you come bring it to me.' We know that a grace is always brought by him. It is he who comes and gives it to us. Let's not make the bad impression of taking the grace and not recognizing the One who brings it to us, the One who gives it to us: the Lord. May the Lord give us the grace of giving us himself, always, in every grace. And that we may recognize him, and that we may praise him like those sick people healed in the Gospel. Because we have, in that grace, found the Lord."

October 10, 2013   *Malachi 3:13–20b ✤ Luke 11:5–13*

110

Following Jesus means no half measures

Jesus casts out the demons, and some people in the crowd begin to make explanations "to downplay the power of the Lord." There is always the temptation of wanting to diminish the figure of Jesus as if he were "at the most a healer," not to take him "so seriously." An attitude that has "continued in our time.

"There are some priests who when they read this passage of the Gospel, this and others, they say: 'But Jesus healed a person from a psychological illness.' This is how they interpret it, right? It is true that at that time there was some confusion between epilepsy and demonic possession; but it's also true that there was the devil! And we do not have the right to make things so simple, as if to say: 'None of them were possessed; they were mentally ill.' No! The presence of the devil is on the first page of the Bible, and the Bible also finishes with the presence of the devil, with the victory of God over the devil."

So "we must not be naïve." The Lord gives us some criteria for "discerning" the presence of evil and for going by the "Christian path when there are temptations." One of these criteria is that we not "follow the victory of Jesus over evil" only "halfway. 'Either you are with me'—the Lord says—'or you are against me.'" Jesus came to destroy the devil, "to give us freedom" from "slavery to the devil." And it cannot be said that "we are exaggerating. There's no dressing this up. This is a fight, and a fight in which our health is at stake, our eternal health, our eternal salvation." Then there is the criterion of vigilance. "We must always be vigilant, vigilant against deception, against the seduction of the evil one.

"And we can ask ourselves this question: Do I watch over myself, over my heart, over my feelings, over my thoughts? Do I guard the treasure of grace? Do I guard the presence of the Holy Spirit in me? Or do I leave it as it is, confident, thinking everything's okay? But if you don't watch out, someone is coming who is stronger than you. But if someone comes who is stronger than you and overcomes you, he takes away the weapons in which you trusted and divides the spoils. Vigilance! But, three criteria. Do not confuse the truth. Jesus fights against the devil: first criterion. Second criterion: He who is not with Jesus is against Jesus. There are no half measures. Third criterion: vigilance over our hearts, because the devil is shrewd. He's never gone for good! Not until the last day."

When the unclean spirit goes out of a man, "he wanders through deserted places seeking relief, and not finding it says: 'I will return to the house from which I came.'" And when he finds it "swept and tidied," then he goes, "gets seven other spirits worse than him, and they come and dwell there." So "the last condition of that man becomes worse than the first.

"Vigilance, because his strategy is this: 'You have become Christian, go ahead in your faith. I'll leave you alone, I'll leave you in peace. But when you're used to it and you're not looking out and you feel confident, then I'll come back.' The Gospel today begins with the devil being cast out and ends with the devil returning! Saint Peter said this: 'He is like a roaring lion looking for [someone] to devour.' That's the way it is. 'But, Father, you're a bit old-fashioned! These things scare us.' No, it's not me! It's the Gospel! And these are not lies. This is the word of the Lord! Let's ask the Lord for the grace of taking these things seriously. He came to fight for our salvation. He has conquered the devil! Please, let's not make deals with the devil! He is trying to come back home, to take possession of us. Don't relativize, be vigilant! And always with Jesus!"

October 11, 2013   *Joel 1:13–15; 2:1–2 ✠ Luke 11:15–26*

111

Christians need to leave behind the "Jonah syndrome"

The "Jonah syndrome" and the "sign of Jonah." Jesus speaks in today's Gospel of "an evil generation." His words are very strong. He is not referring to the people "who followed him with such great love" but rather to the "scholars of the law" who "were seeking to put him to the test and to make him fall into a trap." These people, in fact, "were asking him for signs," and Jesus responds that they will be given only "the sign of Jonah." But there is also the "Jonah syndrome." The Lord asks Jonah to go to Nineveh, and he runs away to Spain. Jonah "had everything clear: the doctrine is this, you have to do this," and sinners "need to look out for themselves; I'm getting out of here." Those who "live according to this Jonah syndrome," Jesus "calls them hypocrites, because they do not want the salvation" of the "poor people," of the "ignorant and the sinners."

"The Jonah syndrome has no zeal for the conversion of the people; it is looking for a sanctity—let me put it this way—a 'dry-cleaned' sanctity, everything beautiful, everything done well, but without that zeal of going to preach the Lord. But in the face of this generation sickened by the Jonah syndrome, the Lord promises this sign of Jonah. The other version, that of Matthew, says: Jonah was in the whale for three nights and three days, a reference to Jesus in the tomb—to his death and Resurrection—and that is the sign that Jesus promises, against hypocrisy, against this attitude of perfect religiosity, against this attitude of a group of Pharisees."

There is a parable in the Gospel that depicts this aspect very well: that of the Pharisee and the tax collector who were praying in the Temple. The Pharisee, "so sure of himself," in front of the altar thanks God that he is not like the tax collector, who instead asks only for the mercy of the Lord, recognizing that he is a sinner. So this is "the sign that Jesus promises for his forgiveness, through his death and Resurrection; it is his mercy: 'I desire mercy, not sacrifice.'

"This sign of Jonah, the real one, is that which gives us the confidence of being saved by the blood of Christ. How many Christians, how many there are who think that they will be saved only because of what they do, by their works. Works are necessary, but they are a consequence, a response to that merciful love which saves us. But works alone, without this merciful love, are not enough. The Jonah syndrome, instead, trusts only in its personal justice, in its works."

So Jesus speaks of a "wicked generation" and "the pagan, the Queen of Sheba, he almost appoints as judge; she will rise up against the men of this generation." And this "because she was a restless woman, a woman seeking the wisdom of God.

"So the Jonah syndrome leads us to hypocrisy, to that self-sufficiency, to being pure Christians, perfect, 'because we do these works: we fulfill the commandments, everything.' It is a serious disease. The sign of Jonah is that mercy of God in Jesus Christ, who died and rose for us, for our salvation. There are a couple of words in the first reading that are connected to this. Paul says of himself that he is an apostle not because he had studied this, no; he is an apostle by calling. And to the Christians he says: You 'are called to belong to Jesus Christ.' The sign of Jonah calls us: follow the Lord, we are all sinners, with humility, with meekness. There is a call, and also a choice.

"Let's take advantage of this liturgy today to ask ourselves and make a choice: Which do I prefer? The Jonah syndrome, or the sign of Jonah?"

October 14, 2013   *Romans 1:1–7 ✤ Luke 11:29–32*

112

Let's worship God to keep from being idolaters or hypocrites

Becoming an apostle of one's own ideas, or a devotee of one's own well-being, rather than of God. Bad-mouthing someone because he doesn't fall into line with a certain formalism, forgetting that the "new" commandment of Christianity is love of neighbor with no ifs, ands, or buts. Once again the liturgy of the Mass urges a reflection on the traps that are strewn across the path of the life of faith. The words of Saint Paul stigmatize the sin of idolatry, that of persons who—in the words of the apostle—"in spite of having come to know God, have not glorified him or thanked him as God," preferring to worship "the creature rather than the creator." It is idolatry that comes to the point of "suffocating the truths of faith," in which "the justice of God is revealed.

"But since we all need to worship—because we have the imprint of God within us—when we do not worship God, we worship creatures. And this is the passage from faith to idolatry. They, the idolaters, have no excuse. In spite of having come to know God, they have not glorified him or thanked him as God. And what is the way of idolatry? He says this very clearly: 'They became vain in their reasoning, and their senseless minds were darkened.' The egoism of my own thought, omnipotent thought, what I think is true: I think the truth, I make the truth with my thought . . ."

Two thousand years ago Saint Paul was criticizing the idolaters who prostrated themselves in front of reptiles, birds, mammals. And here the objection is immediately raised that this problem no longer exists, because no one goes around worshiping statues. This is not true; idolatry has found other forms and modes.

"Today as well there are many idols, and today as well there are many idolaters, many who believe themselves wise. Even among us, among Christians! I respect those who are not Christian. But among us—speaking in the family—they think they're smart, they think they know everything. And they have become fools and have exchanged the glory of the incorruptible God for an image: my ego, my ideas, my comfort . . . Today, all of us—I'm moving on, this is not just a historical thing—today as well there are idols in the street, and even a step further . . . We all have some idol hidden within us. We can ask ourselves before God: What is my hidden idol? The one that takes the place of the Lord!"

If Saint Paul calls idolaters fools, in the Gospel, Jesus does the same thing with the hypocrites, embodied by the Pharisee who is scandalized because the Teacher did not wash himself according to the regulations before sitting down at the table. "Oh, you Pharisees!" Jesus replies. "Although you cleanse the outside of the cup and the dish, inside you are filled with plunder and evil." And he adds: "But as to what is within, give alms, and behold, everything will be clean for you.

"Jesus advises us: don't look at appearances, go right to the truth. The dish is a dish, but what is more important is what is inside the dish: the food. But if you are vain, if you are a careerist, if you are ambitious, if you are a person who always boasts about yourself or you like to brag, because you think you're perfect, do a bit of alms-giving and that will heal your hypocrisy. This is the way of the Lord: it is worshiping God, loving God above everything, and loving our neighbor. This is so simple, but so difficult! This can be done only with grace. Let's ask for that grace."

October 15, 2013   *Romans 1:16–25 ✢ Luke 11:37–41*

113

"Ideological Christians" are a grave illness

"Woe to you, scholars of the law. You have taken away the key of knowledge!" This is the warning of Jesus. "When we go down the street and find ourselves in front of a church that is locked, we feel something strange," because "a locked church makes no sense." Sometimes "they give us explanations" that are nothing of the kind. "They are pretexts, justifications, but the reality is that the church is locked and the people walking by cannot go in." And even worse, "the Lord is inside and he can't get out." In the Gospel, Jesus speaks to us of this "image of closure"; it is "the image of those Christians who have the key in hand, but they take it away, they don't open the door." On the contrary, and even worse, "they lock the door" and "do not allow others to enter," and in doing this "they do not even enter themselves." The "lack of Christian testimony does this," and "when that Christian is a priest, a bishop, or a pope, it is worse." But how does it happen that a "Christian falls into this attitude of keeping the door locked and the key in his pocket?

"Faith passes through a still, so to speak, and becomes ideology. And ideology doesn't share. There is no room for Jesus in the ideologies: his tenderness, love, meekness. And the ideologies are rigid, always. In every way: rigid. And when a Christian becomes the disciple of an ideology, he has lost his faith. He is no longer a disciple of Jesus, he is a disciple of this attitude of thought . . . This is why Jesus says to them: 'You have taken away the key of knowledge.' The knowledge of Jesus is turned into an ideological and even moralistic knowledge, because these people close the door with their many prescriptions."

Jesus said it: "'[You load many things onto the] people's shoulders,' but only one thing is necessary." So this is the "spiritual, mental" process of someone who wants the key in his pocket and the door locked.

"Faith becomes ideology, and ideology is frightening. Ideology drives people away; it distances the people and it distances the

Church from the people. This is a serious illness, that of ideological Christians. It is an illness, but it is not new. The apostle John, in his first letter, spoke of this. Christians who lose the faith and prefer ideologies. His attitude is that they become rigid, moralists, ethicists, but without goodness. The question could be this, right? But how can a Christian become like this? What happens in the heart of that Christian, of that priest, of that bishop, of that pope, that he becomes like this? Only one thing: that Christian does not pray. And if there is no prayer, you always close the door.

"The key that opens the door to faith is prayer. When a Christian does not pray, this is what happens. And his testimony is an arrogant testimony." He who does not pray is "arrogant, prideful; he is sure of himself. He is not humble. He is looking for his own promotion." But "when a Christian prays, he does not distance himself from faith, he speaks with Jesus." And "I say praying, not reciting prayers, because these scholars of the law recited many prayers" to show off. But Jesus says: "When you pray, go to your room and pray to your Father in secret, from heart to heart. It is one thing to pray, and another thing to recite prayers."

"These do not pray, they abandon the faith and turn it into a moralistic, casuistic ideology, without Jesus. And when a prophet or a good Christian reproves them, they do the same thing that they did with Jesus: 'After he went out, the scribes and Pharisees began to treat him in a hostile way—these ideologues are hostile—and to make him speak on many topics, laying traps for him—they are tricky—to catch him in some word from his own mouth.' They are not transparent. Poor little things, they are people dirtied by their arrogance.

"Let's ask the Lord for the grace, first: not to stop praying, not to lose the faith, to remain humble. And so we will not become closed, like those who close off the way to the Lord."

October 17, 2013   *Romans 3:21–30* ✦ *Luke 11:47–54*

114

Let's not forget about priests and sisters in retirement homes

The beginning of the apostolic life and the beginning of the end for the apostle Paul. At the beginning of the apostolic life, the Gospel reminds us, the disciples were "young" and "strong" and even "the demons fled" from "their preaching." The first reading, however, shows us Saint Paul at the end of his life. "It is the decline of the Apostle.

"The apostle has a joyful beginning, enthusiastic, an enthusiast with God inside him, right? But even he was not spared the decline. And it does me good to think about the decline of the apostle . . . These three icons come to mind: Moses, John the Baptist, and Paul. Moses is the one who is the head of the People of God; courageous, he fought against their enemies and even fought with God to save the people: strong! And at the end he is alone, on Mount Nebo, looking at the promised land but prevented from entering into it. He could not enter into the promise."

John the Baptist: in his last moments he was not spared from anguish. John the Baptist even has to confront an "anguish of doubt that tormented him" and "ends up under the power of a weak governor, drunken and corrupt, under the power of an adulteress's envy and the whims of a dancing girl."

And even the apostle Paul, in the first reading, speaks to us of those who have abandoned him, of those who have harmed him by hammering away against his preaching. He recalls that no one assisted him in the tribunal. Everyone abandoned him. But, says Saint Paul, "the Lord was close to me. He gave me strength so that I could bring the proclamation of the Gospel to completion.

"This is what is so great about the apostle, who with his life does what John the Baptist said: 'He must increase, and I must decrease.' The apostle is the one who gives his life so that the Lord may increase. And in the end, this is how he fades away . . . And Peter too, with the Lord's promise 'When you are old, they will take you where you do not want to go.' And when I think about the decline of the apostle, what comes into my heart is the memory of those shrines of apostolic life and holiness that are the retirement homes of priests and sisters: good priests, good sisters, elderly, with the burden of solitude, waiting for the Lord to come knock on the doors of their hearts. These are true shrines of apostolic life and holiness that we have in the Church. Let's not forget about them!"

If we look "deeper," we see that these places "are beautiful. I think so often about how we make a pilgrimage to the shrine of the Blessed Mother, of Saint Francis, of Saint Benedict, so many pilgrimages.

"But I ask myself if we Christians have the urge to pay a visit—which would be a true pilgrimage!—to these shrines of holiness and apostolic life, which are the retirement homes of priests and sisters. One of you was telling me a few days ago that when he went into a mission territory he went to the cemetery and saw all the graves of the old missionaries, priests, and sisters, there for fifty, a hundred, two hundred years, unknown. And he said to me: 'But all of them could be canonized, because in the end the only thing that counts is this everyday holiness, this holiness of every day.' In the retirement homes, these sisters and these priests are waiting for the Lord a little bit like Paul. A bit sad, that's true, but also with a certain peace, with joy on their faces.

"It would do all of us good to think about this stage of life that is the decline of the apostle, and pray to the Lord: 'Take care of those who are in that moment of final destitution, that they may say just one more time: Yes, Lord, I want to follow you!'"

October 18, 2013   *2 Timothy 4:10–17b ❧ Luke 10:1–9*

115

Attachment to money destroys persons and families

A passage of the Gospel in which a man asks Jesus to intervene to resolve a question of inheritance with his brother allows us to develop the problem of our relationship with money.

"This is a problem we see all the time. How many families have we seen destroyed over the problem of money: brother against brother; father against son . . . This is the first thing that this attitude of being attached to money does: it destroys! When a person is attached to money, he destroys himself, he destroys his family! Money destroys! That's what it does, right? It attaches itself to you. Money is useful for accomplishing many good things, many projects for the development of humanity, but when your heart is attached like this, it destroys you."

Jesus recounts the parable of the rich man who lives to accumulate "treasures for himself" and "does not grow wealthy in the sight of God." Jesus is warning us to stay far away from every form of greed.

"That's what does the damage: greed in my relationship with money. Having more, having more, having more . . . It leads you to idolatry, it destroys your relationship with others! Not the money, but the attitude that is called greed. Then this greed makes you sick, because it makes you think of everything only as a function of money. It destroys you, it makes you sick. And in the end—this is the most important thing—greed is a tool of idolatry, because it moves in the opposite direction of the road that God has taken with us. Saint Paul tells us that Jesus Christ, who was rich, made himself poor in order to enrich us. That is the way of God: humility, self-abasement in order to serve. But greed leads you down the opposite road; you, who are a poor man, make yourself God out of vanity. It is idolatry!"

This is why Jesus says things "that are so tough, so strong against this attachment to money. He tells us that we cannot serve two masters: either we serve God or money. He tells us not to worry, that the Lord knows what we need," and he invites us "to trustful abandonment to the Father, who makes the lilies of the field grow and gives the birds the food that they eat." The rich man of the parable continues to think only of wealth, but God says to him: "Fool, this night your life will be demanded of you!" "This way that goes against the way of God is foolishness; it leads us far from life, it destroys all human fraternity.

"The Lord teaches us what is the way. It is not the way of poverty for the sake of poverty. No! It is the way of poverty as a tool, so that God may be God, so that he may be the only Lord! No idol of gold! And all of the goods that we have, the Lord gives them to us for the advancement of the world, for the advancement of humanity, to help, to help others. May the word of the Lord remain in our hearts today: 'Pay heed and keep yourselves far from all greed, because even if one is in abundance, his life does not depend on what he possesses.'"

October 21, 2013   *Romans 4:20–25 ✤ Luke 12:13–21*

116

God does not save us by decree

I ntelligence is not enough to enter into the mystery of God, but what is needed is "contemplation, closeness, and abundance." This is what is suggested by a passage from the letter of Saint Paul to the Romans. The Church, "when it wants to tell us something" about the mystery of God, "uses just one word: wonderful." This mystery is "a wonderful mystery."

"To contemplate the mystery, what Paul is saying to us here about our salvation, about our redemption, this can be understood only on our knees, in contemplation. Not only with the intelligence. When the intelligence wants to explain a mystery, always—always!—it goes crazy! This is what has happened in the history of the Church. 'Contemplation': intelligence, heart, knees, prayer . . . all together enter into the mystery. That is the first word that may help us here."

The second word that helps us to enter into the mystery is "closeness. A man committed the sin, a man has saved us. It is God who is close!" He is "close to us, to our history." From the first moment, "when he chose our father Abraham, he has walked with his people." And this can also be seen with Jesus, who does "the work of an artisan, of a laborer.

"The image that comes to me is that of a nurse, of a nurse in a hospital, healing wounds one after another, but with her hands. God gets involved, he intervenes in our misery, he draws near to our wounds and heals them with his hands, and in order to have hands he became man. This is a labor of Jesus, it is personal. A man committed sin, a man comes to heal it. Nearness. God does not save us only by a decree, a law; he saves us with tenderness, he saves us with caresses, he saves us with his life, for us."

The third word is "abundance." "Where sin abounded, grace abounded all the more. Each of us knows his miseries, he knows them well. And they abound!" But "the challenge of God is to overcome this, to heal the wounds" as Jesus did. And even more than that: "to give that superabundant gift of his love, of his grace." And in this way "we can understand Jesus' preference for sinners.

"In the hearts of these people there was an abundance of sin. But he went to them with that superabundance of grace and love. The grace of God always conquers, because it is he himself who gives, who draws near, who caresses us, who heals us. And because of this—although some of us may not like to say so—those who are closest to the heart of Jesus are the most sinful, because he goes to seek them out, he calls everyone: 'Come, come!' And when they ask him for an explanation, he says: 'Those who are in good health do not need the doctor. I have come to heal, to save.'

"Some of the saints say that one of the ugliest sins is distrust: to distrust God." But "how can we distrust a God who is so close, so good, who prefers our sinful heart?" This mystery "is not easy to understand; we can't understand it well with our intelligence." Only, "perhaps, these three words may help us": contemplation, closeness, and abundance. He is a God "who always conquers with this superabundance of his grace, with his tenderness, with his richness of mercy."

October 22, 2013   *Romans 5:12, 15b, 17–19, 20b–21* ✤ *Luke 12:35–38*

117

Christian life shouldn't be watered down

Before and after Jesus. In the passage from the letter to the Romans centered on the mystery of our redemption, the apostle Paul "tries to explain this to us with this logic of before and after: before Jesus and after Jesus." Saint Paul considers the before as "trash," while the after is like a new creation. And he points out "a way to live according to this logic of before and after.

"We have been remade in Christ! What Christ has done in us is a re-creation: the blood of Christ has re-created us. It is a second creation! If before our whole life, our body, our soul, our habits were on the path of sin, of iniquity, after this re-creation we must make the effort to walk in the way of justice, of sanctification. Use this word: 'sanctity.' All of us have been baptized. At that moment, our parents—we were children—made the act of faith in our name: 'I believe in Jesus Christ, who has forgiven our sins.' I believe in Jesus Christ!

"We have to take up" this faith in Jesus Christ and "carry it forward in our different ways of life." "Living as Christians means carrying forward this faith in Christ, this re-creation." And with faith, carrying forward the works that arise from this faith, "works for sanctification." We have to carry forward "the first sanctification that all of us received in Baptism.

"We are truly weak, and many times, many times, we commit sins, imperfections . . . And this is on the path of sanctification? Yes and no! If you get used to it: 'This is just the way my life is; I believe in Jesus Christ, but I live how I want.' No, that does not sanctify you; that doesn't work! It makes no sense! But if you say, 'Yes, I am a sinner; I am weak,' and you always go to the Lord and tell him: 'Lord, you have the strength. Give me faith! You can heal me!' And in the sacrament of Reconciliation you get yourself healed, then yes, even our imperfections serve a purpose on this path of sanctification. But this is always before and after.

"Before the act of faith, before accepting Jesus Christ, who has re-created us with his blood, we were on the way of injustice." After, however, "we are on the path of sanctification, but we have to take it seriously!" And in order to take it seriously we have to do works of justice, "simple" works. "Worship God: God always comes first! And then do what Jesus advises us: help others." These works "are the works that Jesus did in his life: works of justice, works of re-creation. When we give food to someone who is hungry, we are re-creating hope in him. And so on with the others." But if "we accept the faith and then do not live it, we are Christians in memory only.

"Without this awareness of before and after of which Paul is speaking, our Christianity doesn't help anyone! And more than that, it goes by the way of hypocrisy. 'I call myself Christian, but I live like a pagan!' Sometimes we say 'Christians stuck halfway,' who don't take this seriously. We are holy, justified, sanctified by the blood of Christ. Take up this sanctification and carry it forward! And this is not taken seriously! Lukewarm Christians say, 'But, yes, yes; but, no, no.' A little bit like what our mothers used to say: 'Milk and water Christians, no!' A little like that . . . A bit of Christian whitewash, a bit of catechism whitewash. But inside there is no real conversion, there is not this conviction of Paul: 'I have let everything go and consider it trash, to gain Christ and be found in him.'"

This "was Paul's passion, and this is the passion of a Christian!" We have to "let go of everything that distances us from Jesus Christ" and "make everything new: everything is new in Christ!" And this "can be done." Saint Paul did it, but also many Christians. "Not only the saints, those we know; also the anonymous saints, those who live Christianity seriously." So the question we can ask ourselves today is if we really want to live Christianity seriously, if we want to carry this re-creation forward. "Let's ask Saint Paul to give us the grace to live as serious Christians, to truly believe that we have been sanctified by the blood of Jesus Christ."

October 24, 2013   *Romans 6:19–23 ✚ Luke 12:49–53*

118

The struggle against evil also means confessing sins

For many adult believers, confessing to a priest is an unmanageable effort—which often leads them to neglect the sacrament—or such an agony that it turns a moment of truth into an exercise of fiction. Saint Paul, in the letter to the Romans, does exactly the opposite: he publicly admits in front of the community that "good does not dwell in me, that is, in my flesh." He affirms that he is a "slave" who does not do the good that he wants but commits the evil that he does not want. This happens in the life of faith, according to which "when I want to do right, evil is at hand.

"And this is the struggle of Christians. It is our struggle every day. And we do not always have the courage to speak as Paul speaks about this struggle. We are always looking for justification: 'Well, sure, we're all sinners.' That's how we talk, right? This says it dramatically: it is our struggle. And if we do not recognize this, we can never have God's forgiveness. Because if being a sinner is a word, a manner of speaking, we don't need God's forgiveness. But if it is a reality that makes us slaves, we need this inner liberation of the Lord, that strength. But what is more important here is that to find the way out, Paul confesses his sin to the community, his tendency to sin. He does not hide it."

The confession of sins made with humility is what "the Church asks of all of us." Let's think of the entreaty of Saint James that we confess our sins among one another. But not for publicity," rather "to give glory to God" and recognize that "he is the one who saves me." This is why for confession we go to our brother, "our brother priest"; it is to do as Paul did. Above all with the same "concreteness.

"Some say: 'Well, I confess to God.' But that's easy, it's like confessing by e-mail, isn't it? God is far away; I say things and it is not a face-to-face, it is not an eye to eye. Paul confesses his weakness to his brothers face-to-face. Others say: 'No, I go to confession,' but the things confessed are so ethereal, so up in the air, that they have no concreteness. And this is the same as not doing it. Confessing our sins is not going to a therapy session, nor is it going to a torture chamber. It is telling the Lord, 'Lord, I am a sinner,' but saying it through our brother, so that even this saying it may be concrete. 'And I am a sinner for this, for this, and for this.'"

Concreteness, honesty, and also a sincere capacity to be ashamed of our mistakes. There are no shortcuts on the open road that leads to God's forgiveness, to perceiving in the depths of our heart his forgiveness and love. And whom should we imitate, if not children?

"The little ones have this wisdom. When a child comes to confession, he never says anything vague. 'But, Father, I did this and I did this to my aunt, I said this word to someone else,' and they say the word. They are concrete, they have the simplicity of the truth. And we always have the tendency to hide the reality of our miseries. But there is a beautiful thing: when we confess our sins as they are in the presence of God, we always feel this grace of shame. Being ashamed before God is a grace. It is a grace to say: 'I am ashamed of myself.' Let's think of Peter, after the miracle of Jesus on the lake: 'But, Lord, go away from me, I am a sinner.' He was ashamed of his sin before the holiness of Jesus Christ."

October 25, 2013   *Romans 7:18–25a ❧ Luke 12:54–59*

119

Jesus continues to pray for us even today

Before choosing the twelve apostles, Jesus spends the whole night praying to the Father. "Jesus sets up his team," and immediately afterward he is surrounded by a great multitude of people "who have come to listen to him and to be healed" because "from him went out a power that healed all." These are "the three relationships of Jesus: Jesus with the Father, Jesus with his apostles, and Jesus with the people." Jesus prayed to the Father for the apostles and for the people. But he's still praying today.

"He is the intercessor, the one who prays, and he prays to God with us and in front of us. Jesus has saved us, he has made this great prayer, his sacrifice, his life, to save us, to justify us; we are justified thanks to him. Now he has gone away, and he prays. But is Jesus a spirit? Jesus is not a spirit! Jesus is a person, he is a man, with flesh like ours, but in glory. Jesus has wounds on his hands, on his feet, in his side, and when he prays he shows to the Father this price of justification, and he prays for us, as if he were saying: 'But, Father, don't let all this be for nothing!'"

Jesus "has our prayers in mind" because "he is the first to pray," and like "our brother" and "a man like us," he intercedes for us.

"In the first phase, he worked our redemption, he justified all of us. But what is he doing now? He is interceding, praying for us. I think about what Peter must have felt when he denied Jesus, and then Jesus looked at him and he wept. He felt that what Jesus had done for him was true. He had prayed for him, and this was why he was able to weep, he was able to repent. So many times we say to each other, 'Well, pray for me, I need it, I have so many problems, so many things: pray for me.' And that is good, because we have to pray for each other."

And we have to ask: "Pray for me, Lord: you are the intercessor.

"He prays for me; he prays for all of us. And he prays courageously, because he shows the Father the price of our justice: his wounds. Let's really think about this and thank the Lord. Let's be thankful for having a brother who prays with us, and prays for us, intercedes for us. And let's talk with Jesus, saying to him: 'Lord, you are the intercessor, you have saved me, you have justified me. But now, pray for me.' And let's entrust our problems, our lives, so many things to him, that he may take them to the Father."

October 28, 2013   *Ephesians 2:19–22 ✣ Luke 6:12–16*

120

Hope is dynamic and life-giving

Wmat is hope for a Christian? The words of Saint Paul, in the first reading, emphasize the unique dimension of Christian hope. This is not a matter of optimism but of "an ardent expectation" lifted up toward the revelation of the Son of God. Creation "was made subject to futility," so the Christian lives in tension between hope and slavery. "Hope," to echo Saint Paul, "does not disappoint, it is sure." Nonetheless, "it is not easy to understand hope." Sometimes "we think that being people of hope means being optimists." But that's not true.

"Hope is not optimism, it is not that ability to look at the bright side and keep going. No, that is optimism, it is not hope. Nor is hope a positive attitude toward things. Those sunny, positive people . . . Sure, this is good! But it's not hope. It's not easy to understand what hope is. It is called the most humble of the three virtues, because it is hidden within life. Faith can be seen, it makes itself felt, we know what it is. Charity acts, we know what it is. But what is hope? What is this attitude of hope? To get an idea of this, we could first say that hope is a risk, it is a risky virtue; it is a virtue, as Saint Paul says, 'of an ardent expectation for the revelation of the Son of God.' It is not an illusion."

Having hope is precisely this: "being in tension toward that revelation, toward this joy that will put smiles on all our faces." Saint Paul is careful to emphasize that hope is not optimism, "it is something more." It is "another thing, different." The first Christians "depicted it as an anchor; hope was an anchor, an anchor fixed in the shore" of the afterlife. And our life is precisely a journey toward this anchor.

"The question occurs to me: Where are we anchored, each one of us? Are we anchored in the shore of that faraway ocean, or are we anchored in an artificial lagoon that we have made, with our rules, our behaviors, our schedules, our clericalism, our ecclesiastical and non-ecclesial attitudes? That is not hope. Where my heart is anchored, there in that artificial lagoon, with my ever so impeccable behavior . . ."

Saint Paul then points to another icon of hope, that of childbirth. "We are in waiting, this is childbirth. And hope is in this dynamic," of "giving life." But "the firstfruits of the Spirit are not seen." And yet "I know that the Spirit is working." He is working in us "as if he were a tiny mustard seed, but inside he is full of life, of strength, that keeps going" until it becomes a tree. The Spirit works like leaven. This is "how the Spirit works: we don't see him, but he's there. We must ask for this grace.

"It is one thing to live in hope, because in hope we have been saved, and another thing to live as good Christians and nothing more. Living in anticipation of the revelation or living the commandments well versus being anchored in the shore over there or moored in the artificial lagoon. I think of Mary, a young woman, who after she heard she was a mother changed her attitude and went, helped, and sang that canticle of praise. When a woman becomes pregnant she is a woman, but she is no longer just a woman; she is a mother. And hope has something of this about it. It changes our attitude; we are ourselves, but we are not ourselves; we are ourselves, seeking the other side, anchored in the other side."

October 29, 2013   *Romans 8:18–25 ✠ Luke 13:18–21*

121

We are all invited to the feast by the Lord

The readings of the day "show us the Christian's identity card." "First of all, the essence of being a Christian is an invitation; we become Christian only if we are invited." This is "a gratuitous invitation" to participate, which comes from God. Admission to this celebration is "not something you can buy; either you are invited or you can't get in." If "in our conscience we do not have this certainty of being invited," then "we have not understood what a Christian is.

"A Christian is someone who is invited. Invited to what? To a deal? Invited to go for a stroll? The Lord wants to tell us something more: 'You are invited to a celebration!' The Christian is the one who is invited to a celebration, to joy, to the joy of being saved, to the joy of being redeemed, to the joy of participating in life with Jesus. This is a joy! You are invited to a celebration! We understand, a celebration is a gathering of people who talk, laugh, celebrate; they are happy. It is a gathering of people. Among normal people, mentally normal, I have never seen someone celebrating alone, have you? That would be boring! Open the bottle of wine . . . This is not a celebration, it's something else. We celebrate with others, we celebrate in the family, we celebrate with friends, we celebrate with people who have been invited, as I have been invited. In order to be Christian we need to belong to something, and what we belong to is this Body, these people who have been invited to the celebration: this is Christian belonging."

So in terms of the letter to the Romans, it must therefore be affirmed that this celebration is a "celebration of unity." And all are invited, "good and bad." And the first to be called are the marginalized.

"The Church is not a Church only for the good people. Do we want to say who belongs to the Church, to this celebration? Sinners do; all of us sinners have been invited. And what do we do here? We make up a community that has different gifts: one has the gift of prophecy, the other of ministry, here is a teacher . . . This is where it comes from. Everyone has some quality, some virtue. But the celebration happens when we share what we have with everyone else. We participate in the celebration; we participate completely. We cannot understand Christian existence without this participation. It is a participation of all of us. 'I'm going to the party, but I'll just stay in the living room, because I have to be with the three or four I know already, and the others . . .' You can't do this in the Church! Either you enter with everyone or you're out! You can't pick and choose. The Church is for all, starting with these I have mentioned, the most marginalized. It is the Church of all!"

It is the "Church of the invited," "being invited, being participants in a community with all." But in the parable narrated by Jesus, we read that those invited, one after the other, began to find excuses not to go to the banquet. "They don't accept the invitation! They say yes, but they don't go." These "are the Christians who just content themselves with being on the guest list: listed Christians." But this "is not enough," because if you don't go into the banquet you are not Christian. "You may be on the list, but this isn't enough for your salvation! This is the Church. Entering into the Church is a grace; entering into the Church is an invitation." And this right "cannot be bought." Entering into the Church is being part of the community, the community of the Church; entering into the Church is participating with all that we have of the virtues, of the qualities that the Lord has given us, in our service for one another. "Entering into the Church means being available for what the Lord Jesus asks of us." Ultimately, "entering into the Church means entering into this People of God that is walking toward eternity. No one is a protagonist in the Church, but we have One," who has done everything. God "is the protagonist"! All of us are "behind him, and anyone who is not behind him is one who makes excuses" and does not go to the banquet.

"The Lord is very generous. The Lord opens the doors for all. The Lord even understands what is said to him: 'No, Lord, I don't want to go to you!' He understands and waits, because he is merciful.

"But the Lord is not pleased with that person who says yes and does no; who pretends to thank him for so many wonderful things but in reality goes his own way; who has good manners, does his own will and not that of the Lord. Those who are always excusing themselves, those who do not know joy, who do not experience the joy of belonging. Let's ask the Lord for this grace: to understand well how beautiful it is to be invited to the feast, how beautiful it is to be with everyone and share with everyone our qualities, how beautiful it is to be with him, and how ugly it is to play with yes and no, to say yes but simply content myself with being on the Christian guest list."

November 5, 2013   *Romans 12:5–16ab ✣ Luke 14:15–24*

122

God's weakness for love is the joy of mercy

The parable of the lost sheep and of the lost coin helps to explain the attitude of the scribes and Pharisees who were scandalized by the things that Jesus did and grumbled against him. "This man is a threat," he eats with tax collectors and sinners, "he offends God, he desecrates the ministry of the prophet . . . to be close to these people." Jesus says that this "is the music of hypocrisy," and "he responds to this grumbling hypocrisy with a parable.

"He responds to the grumbling with a joyful parable. Many times, in this brief passage, we come across the word 'joy' or 'gladness.' 'And you'—it is as if he were saying this—'you are scandalized by this, but my Father rejoices.' This is the deeper message here: the joy of God, who is a God who does not like to lose. He is not a good loser, and for this reason, in order not to lose, he goes out from himself and goes, seeks. He is a God who seeks; he seeks all those who are far from him. Like the shepherd who goes to look for the lost sheep."

The work of God is "to go and seek," to "invite all to the feast, good and bad.

"He does not tolerate losing one of his own. But this will also be the prayer of Jesus on Holy Thursday: 'Father, let none of those you have given to me be lost.' He is a God who walks to seek us and has a certain weakness of love for those who are farthest from him, who have gotten lost . . . He goes and seeks them. And how does he seek? He seeks until the end, like that shepherd who goes into the darkness, seeking until he finds the lost sheep; or like the woman, who when she loses that coin lights the lamp, sweeps her house, and searches carefully. This is how God seeks. 'But I am not losing this child, he is mine! And I do not want to lose him.' This is our Father: he always seeks us."

Then, "when he has found the sheep" and has brought it back into the sheepfold with the others, no one must say: "You're a lost cause," but "You are one of us," because he restores all of its dignity. "There is no difference" because God "restores all those he has found. And when he does this he is a God who rejoices.

"God's joy is not the death of the sinner but his life; that is joy. How far away were these people who were grumbling against Jesus, how far from the heart of God! They didn't know him. They believed that being religious, being good people meant always being in the right, following the customs and sometimes pretending to follow the customs. This is the hypocrisy of grumbling. But the joy of the Father, of God, is that of love: he loves us. 'But I am a sinner, I have done this, this, this!' 'But I love you just the same, and I am going to seek you out and bring you home.' This is our Father. Let's think about it."

November 7, 2013   *Romans 14:7–12 ✦ Luke 15:1–10*

123

Corruption destroys dignity

The parable of the dishonest steward brings up a chance to talk "about the spirit of the world, about worldliness," about "how this worldliness acts and how dangerous it is." Jesus "prayed to the Father that his disciples might not fall into worldliness. It is the enemy.

"When we think about our enemies, let's really think about the devil first, because he is the one who hurts us. The atmosphere, the way of life that is so pleasing to the devil is this worldliness: living according to the 'values' of the world. And this steward is an example of worldliness."

In the parable, the master praises the dishonest steward for his cunning. "Yes, this is a praise of bribery! And the habit of bribery is a worldly and strongly sinful habit. It is a habit that does not come from God. God has commanded us to bring bread home with our honest labor! And this man, the steward, he brought it home, but how? He was giving his children dirty bread to eat! And although they may have been educated at expensive schools and may have grown up in cultured environments, his children have received from their father, as their food, filth, because their father, bringing dirty bread home, had lost his dignity! And this is a grave sin! Because it may begin with a little kickback, but it's like a drug!"

So the habit of taking bribes becomes an addiction. But if there is a "worldly cunning," there is also a "Christian cunning, a way of moving things along, not with the spirit of the world" but honestly. This is what Jesus says when he tells us to be as sly as serpents and as innocent as doves. Putting these two dimensions together "is a grace of the Holy Spirit," a grace that we must ask for. Finally, a prayer:

"Perhaps it would do all of us good today to pray for the many children and young people who receive dirty bread from their parents. These too are hungry, they are hungry for dignity! Pray that the Lord may change the hearts of these devotees of bribery, and that they may realize that dignity comes from worthy work, from honest work, from the work of every day, and not from these shortcuts that take everything away from you in the end. And then you would end up like that other man in the Gospel who had so many granaries, so many silos crammed full and didn't know what to do with them. 'This night you must die,' the Lord said. These poor people who have lost their dignity in the practice of bribery, all they take with them is not the money they have gained but their lack of dignity! Let's pray for them!"

November 8, 2013   *Romans 15:14–21 ☙ Luke 16:1–8*

Ecclesia semper reformanda

Three icons" speak to us of the Church. From the first reading from Ezekiel and from Psalm 46, the icon of the river of water that flows from the Temple and gladdens the city of God, an image of the grace that sustains and nourishes the life of the Church. From the second reading, from the first letter of Saint Paul to the Corinthians, the icon of the rock, which is Jesus Christ, the foundation on which the Church is built.

From the Gospel passage of the purification in the Temple, the icon of the reform of the Church: *"Ecclesia semper reformanda,"* because the members of the Church are always sinners and need conversion. The call to the faithful is to pray that the Church may always flow with the water of grace, may always be founded on Christ, may remain faithful to him, and that its members may always allow themselves to be converted by Jesus.

November 9, 2013   *Ezekiel 47:1–2, 8–9, 12* ✢
1 Corinthians 3:9c–11, 16–17 ✢ *John 2:13–22*

No to Christians with a double life

Jesus "does not tire of forgiving, and he advises us" to do the same. The Gospel speaks to us of the Lord's exhortation to forgive our repentant brother. When Jesus asks us to forgive seven times a day, "he is giving us a portrait of himself." Jesus "forgives," but in this passage from the Gospel he also says, "Woe to those on account of whom scandals come." He does not speak of sin but of scandal, which is another thing. And he adds that "it would be better for him to have a millstone tied around his neck and be thrown into the sea rather than to scandalize one of these little ones." But what is the difference "between sinning and scandalizing?

"The difference is that the one who sins and repents asks for forgiveness. He feels weak, he feels like a child of God, he humbles himself and asks for salvation from Jesus. But that other, who scandalizes, what is scandalous about him? That he doesn't repent. He continues to sin, but he pretends to be Christian: a double life. And the double life of a Christian does so much harm, so much harm. 'But I am a benefactor of the Church! I put my hand into my pocket and I give to the Church.' But with the other hand he steals: from the state, from the poor . . . He steals. He is unrighteous. This is a double life. And what he deserves—Jesus says this; I'm not the one who says it—is to have a millstone tied around his neck and to be thrown into the sea. He doesn't speak of forgiveness here."

And this "is because this person deceives," and "where there is deception, there is not the Spirit of God. This is the difference between the sinner and the corrupt." Anyone "living a double life is corrupt." It is different when someone "sins and would like not to sin, but is weak" and "goes to the Lord" and asks for forgiveness. "The Lord loves this one! He accompanies him, he is with him.

"And we must say that we are sinners, yes, all of us, right here! We all are. Corrupt, no. The corrupt are stuck in a state of self-sufficiency; they don't know what humility is. Jesus said of these corrupt: 'the beauty of being whitewashed tombs,' which look beautiful on the outside but inside are full of dead bones and putrefaction. And a Christian who boasts of being Christian but does not live as a Christian is one of these corrupt. We all know someone who is in this situation, and how much harm they do to the Church! Corrupt Christians, corrupt priests . . . How much harm they do to the Church! Because they do not live in the spirit of the Gospel but in the spirit of worldliness."

Saint Paul says this clearly in the letter to the Christians of Rome: "Do not conform yourselves to this world." In fact, the "original text is stronger" because it says "not to enter into the mind-set of this world, into the parameters of this world." A mind-set that "is this worldliness that leads you to a double life.

"A whitewashed putrefaction: this is the life of the corrupted. And Jesus did not simply call these people sinners, he called them hypocrites. But how beautiful is that other part, right? 'If he commits a fault against you seven times in one day and seven times returns saying: "I repent, I am a sinner," you will forgive him.' This is what he does with sinners. He does not tire of forgiving, only on the condition that they do not want to live this double life, that they go to him with repentance: 'Forgive me, Lord, I am a sinner!' Today let's ask the Holy Spirit for the grace to flee from all deception. Let's ask for the grace to recognize that we are sinners. We are sinners. Sinners, yes. Corrupt, no."

November 11, 2013   *Wisdom 1:1–7 ✤ Luke 17:1–6*

126

Even when he scolds us, God caresses us

God created man for incorruptibility," but "by the envy of the devil, death entered the world." A passage from the book of Wisdom reminds us of our creation. The envy of the devil brought the beginning of this war, "this road that ends with death." This latter "has entered the world, and is experienced by those who belong to it." It is an experience we all have.

"We all have to pass through death, but it is one thing to pass through this experience while belonging to the devil and another thing to pass through this experience in the hand of God. And I like to hear this: 'We are in the hands of God from the beginning.' The Bible explains the Creation to us using a wonderful image: God who, with his hands, makes us from mud, from the earth, in his image and likeness. It is the hands of God that have created us: God the craftsman. Like a craftsman he has made us. These hands of the Lord . . . the hands of God, which have not abandoned us."

The Bible tells us that the Lord says to his people: "I have walked with you, like a father with his son, holding him by the hand." It is precisely the hands of God "that accompany us on the journey.

"Our Father, like a father with his son, teaches us to walk. He teaches us to go the way of life and salvation. It is the hands of God that caress us in our moments of sorrow; they comfort us. It is our Father who caresses us! He loves us so much. And also in these caresses, so many times, there is forgiveness. There is one thing that really makes me think about this. Jesus, God, took his wounds with him; he shows them to the Father. This is the price: the hands of God are hands wounded out of love! And this consoles us so much."

So many times we hear people say that they don't know where to turn. "I entrust myself to the hands of God!" This "is beautiful" because "there we are safe. It is the greatest safety, because it is the safety of our Father who loves us. The hands of God also heal us from our spiritual illnesses.

"Let's think about the hands of Jesus, when he touched the sick and healed them . . . They are the hands of God; they heal us! I cannot imagine God hitting us! I can't imagine it. Scolding us, yes, I can imagine that, because he does it. But he never, ever hurts us. Never! He caresses us. Even when he has to scold us, he does it with a caress, because he is Father. 'The souls of the righteous are in the hands of God.' Let's think about the hands of God, who created us like a craftsman, who has given us eternal health. They are wounded hands, and they accompany us on the path of life. Let's entrust ourselves to the hands of God, as a child entrusts himself to the hand of his father. That is a sure hand!"

November 12, 2013   *Wisdom 2:23–3:9 ✤ Luke 17:7–10*

127

The spirit of curiosity pulls us away from the wisdom and peace of God

The first reading, taken from the book of Wisdom, describes "the mind-set of the spiritual person," of the true Christian, who lives "in the wisdom of the Holy Spirit. And this wisdom leads him forward with this spirit that is intelligent, holy, one, manifold, subtle.

"This is walking in life with this spirit, the Spirit of God, which helps us to judge, to make decisions according to the heart of God. And this spirit gives us peace, always! It is the spirit of peace, the spirit of love, the spirit of fraternity. And holiness is precisely this. What God asks of Abraham—'Walk in my presence and be blameless'—is this: this peace. Going along with the movement of the Spirit of God and this wisdom. And the person who walks like this, it can be said that he is a wise person. A wise person, because he moves with the motion of God's patience."

But in the Gospel "we find ourselves facing another spirit, contrary to this wisdom of God: the spirit of curiosity.

"It is when we want to take control of God's plans, of the future, of things, to know everything, to take everything in hand. The Pharisees asked Jesus 'when the Kingdom of God would come.' Curious! They wanted to know the date, the day . . . The spirit of curiosity distances us from the spirit of wisdom, because it is interested only in details, news, the petty news of every day. Oh, how will this get done? It is the how; it is the spirit of the how! And the spirit of curiosity is not a good spirit. It is the spirit of dispersion, of withdrawing from God, the spirit of talking too much. And Jesus goes on to tell us something else that is interesting: this spirit of curiosity, which is worldly, leads us to confusion."

Curiosity drives us to want to feel that the Lord is here or there. Or it makes us say: "'But I know a mystic, a mystic who receives letters from the Blessed Mother, messages from the Blessed Mother.'

"But look, the Blessed Mother is our Mother. And she loves us all.

But she's not some postal official, to be sending messages out every day. These innovations distance us from the Gospel; they distance us from the Holy Spirit; they distance us from peace and hope, from the glory of God, from the beauty of God." Because "Jesus says that the Kingdom of God does not come in a way to attract attention; it comes in wisdom. The Kingdom of God is among you!" Jesus says. It is "this action of the Holy Spirit that gives us wisdom, that gives us peace. The Kingdom of God does not come in confusion, as God did not speak to the prophet Elijah in the wind, in the storm" but "spoke in the gentle breeze, the breeze of wisdom.

"So Saint Thérèse of the Child Jesus said that she always had to stop herself when the spirit of curiosity came to her. When she was speaking with another sister and this sister was telling her a story, something about her family, about people, sometimes she went on to another topic and Thérèse wanted to hear the end of the story. But she felt that that was not the spirit of God, because it was a spirit of dispersion, of curiosity. The Kingdom of God is among us. Don't seek out strange things, don't seek out innovations with this worldly curiosity. Let's let the Spirit lead us forward, with that wisdom which is a gentle breeze. This is the Spirit of the Kingdom of God, of which Jesus speaks."

November 14, 2013   *Wisdom 7:22b–8:1 ✛ Luke 17:20–25*

Man's prayer is God's weakness

Jesus urges us to pray without tiring, recounting the parable of the widow who insistently asks a dishonest judge to give her justice. This is how "God does and will do justice for his chosen, who cry out to him day and night," as happened when Moses guided Israel out of Egypt.

"When he calls Moses, God says he has heard the weeping, the lamentation of his people. The Lord listens. And in the first reading we hear what the Lord has done, that omnipotent word: 'From heaven he comes like a relentless warrior.' This is what the Lord is like when he comes to the defense of his people; he is a relentless warrior, and he saves his people. He saves, he renews all. 'All of creation was molded anew in its proper nature as before.' 'The Red Sea became a road without obstacles . . . And those whom your hand protected passed there with all of the people.'"

The Lord "has heard the prayers of his people, because he felt in his heart that his chosen were suffering" and saved them in a powerful way.

"This is the power of God. And what is the power of men? What is the power of man? It is what the widow does: to knock at God's heart, to knock, ask, lament over our many problems, over our many sorrows, and ask the Lord for liberation from these sorrows, from these sins, from these problems. The power of man is prayer, and the prayer of a humble man is God's weakness. The Lord is weak only in this: he is weak in the face of the prayer of his people."

November 16, 2013   *Wisdom 18:14–16; 19:6–9 ✢ Luke 18:1–8*

God save us from the worldly spirit and from uniform thinking

The People of God prefer to withdraw from the Lord when offered a proposal of worldliness. The first reading, a passage from the first book of Maccabees, provides an opportunity to ponder the "perverse root" of worldliness. The leaders of the people don't want Israel to be isolated from the other nations anymore, so they abandon their own traditions in order to go negotiate with the king. They go to "bargain," and they are enthusiastic about this. It is as if they were saying, "We are progressives, we are going with progress where all the people are going." This is the "spirit of adolescent progressivism," which "believes that going forward in any choice is better than remaining in the habits of fidelity." These people, therefore, negotiate with the king over "fidelity to the God who is always faithful. This is called apostasy, adultery." They are not negotiating, in fact, over just a few values, "they are negotiating over the essence of their being: faithfulness to the Lord.

"And this is a contradiction. We do not negotiate over values, but we negotiate over faithfulness. And this is the fruit of the devil, of the prince of this world, who leads us forward with the spirit of worldliness. And then come the consequences. They have taken on the habits of the pagans, and then one step further: the king ordered that throughout his kingdom all should form only one people and everyone should abandon his own customs. This is not the good globalization of the unity of all nations, each with his own customs but united, but it is the globalization of hegemonic uniformity; it is uniform thinking. And this uniform thinking is the fruit of worldliness."

And after this, "the people complied with the orders of the king; they even accepted his religious worship, sacrificing to idols and profaning the Sabbath." Step after step, "they went forward on this road." And in the end "the king erected upon the altar 'the desolating abomination.'

" 'But, Father, does this still happen today?' Yes. Because the spirit of worldliness is still there today, still today it leads us on with this desire to be progressives in line with uniform thinking. If anyone was found with a scroll of the covenant and if anyone obeyed the law, the king condemned him to death. And this is what we have read in the newspapers in recent months. These people bargained away their faithfulness to their Lord; these people, moved by the spirit of the world, bargained away their identity, bargained away their membership in a people, a people that God loves so much, that God wants as his people."

Lord of the World, a novel of the early twentieth century, dwells precisely on "that spirit of worldliness that leads us to apostasy." Today we think that "we have to be like everyone else, we have to be more normal, do as everyone does, which is adolescent progressivism." And then "the story goes on: the death sentences, the human sacrifices. But do you think these are not done today, human sacrifices? There are so many, so many! And there are laws that protect them.

"But what consoles us is that in the face of this advancement of the spirit of the world, the prince of this world, the advancement of unfaithfulness, there always remains the Lord, who cannot deny himself, the Faithful One. He is always waiting for us, he loves us so much, and he forgives us when we, repentant over some step, over some little step in this spirit of worldliness, go to him, the God who is faithful before his people who are not faithful. With the spirit of children of the Church, let us pray to the Lord that with his goodness, with his faithfulness he may save us from this worldly spirit that negotiates over everything; that he may protect us and lead us forward as he led his people forward in the desert, taking them by the hand as a father does with his child. With the Lord holding our hand, we will walk in safety."

November 18, 2013   *1 Maccabees 1:10–15, 41–43, 54–57, 62–63*

✤ *Luke 18:35–43*

In the memories of grandparents is the future of our people

Choosing death, instead of escaping it with the help of sympathetic friends, in order to keep from betraying God: this is at the heart of the story of the noble Eleazar. This figure of the book of Maccabees told his persecutors who wanted to force him into apostasy that he preferred martyrdom, the sacrifice of his life, rather than a salvation procured through hypocrisy. "In the face of the choice between apostasy and faithfulness this man had no doubt," rejecting "that attitude of faking, of faking piety, of faking religiosity." On the contrary, instead of looking out for himself, he "thinks of the young people," of what legacy his act of courage could leave behind.

"The consistency of this man, the consistency of his faith, but also the responsibility of leaving behind a noble inheritance, a true inheritance. We are living at a time when the elderly don't matter. It is horrible to say this, but they are discarded. Because they are a nuisance. The elderly are those who bring us history, who bring us doctrine, who bring us faith and give it to us as an inheritance. They are those who, like good aged wine, have this strength inside to give us a noble inheritance."

This brings a joke to mind. A family—"mom, dad, lots of kids"—and Grandpa are at the table eating soup, and Grandpa "is getting his face all messy." Upset, the dad explains to the children why their grandpa acts like this and then gets a little table to put his father off to the side. One day the dad comes home and sees one of the children playing with some pieces of wood. "'What are you making?' he asks him. 'A table,' the child replies. 'And why?' 'For you, Dad, for when you get old like Grandpa.'

"This story has done me so much good, my whole life. Grandparents are a treasure. The letter to the Hebrews tells us: Remember your leaders, those who have preached to you, those who have preached the Word of God to you. And consider the outcome of their way of life and imitate their faith. The memory of our forefathers leads us to the imitation of faith. Getting old really is lousy sometimes. Because of the illnesses it brings and all of that. But the wisdom of our grandparents is the inheritance that we must receive. A people that does not take care of grandparents, a people that does not respect grandparents has no future because it has no memory; it has lost memory.

"It would do us good to think of the many elderly, many of whom are in retirement homes, and also many who are—it is a terrible word, but let's say it—abandoned by their families. They are the treasure of our society.

"Let's pray for our grandfathers, our grandmothers, who many times have played a heroic role in the transmission of the faith in times of persecution. When Mom and Dad weren't home and even had strange ideas taught by the politics of the time, it was the grandmothers who transmitted the faith. The fourth commandment: it is the only one that promises something in exchange. It is the commandment of piety. Being compassionate with our ancestors. Today let's ask for grace from the elderly saints—Simeon, Anne, Polycarp, and Eleazar—from the many elderly saints. Let's ask for the grace to protect, listen to, and venerate our ancestors, our grandparents."

November 19, 2013   *2 Maccabees 6:18–31* ✤ *Luke 19:1–10*

131

We go to the Temple not to celebrate a ritual but to worship God

The Temple is the house of stone where a people guards its soul before God. But another sacred temple is the body of an individual, in which God speaks and the heart listens. These two dimensions run parallel in the Christian life. The jumping-off point is offered by the liturgical passage from the Old Testament in which Judas Maccabeus reconsecrates the Temple destroyed during the wars. "The Temple as a place of reference for the community, a place of reference for the People of God," where they go for various reasons, one of which surpasses all the others.

"The Temple is the place where the community goes to pray, to praise the Lord, to give thanks, but above all to worship. The Temple is a place for worshiping the Lord. And this is the most important point. This is also valid for liturgical ceremonies; in this liturgical ceremony, what is the most important thing? The songs, the rituals—beautiful, is that all . . . ? The most important thing is worship: the whole community gathered together looks to the altar, where the sacrifice is celebrated, and worships. But I believe— humbly I say this—that we Christians have perhaps lost the sense of worship a little, and we think: Let's go to the Temple, let's gather as brothers. That's wonderful, it's wonderful! But the center is there where God is. And we worship God.

"From this statement a direct question arises: Are our temples places of worship, do they foster worship? Do our celebrations foster worship?" In today's Gospel, Jesus casts out the "dealers" who had taken the Temple for a place for trading goods rather than of worship. But there is another "Temple" and another sacrality to be considered in the life of faith.

"Saint Paul tells us that we are temples of the Holy Spirit. I am a temple. The Spirit of God is in me. And he also tells us not to sadden the spirit of the Lord who is within us. And here as well, perhaps we cannot speak of worship as before, but of a sort of worship that is the heart that seeks the Spirit of the Lord within itself and knows that God is within it, that the Holy Spirit is within it. It listens to him and follows him."

Of course, following God presupposes a continual purification, "because we are sinners"; we therefore need "to purify ourselves with prayer, with penance, with the sacrament of Reconciliation, with the Eucharist." And so "in these two temples—the material temple, the place of worship, and the spiritual temple within me, where the Holy Spirit dwells—in these two temples our attitude must be that of the piety that worships and listens, that prays and asks for forgiveness, that praises the Lord.

"And when we talk about the joy of the Temple, we are talking about this: the whole community in worship, in prayer, in thanksgiving, in praise. Me, in prayer with the Lord, who is within me because I am a 'temple.' Me listening, me open and in readiness. May the Lord grant us this true sense of the Temple, in order to be able to go forward in our life of worship and listen to the Word of God."

November 22, 2013   *1 Maccabees 4:36–37, 52–59* ✤ *Luke 19:45–48*

132

Like the martyrs, Christians must make definitive choices

Choosing the Lord "in an extreme situation." The occasion for reflection is offered by the figures presented to us in the first reading, taken from the book of Daniel, and in the Gospel: the young Jewish slaves in the court of Nebuchadnezzar, and the widow who goes to the Temple to worship the Lord. In both cases they are in extreme circumstances: the widow in a condition of misery, the young men in one of slavery. The widow puts everything she has into the treasury of the Temple; the young men remain faithful to the Lord at the risk of their lives.

"Both of these—the widow and the young men—took a risk. In their risk they opted for the Lord, with a great heart, without personal interests, without pettiness. They didn't have a petty attitude. The Lord, the Lord is all. The Lord is God, and they entrusted themselves to the Lord. And they did not do this through—if I may put it this way—a fanatical effort, no. 'We have to do this, Lord,' no! There is another way: they trusted, because they knew that the Lord is faithful. They trusted in that faithfulness which is always there, because the Lord cannot change, he cannot. He is always faithful, he cannot be unfaithful, he cannot deny himself."

This trust in the Lord led them "to make this choice, for the Lord," because they know that he "is faithful." A choice that applies to the little things as well as to the big and difficult decisions.

"Also in the Church, in the history of the Church there are men, women, elderly, young people who make this choice. When we hear about the lives of the martyrs, when we read in the newspapers about persecutions against Christians, today, let's think about these brothers and sisters in extreme situations, who make this choice. They are living at this time. They are an example for us, and they encourage us to put into the treasury of the Church all that we have to live on."

The Lord helps the young Jews in slavery to escape from their difficulties, and the widow is also helped by the Lord. Jesus has words of praise for her, and behind the praise there is also a victory.

"It would do us good to think about these brothers and sisters who, in our whole history, even today, make definitive choices. But let's also think about the many mothers, about the many fathers of families who every day make definitive choices to go forward with their families, with their children. And this is a treasure in the Church. They give us testimony, and in the face of so many who are giving this testimony, let's ask the Lord for the grace of courage, for the courage to go forward in our Christian life, in the usual, ordinary situations of every day and also in the extreme situations."

November 25, 2013   *Daniel 1:1–6, 8–20 ✤ Luke 21:1–4*

133

The moment belongs to man; time belongs to God

There are two principles for understanding the unfolding of the present and preparing for the end of time: prayer and hope. Prayer, together with discernment, helps us to decipher the individual moments of life and direct them to God. Hope is the far-reaching lighthouse that illuminates the final harbor, that of an individual life and at the same time—in the eschatological sense—that of the end of time. Jesus explains to the faithful in the Temple what will happen before the end of humanity, reassuring them that even the worst drama does not have to cast into desperation one who believes in God. "On this road toward the end of our journey, of each one of us and also of all humanity, the Lord gives us two principles, two things that are different; they are different according to how we live, because living in the moment is different from living in time.

"And the Christian is a man or woman who knows how to live in the moment and knows how to live in time. The moment is what we have at hand right now. But this is not time, this passes! We may feel that we are in charge of the moment, but the deception lies in believing we are in charge of time. Time is not ours, time belongs to God! The moment is in our hands, and so is the freedom we have in how we seize it. Now we may become sovereigns of the moment, but time has only one sovereign, only one Lord, Jesus Christ."

So, citing the words of Jesus, we must not allow ourselves "to be deceived in the moment," because there will be those who will take advantage of our confusion to present themselves as Christ. "The Christian who is a man or woman of the moment must have two virtues, those two attitudes for living in the moment: prayer and discernment.

"And in order to know the true signs, to know the road that I must take at this moment, I must have the gift of discernment and prayer to do it well. But when it comes to taking hold of time, the only master of which is the Lord, Jesus Christ, we have no human virtue there. The virtue for taking hold of time must be given, bestowed by the Lord. It is hope! Prayer and discernment for the moment; hope for time.

"So the Christian moves down this road, moment after moment, with prayer and discernment, but leaves time to hope.

"The Christian knows how to wait for the Lord in every moment, but hopes in the Lord at the end of time. A man and woman of the moment and of time: of prayer and discernment, and of hope. May the Lord give us the grace to walk with the wisdom that is also a gift from him: the wisdom that in the moment may lead us to pray and to discern. And in time, which is God's messenger, may he make us live with hope."

November 26, 2013   *Daniel 2:31–45 ✢ Luke 21:5–11*

134

Faith is not a private affair

In the final struggle between God and the evil one, there is a great snare: "the universal temptation." The temptation of giving in to the persuasion of one who would have us believe he has beaten God, having gotten the better of those who believe in him. But those who believe have a crystal-clear example to hold on to. It is the story of Jesus with the sufferings he endured in the desert and then the "many" sorrows he bore in his public life, accompanied by "insults" and "calumnies," ending with the ultimate affront, the Cross, where, however, the prince of the world loses his battle before the Resurrection of the Prince of Peace. In the final upheaval of the world, described in the Gospel, what is at stake is the highest of dramas, represented by natural catastrophes.

"When Jesus speaks of this calamity in another passage, he tells us that it will be a profanation of the Temple, a profanation of the faith, of the people. It will be the abomination, it will be the abomination of desolation. What does this mean? It will be like the triumph of the prince of this world: the defeat of God. He will seem in that final moment of calamity, he will seem to take possession of this world, he will be the master of the world."

This is the heart of the "final trial": the profanation of the faith. Which is also quite clear from what the prophet Daniel suffers in the account of the first reading: thrown into the lions' den for having worshiped God instead of the king. So "the abomination of desolation" has a precise name, "the prohibition of worship.

"We can't talk about religion; it's a private matter, right? We don't talk about this in public. Religious signs are taken away. We have to obey orders that come from worldly powers. We can do many things, wonderful things, but not worship God. The prohibition of worship. This is at the heart of this end [of time]. And when the fullness comes—when this time is fulfilled—then yes, he will come: 'And then they will see the Son of Man coming in a cloud with power and great glory.' The Christians who suffer through times of persecution, times of the prohibition of worship are a prophecy for what will happen to all of us."

And yet, when the "times of the pagans are fulfilled," that is the time to lift up our heads, because the "victory of Jesus Christ" is near.

"Let's not be afraid; he is only asking us for faithfulness and patience. Faithfulness like that of Daniel, who was faithful to his God and worshiped God to the end. And patience, because even the hairs of your head have all been counted. This is what the Lord has promised us. This week it would do us good to think about this general apostasy, which is called the prohibition of worship, and ask ourselves: Do I worship the Lord? Do I worship Jesus Christ, the Lord? Or a little half and half, am I playing the game of the prince of this world? To worship to the end, with trust and faithfulness: this is the grace we must ask for."

November 28, 2013   *Daniel 6:12–28 ✢ Luke 21:20–28*

135

The Christian does not give in to "weak thinking"

The Lord teaches his disciples to understand the "signs of the times," signs that the Pharisees are not able to grasp. We need to dwell upon "thinking as Christians." Those who follow Jesus think not only with their heads but also with their hearts and "the spirit they have within." Otherwise "God's stride through history" makes no sense.

"Jesus does not get angry in the Gospel, but he pretends to when the disciples don't understand things. To those on the way to Emmaus he says: 'Foolish and slow of heart.' 'Foolish and slow of heart.' That's what a person who doesn't understand the things of God is like. The Lord wants us to understand what is happening: what is happening in my heart, what is happening in my life, what is happening in the world, in history . . . what does it mean, this that is happening now? These are the signs of the times! But the spirit of the world offers us other things, because the spirit of the world does not want us to be a people; it wants us to be a mass, without thought, without freedom."

The spirit of the world "wants us to go by a path of uniformity," but Saint Paul warns us that the spirit of the world treats us as if we did not have the capacity to think for ourselves; it treats us like persons who are not free.

"Uniform thinking, the same thinking, weak thinking, a thinking that is so widespread. The spirit of the world does not want us to ask ourselves before God: But why is this, why that, why is this happening? Or it even presents us with 'thinking to-go,' according to one's own tastes: I think the way I like! That's fine, they say. But what the spirit of the world does not want is what Jesus is asking of us: free thought, the thought of a man and a woman who are part of the People of God. Salvation was precisely this! Think about the prophets . . . You were not my people, and now I call you my people; this is what the Lord says. And this is salvation: making us a people, the People of God, to have freedom.

"And Jesus is asking us to think freely, to think in order to understand what is happening." The truth is that "we cannot think on our own! We need the Lord's help." We need this "in order to understand the signs of the times," and "the Holy Spirit gives us this gift: the intelligence to understand, and not so that others may tell me what is happening.

"What is the path that the Lord wants? Always with the spirit of intelligence to understand the signs of the times. It is wonderful to ask the Lord Jesus for this grace, that he may send us his spirit of understanding, so that we may not indulge in weak thinking, uniform thinking, and not think according to our own tastes; so that we may have only a thinking according to God. With this thought, which is a thought of mind, heart, and soul. With this thought, which is the gift of the Spirit, to seek what things mean and understand the signs of the times."

So this is the grace that we must ask of the Lord today: "the capacity that the Spirit gives us" to "understand the signs of the times."

November 29, 2013   *Daniel 7:2–14 ✛ Luke 21:29–33*

136

Christmas means letting Jesus encounter us with open hearts

The passage of the Gospel in which the Roman centurion asks Jesus with great faith for the healing of his servant reminds us that in these days "we are beginning a new journey," a "journey as Church . . . toward Christmas." Let's go to meet the Lord, "because Christmas is not only a date on the calendar or a memory of something nice.

"Christmas is more than that; we are going on this path to meet the Lord. Christmas is an encounter! And let us walk so as to meet him: to meet him with our hearts, with our lives; to meet him as living, as he is; to meet him with faith. And it is not easy to live with faith. The Lord, in the word we have listened to, was amazed by this centurion; he was amazed at the faith that he had. He had made a journey to encounter the Lord, but he had done so with faith. This is why he not only encountered the Lord but felt the joy of being encountered by the Lord. And this is exactly the encounter that we want: the encounter of faith!"

And more than being the ones to encounter the Lord, we must "allow him to encounter us.

"When we encounter the Lord on our own, we are—so to speak—the masters of this encounter. But when we allow him to encounter us, it is he who enters within us, it is he who makes us entirely new, because this is the coming, this is what it means when Christ comes: to make everything anew, remake the heart, the soul, life, hope, the journey. We are on a journey of faith, with the faith of this centurion, to encounter the Lord, and mainly to allow him to encounter us!"

But we need to have open hearts.

"An open heart, so that he may encounter me! And so that he may tell me what he wants to tell me, which is not always what I want him to say! He is the Lord, and he will tell me what he has for me, because the Lord does not look at us all together, as a mass. No, no! He looks each one of us in the face, in the eyes, because love is not like that, abstract: it is concrete love! Person to person: the Lord, a person, looks at me, a person. Allowing the Lord to encounter us is precisely this: allowing the Lord to love us!"

On this journey toward Christmas there are a few attitudes that can help us: "perseverance in prayer, praying more; diligence in fraternal charity, getting a little closer to those who are in need; and joy in praising the Lord." So "prayer, charity, and faith," with open hearts "so that the Lord may encounter us."

December 2, 2013   *Isaiah 4:2–6 ✢ Matthew 8:5–11*

137

A Church without joy is unthinkable

Peace and joy. In the first reading, taken from the book of Isaiah, we hear about the desire for peace that we all have. A peace that, Isaiah says, the Messiah will bring us. In the Gospel, instead, "we get a glimpse of the soul of Jesus, the heart of Jesus: a joyful heart.

"We always think about Jesus when he was preaching, when he was healing, when he was walking, going along the roads, even during the Last Supper . . . But we are not so accustomed to thinking about Jesus smiling, joyful. Jesus was full of joy: full of joy. In that intimacy with his Father, 'he exulted with joy in the Holy Spirit and praised the Father.' This is precisely the inner mystery of Jesus, that relationship with the Father in the Spirit. It is his inner joy, his interior joy that he gives to us.

"And this joy is true peace: not a static, quiet, tranquil peace." No, "Christian peace is a joyful peace, because our Lord is joyful." And he is also joyful "when he talks about the Father. He loves the Father so much that he cannot talk about the Father without joy." Our God "is joyful." And Jesus "wanted his bride, the Church, to be joyful too.

"A Church without joy is unthinkable, and the joy of the Church is precisely this: proclaiming the name of Jesus. Saying: 'He is the Lord. My bridegroom is the Lord. He is God. He saves us, he walks with us.' And that is the joy of the Church, and in this joy as bride she becomes mother. Paul VI said: The joy of the Church is precisely to evangelize, to go forward and speak of her Bridegroom. And also to transmit this joy to the children to whom she gives birth, whom she raises."

So let us contemplate that the peace Isaiah is talking about "is a peace that is dynamic; it is a peace of joy, a peace of praise," a peace that we can call "noisy, in praise, a peace fruitful in the bearing of new children." A peace "that comes precisely in the joy of praising the Trinity and in evangelization, of going to the peoples to tell them who Jesus is. Peace and joy." Jesus makes "a dogmatic declaration" when he affirms that this is what he decided, to reveal himself not to the wise but to the simple.

"Even in things as serious as this, Jesus is joyful, the Church is joyful. She has to be joyful. Even in her widowhood—because the Church has an aspect of the widow waiting for her bridegroom to return—even in her widowhood, the Church is joyful in hope. May the Lord give all of us this joy, this joy of Jesus, praising the Father in the Spirit. This joy of our Mother Church in evangelizing, in proclaiming her Bridegroom."

December 3, 2013   *Isaiah 11:1–10 ✤ Luke 10:21–24*

138

Not putting the Word of God into practice is harmful

Listening to the word of the Lord and putting it into practice is like building a house on rock. Jesus reproves the Pharisees for knowing the commandments but not carrying them out in their lives. "They are good words," but if they are not put into practice, "not only are they not helpful but they are harmful, they deceive us; they make us believe we have a great house, but it is without foundation." A house that is not built on rock.

"This figure of the rock points us to the Lord. Isaiah, in the first reading, says this: 'Trust in the Lord forever! For the Lord is an eternal Rock!' The rock is Jesus Christ! The rock is the Lord! A word is strong, it gives life, it can move things forward, it can withstand all attacks, if this word has its roots in Jesus Christ. A Christian word that does not have its vital roots, its personal roots, in Jesus Christ is a Christian word without Christ! And Christian words without Christ are deceptive, they are harmful! An English writer, speaking of heresy, once said that a heresy is a truth that has gone mad. When Christian words are without Christ they begin to go down the road of madness."

It is a madness that brings arrogance.

"A Christian word without Christ leads you to vanity, to complacency, to pride, to power for power's sake. And the Lord strikes these people down. This is a constant in the history of salvation. Samuel's mother, Anna, says it; Mary says it in the Magnificat: the Lord strikes down the vanity, the pride of those persons who believe themselves to be rock. These persons who follow only after a word but without Jesus Christ. It may be a Christian word, but it is without Jesus Christ, without the relationship with Jesus Christ, without prayer with Jesus Christ, without the service of Jesus Christ, without love for Jesus Christ. This is what the Lord is telling us today: to build our lives on this rock, and the rock is him.

"It would do us good to make an examination of conscience to understand what our words are like," if they are words "that we ourselves believe are powerful," capable "of giving us salvation," or if "they are words with Jesus Christ.

"I am referring to Christian words, because when Jesus Christ is not there, this too divides us, it makes divisions in the Church. Let's ask the Lord for the grace to help us in this humility, which we must always have, to speak Christian words in Jesus Christ, not without Jesus Christ. With this humility of being saved disciples and of going forward not with words that we believe will make us powerful, that end up in the madness of vanity, in the madness of pride. May the Lord give us this grace of humility to speak words with Jesus Christ, founded on Jesus Christ!"

December 5, 2013   *Isaiah 26:1–6 ✢ Matthew 7:21, 24–27*

139

Praying means "bothering" God until he listens to us

Prayer, when it is really Christian, oscillates between the need that it always contains and the certainty that it will be answered, even if we do not know exactly when. This is because the one who prays is not afraid of bothering God and fosters a blind trust in his love as Father. Blind like the two men in the Gospel passage who cry out after Jesus in their need to be healed. Or like the blind man of Jericho, who calls out for the help of the Teacher in a voice louder than those of the people who want to silence him. Because Jesus himself has taught us to pray like the "annoying friend" who begs for food in the middle of the night, or like "the widow with the corrupt judge.

"I don't know if this might sound bad, but praying is a little bit like bothering God to listen to us. But this is what the Lord says: like a friend who comes in the middle of the night, like the widow with the judge . . . It means drawing the eyes, drawing the heart of God to us . . . And this is what those lepers did who drew near to him: 'If you wish, you can heal us!' They did this with a certain confidence. This is how Jesus teaches us to pray. When we pray, we sometimes think: Well, sure, I'll tell the Lord about this need, once, twice, three times, but not very forcefully. Then I'll get tired of asking for it and forget about it. But these people cried aloud, and they did not get tired of crying out. Jesus tells us: 'Ask,' but he also tells us: 'Knock at the door,' and the one who knocks at the door makes noise, disturbs, bothers."

Insistence at the limits of annoyance then. But also an unshakable certainty. The blind men of the Gospel are again an example. "They feel sure about asking the Lord for healing," because when Jesus asks them if they believe that he can heal them, they reply: "Yes, Lord, we believe! We are sure!"

"And prayer has these two attitudes: it is needy and it is sure. Needy prayer always. Prayer, when we are asking for something, is needy: 'I have this need, listen to me, Lord.' But also, when prayer is true, it is sure: 'Listen to me! I believe that you can do it because you have promised.'

"He has promised"; this is the cornerstone on which the certainty of prayer is based. "With this confidence let us tell the Lord of our needs, really sure that he can do it." Praying means that we hear Jesus ask us the same question he asked the two blind men: "Do you believe that I can do this?"

"He can do it. When he will do it, how he will do it we do not know. This is the confidence of prayer. The need to say it with truth, to the Lord, 'I am blind, Lord, I have this need. I have this sickness. I have this sin. I have this pain . . .' But always the truth, as the matter stands. And he hears the need, but he hears that we are asking for his help with confidence. Let's consider whether our prayer is needy and confident: needy, because we are telling the truth to ourselves, and confident, because we believe that the Lord can do what we are asking."

December 6, 2013   *Isaiah 29:17–24 ✢ Matthew 9:27–31*

140

Peace and religious freedom in the Middle East, no more divisions

The division and enmity in the Holy Land and Middle East must come to an end. We think of the Coptic faithful, borrowing the words of the prophet Isaiah, who speaks of a reawakening of hearts in the anticipation of the Lord.

"We feel that the encouragement 'to the fearful of heart' is addressed to those in your beloved Egyptian land who experience insecurity and violence, sometimes on account of the Christian faith. 'Courage: do not be afraid!' These are the consoling words that find confirmation in fraternal solidarity."

The Scriptures present "Christ, who overcomes the paralysis of humanity." And moreover, "the paralysis of conscience is contagious. With the complicity of the poverty of history and our sin, it can expand and enter into social structures and into the community to the point of immobilizing entire peoples." But "the commandment of Christ—'Get up and walk!'"—can shake up the situation.

"Let's pray with trust that in the Holy Land and in the whole Middle East peace may always get up again from its too frequent and sometimes dramatic pauses. But may enmity and division stop forever. May the peace agreements, often paralyzed by opposition and obscure interests, be resumed quickly. May real guarantees of religious freedom finally be given to all, together with the right for Christians to live in peace where they are born, in the country they love as citizens going back two thousand years, to contribute as ever to the good of all."

Jesus experienced flight with the Holy Family, and was taken in by the "generous land" of Egypt. May the Lord "watch over the Egyptians who are seeking their dignity and security in the world.

"And let us go ever onward, seeking the Lord, seeking new paths, new ways to approach the Lord. And if it should be necessary to open a hole in the roof in order for all of us to draw near to the Lord, may our creative imagination lead us to this: to find and to make ways of encounter, paths of fraternity, roads of peace."

December 9, 2013   *Genesis 3:9–15, 20 ❧ Ephesians 1:3–6, 11–12 ❧*

Luke 1:26–38

141

The Lord's door is always open

"Comfort, give comfort to my people." Dwelling on a passage from the book of the prophet Isaiah, the book of the consolation of Israel, we observe how the Lord draws near to his people to comfort them, "to bring them peace." And this "work of consolation" is so powerful that "it remakes all things." The Lord accomplishes a true re-creation.

"He re-creates things. And the Church does not get tired of saying that this re-creation is more wonderful than the creation. The Lord re-creates more wonderfully. And this is how he visits his people: re-creating, with that power. And the People of God have always had this idea, this thought, that the Lord would come to visit them. Let's remember Joseph's last words to his brothers: 'When the Lord visits you, bring my bones with you.' The Lord will visit his people. This is the hope of Israel. But he will visit them with this consolation.

"And the consolation is this remaking of everything not once, but many times, with the universe and also with us." This "remaking by the Lord" has two dimensions that it is important to emphasize. "When the Lord draws near to us he brings us hope; the Lord remakes with hope; he always opens a door. Always. When the Lord draws near to us he does not close doors, he opens them." The Lord "in his nearness gives us hope, this hope that is a true fortress in Christian life. It is a grace, it is a gift.

"When Christians forget hope or, worse, lose hope, their lives have no meaning. It is as if they were living their lives in front of a wall: nothing. But the Lord comforts us and remakes us, with hope, to go forward. And he also does so with a special nearness to each one, because the Lord comforts his people and he comforts each one of us. It is wonderful how the passage today finishes: 'Like a shepherd he feeds his flock; in his arm he gathers the lambs, carrying them in his bosom, and leading the ewes with care.' That image of carrying the lambs in his bosom and gently leading the ewes: that is tenderness. The Lord comforts us with tenderness."

God, who is powerful, "is not afraid of tenderness. He makes himself tenderness, he makes himself a child, he makes himself small." In the Gospel, Jesus himself says this: "This is the will of the Father, that not even one of these little ones should be lost." In the eyes of the Lord, "each of us is very, very important. And he gives himself with tenderness." And so he "leads us onward, giving us hope." This "was the main work of Jesus" in the "forty days between the Resurrection and the Ascension: to comfort the disciples, to draw near and give consolation.

"Drawing near and giving hope, drawing near with tenderness. But let's think about the tenderness that he had with the apostles, with the Magdalene, with those on the way to Emmaus. He drew near with tenderness: 'Give me something to eat.' With Thomas: 'Put your finger here.' This is the way the Lord always is. This is the consolation of the Lord. May the Lord give all of us the grace not to be afraid of his consolation, to be open: to ask for it, to seek it, because it is a consolation that will give us hope and will make us feel the tenderness of God the Father."

December 10, 2013   *Isaiah 40:1–11 ✤ Matthew 18:12–14*

142

Approaching Christmas in silence, in order to listen to the tenderness of God

It is important to emphasize not so much "what the Lord says" but "how he says it." God speaks to us like a mom and dad speaking with their child.

"When a child has a bad dream, he wakes up crying. Dad goes in and says: 'Don't be afraid, don't be afraid, here I am, here.' This is how the Lord speaks to us. The Lord has this way of speaking to us: he draws near . . . When we look at a mom or dad talking to their child, we see that they become small and speak in the voice of a child and make the gestures of children. Someone looking from the outside may think: But they are ridiculous! They hunker down, right on the spot, don't they? Because the love of the mom and dad has this need to get close. I'll put it this way: to stoop down right into the world of the child. Yes: if Mom and Dad speak to him normally, the child will understand all the same; but they want to adopt the child's way of speaking. They get close, they make themselves children. And this is how the Lord is."

Greek theologians explain this attitude of God with "a rather difficult word: *synkatábasis*," or "the condescension of God who descends to become like one of us.

"And then the mom and dad even say silly things to the child: 'O my sweetie, my teddy bear,' things like that. The Lord says this too: 'You worm Jacob.' 'You're like a little worm to me, just a little tiny thing, but I love you so much.' This is the language of the Lord, the love language of a father and mother. The word of the Lord? Yes, let's listen to what he says. But let's also see how he says it. And we must do what the Lord does, do what he says and do as he says, with love, with tenderness, with that compassion for our brothers and sisters."

God—recalling Elijah's encounter with the Lord—is like "the gentle breeze," or—as the original text says—"a sound-stream of silence." In this way "the Lord draws near, with the sonority of silence that is characteristic of love. Without making a show." And "he makes himself small to make me powerful; he goes to death, with that abasement, so that I may live.

"This is the music of the language of the Lord, and in the preparation for Christmas we must listen to it. It will do us good to listen to it, it will do us so much good. Normally, Christmas seems like a very noisy celebration. It would do us good to make room for a bit of silence and listen to these words of love, and to make room for silence at this time in which, as the preface says, we are vigilant in anticipation."

December 12, 2013   *Zechariah 2:14–17 or Revelation 11:19a;*
                                        12:1–6a, 10ab ✦ Luke 1:26–38 or 1:39–47

143

Christians allergic to preachers are closed off to the Spirit

Jesus compares the generation of his time to those always discontented children "who do not know how to play happily, who always reject the invitation of others: if there's music, they do not dance; if there's a song of mourning, they do not weep . . . nothing is right for them." Those people "were not open to the Word of God." They do not reject the message; they reject the messenger. They reject John the Baptist, who "does not eat and does not drink"; they say that "he is possessed by a demon!" They reject Jesus, because they say that "he is a glutton, a drunkard, a friend of tax collectors and sinners." They always have a reason to criticize the preacher.

"And they, the people of that time, preferred to take refuge in a more elaborate religion: in moral precepts, like that group of Pharisees; in political compromise, like the Sadducees; in social revolution, like the Zealots; in Gnostic spirituality, like the Essenes. They stayed with their own system, nice and tidy, nicely made. But a preacher, no. Jesus also reminds them: 'Your fathers did the same with the prophets.' The People of God have a sort of allergy to preachers of the word; they persecuted the prophets, they killed them."

These people, then, say that they accept the truth of revelation, "but the preacher, preaching, no. They prefer to spend their life imprisoned in their precepts, in their compromises, in their revolutionary plans, or in their disembodied spirituality." They are those Christians who are always dissatisfied with what the preachers say.

"These Christians who are closed off, who are caged, these sad Christians . . . they are not free. Why? Because they are afraid of the freedom of the Holy Spirit, which comes through preaching. And this is the scandal of preaching, which Saint Paul was talking about, the scandal of preaching that ends in the scandal of the Cross. It is scandalous that God should speak to us through men with limitations, sinful men: scandalous! And it is even more scandalous that

God should speak to us and save us through a man who says that he is the Son of God but ends up like a criminal. That scandalizes them.

"These sad Christians do not believe in the Holy Spirit; they do not believe in that freedom which comes from preaching, which admonishes you, teaches you, knocks you around a bit, sure. But it is precisely that freedom that makes the Church grow.

"Seeing these children who are afraid of dancing, of weeping, afraid of everything, who want guarantees in everything, I think of these sad Christians who always criticize the preachers of the Truth, because they are afraid of opening the door to the Holy Spirit. Let's pray for them, and let's also pray for ourselves, that we may not become sad Christians, preventing the Holy Spirit from coming to us through the scandal of preaching."

December 13, 2013   *Isaiah 48:17–19 ✤ Matthew 11:16–19*

144

Without prophecy you have clericalism

The prophet is the one who listens to the words of God, is able to see the present moment and project himself into the future. "He has within himself three moments": the past, the present, and the future.

"The past: The prophet is aware of the promise and has within his heart the promise of God; he keeps it alive, remembers it, repeats it. Then he looks at the present, looks at his people, and feels the power of the Spirit to speak a word to them that will help them to get up, to continue the journey toward the future. The prophet is a man of three times: the promise of the past, the contemplation of the present, the courage to point out the path to the future. And with the prophets the Lord has always guarded his people in difficult moments, in moments in which the people were discouraged or devastated, when the Temple wasn't there, when Jerusalem was under the power of the enemy, when the people were asking themselves: 'But, Lord, you promised us this! And now what's going to happen?'"

This is what "happened in the heart of the Blessed Mother when she was at the foot of the Cross." In these moments "a prophet is needed. And the prophet is not always accepted; many times he is rejected. Jesus himself says to the Pharisees that their fathers killed the prophets because they told them things that were not pleasant; they spoke the truth, they remembered the promise! And when the People of God do not have prophecy, something is missing: the life of the Lord is missing! When there is no prophecy, the accent falls on legalism," legalism gets the upper hand. So in the Gospel "the priests went to Jesus to ask him for his papers. 'With what authority do you do these things? We are in charge of the Temple!' They didn't understand the prophecies. They had forgotten the promise! They couldn't read the signs of the moment, they did not have eyes to see or ears to hear the Word of God; all they had was their authority!

"When there is no prophecy among the People of God, the void left behind is taken up by clericalism. This is precisely the clericalism that asks Jesus: 'By what authority are you doing these things?' By what law? And the memory of the promise and the hope of moving forward is reduced only to the present: no past, no hopeful future. The present is where the law is: if it is legal, go ahead."

But when legalism reigns, the Word of God is gone and the faithful People of God weep in their hearts because they cannot find the Lord; they lack prophecy. They weep "as Hannah, the mother of Samuel, wept, asking for the fecundity of the people, the fecundity that comes from the power of God, when he reawakens our memory of his promise and urges us toward the future, with hope. This is the prophet! This is the man with the penetrating eye who hears the words of God.

"In these days during which we are preparing for the Nativity of the Lord, may our prayer be 'Lord, do not leave your people without prophets!' All of us who have been baptized, we are all prophets. 'Lord, do not let us forget your promise! Do not let us get tired of moving forward! Do not let us shut ourselves up in the legalism that closes the doors! Lord, free your people from the spirit of clericalism and help us with the spirit of prophecy.'"

December 16, 2013   *Numbers 24:2–7, 15–17a* ✤ *Matthew 21:23–27*

145

God became history and walks with us

God never leaves us alone, he always walks with us. The passage of the Gospel in today's liturgy focused on the genealogy of Jesus offers the occasion to consider the presence of the Lord in our lives.

"I once heard somebody say: 'This part of the Gospel is like a page from the telephone book!' But it's not, it's something else entirely. This passage of the Gospel is pure history, and it has an important point. It is pure history, because God, as Pope Saint Leo said, God has sent his Son. And Jesus is consubstantial with the Father, God, but he is also consubstantial with his Mother, a woman. And this is that consubstantiality with his Mother. God has become history. God wanted to become history. He is with us. He has made the journey with us."

After the first sin in Paradise, "he got this idea: to make the journey with us." He called Abraham, "the first name on this list," and "invited him to walk." And Abraham "set out on this journey." And then Isaac, Jacob, Judah. "And so goes this journey in history." God "walks with his people. God did not want to come and save us without history. He wanted to make history with us." A history "that goes from holiness to sin. There are saints on this list, but there are also sinners.

"Sinners who were high in the ranks, who committed big sins. And God made history with them. Sinners who did not respond to what God wanted for them. Let's think of Solomon, so great, so intelligent, and he ended up, poor guy, not knowing his own name! But God was with him. This is wonderful, isn't it? God is consubstantial with us. He makes history with us. And more: when God wants to say who he is, he says, 'I am the God of Abraham, of Isaac and Jacob.' But what is God's last name? It is us, each one of us. He takes our name to make it his last name. 'I am the God of Abraham, of Isaac, of Jacob, of Pedro, of Marietta, of Marisa, of Simone, of all!' He takes his last name from us. God's last name is each of us.

"He, our God, has made history with us, has taken his last name from our name; he has allowed us to write his history. We write this history of grace and sin, and he follows after us." This "is the humility of God, the patience of God, the love of God. It is ours!" And this is touching. "So much love, so much tenderness, of having a God like this.

"His joy was to share his life with us. The book of Wisdom says that the joy of the Lord is among the sons of men, with us. With Christmas approaching, this thought comes to us: If he made his history with us, if he took his last name from us, if he allowed us to write his history, let's at least allow him to write our history. And that is holiness, to let the Lord write our history. And this is a Christmas wish for all of us. May the Lord write your history, and may you allow him to write it."

December 17, 2013   *Genesis 49:2, 8–10 ✦ Matthew 1:1–17*

146

Humility makes us fruitful; pride makes us sterile

Many times, in the Bible, we find sterile women to whom the Lord gives the gift of life. The Gospel tells of Elizabeth, who after being sterile had a son, John. "From the impossibility of giving life comes life." And this also "happens to women who are not sterile" but who "had no hope of life," like Naomi, who finally had a grandson.

"The Lord intervenes in the lives of these women to tell us: 'I am capable of giving life.' In the prophets as well there is the image of the desert, the desert land incapable of growing a tree, a fruit, to make something sprout. 'But the desert will be like a forest,' say the prophets, 'it will be great, it will flourish.' But can the desert flourish? Yes. Can a sterile woman bear life? Yes. That promise of the Lord: I can! From dryness, from your dryness, I can make life grow, salvation! From aridity I can make fruits grow!"

And salvation is this: "the intervention of God that makes us fruitful, that gives us the capacity to give life." We "cannot do it on our own." And yet, "so many have given evidence of thinking that we have the capacity to save ourselves.

"Even Christians! Let's think about the Pelagians, for example. All is grace. It is the intervention of God that brings us to salvation. It is the intervention of God that helps us on the journey of holiness. Only he can. But what can we do for our part? First, recognize our dryness, our inability to give life. Recognize this. Second, ask, 'Lord, I want to be fruitful. I want my life to give life, my faith to be fruitful so that I can go forward and give it to others.' 'Lord, I am sterile: I can't do it, you can. I am a desert: I can't do it, you can.'"

And this can be the first prayer of Christmas. "Let's think about how the arrogant, those who think they can do everything themselves, are struck down." Let's think about Michal, Saul's daughter. A woman "who was not sterile, but was arrogant, and she didn't know what it means to praise God"; on the contrary, "she laughed about it." And "she was punished with sterility.

"Humility is necessary for fecundity. How many people think they are righteous, like her, and in the end are poor wretches. The humility of saying to the Lord: 'Lord, I am sterile, I am a desert,' and repeating in these days the beautiful antiphons that the Church has us pray: 'O Key of David, O Adonai, O Wisdom—today—O root of Jesse's stem, O Emmanuel, come to give us life, come to save us, because only you can. On my own I can't!' And with this humility, the humility of the desert, the humility of the sterile soul, to receive grace, the grace of flourishing, of bearing fruit and giving life."

December 19, 2013   *Judges 13:2–7, 24–25a ✠ Luke 1:5–25*

147

Only silence guards the mystery

In the history of salvation, it is not noise or spectacle but shadow and silence that are the "places" in which God has chosen to manifest himself. Evanescent boundaries from which his mystery has sometimes taken visible form, has taken flesh. The reflection is suggested by the Annunciation, in particular the passage in which the angel tells Mary that "the power of the Most High will over-shadow you." Almost exactly like the cloud with which God had protected the Israelites in the desert.

"The Lord has always taken care of the mystery and has sheltered the mystery. He has not made publicity of the mystery. A mystery that makes publicity for itself is not Christian, it is not the mystery of God; it is a phony mystery! And this is what happens to the Blessed Mother here, when she receives her Son: the mystery of her virginal motherhood is covered. It is covered for her whole life! And she knew this. This shadow of God, in our lives, helps us to discover our mystery: the mystery of our encounter with the Lord, the mystery of our journey of life with the Lord.

"Each one of us knows how mysteriously the Lord works in our hearts, in our souls." And what is "the cloud, the power, the style in which the Holy Spirit covers over our mystery?

"This cloud in us, in our lives is called silence. Silence is the cloud that covers the mystery of our relationship with the Lord, of our holiness and our sins. This mystery that we cannot explain. But when there is no silence in our lives, the mystery is lost, it goes away. Protect the mystery with silence! That is the cloud, that is the power of God for us, that is the power of the Holy Spirit."

The Mother of Jesus is the perfect icon of silence. From the proc-lamation of her remarkable maternity to Calvary. "I think of how many times she was silent and did not say what she felt to protect the mystery of her relationship with her Son," to the rawest form of silence, "at the foot of the Cross."

"The Gospel doesn't tell us anything, whether she said a word or not . . . She was silent, but in her heart, how many things she was saying to the Lord! 'You, that day,' this is what we have read, 'you told me that he would be great; you told me that you would give him the Throne of David his father, that he would reign forever, and now I see him there!' The Blessed Mother was human! And perhaps she wanted to say: 'Lies! I was deceived!' John Paul II said this, speaking of the Blessed Mother at that moment. But she, in silence, covered the mystery that she did not understand, and with this silence she allowed that mystery to grow and blossom in hope.

"Silence is what protects the mystery," so that the mystery "of our relationship with God, of our journey, of our salvation cannot be brought out in the open, publicized." May the Lord "give all of us the grace to love silence, to seek it out and have a heart guarded by the cloud of silence."

December 20, 2013   *Isaiah 7:10–14* ✣ *Luke 1:26–38*

148

At Christmas, let's make room for Jesus

In the days preceding the Nativity of the Lord, the Church, like Mary, is awaiting the birth of a child. She too "feels what all women feel at this time." She feels these "perceptions in her body, in her soul" that the child is coming. Mary feels in her heart that she wants to look at the face of her Child. We as the Church "accompany the Blessed Mother on this journey of anticipation" and almost "want to hasten this birth" of Jesus. The Lord comes two times, "the one that we commemorate now, the physical birth," and the one in which "he will come at the end to close history." But as Saint Bernard affirms, there is also a third birth.

"There is a third coming of the Lord: that of every day. The Lord visits his Church every day! He visits each one of us, and our soul also enters into this resemblance; our soul resembles the Church, our soul resembles Mary. The Desert Fathers say that Mary, the Church, and our soul are feminine, and what is said of one can analogously be said of the others. Our soul is also in waiting, in this anticipation for the coming of the Lord; it is an open soul that calls out: 'Come, Lord!'"

And also with each one of us, in these days, "the Holy Spirit is moving us to make this prayer: *Come! Come!*" Every day during Advent, "we have said in the Preface that we, the Church, like Mary, are vigilant in anticipation." And vigilance "is the virtue" of the pilgrim. All of us "are pilgrims!

"And I ask myself: Are we in waiting or are we closed? Are we vigilant or are we holed up in a hotel along the way, not wanting to go any further? Are we pilgrims or are we wanderers? The Church invites us to open our souls and make our souls, during these days, vigilant in expectation. Keep watch! What happens in us if the Lord comes or if he does not come? If there is room for the Lord or there is room for parties, for spending, for making noise . . . Is our soul open, like Holy Mother Church is open, and like the Blessed

Mother was open? Or is our soul closed, and have we put up a sign on the door, very politely, saying: *Please do not disturb*?

"The world does not end with us, and we are not the most important thing in the world; this is the Lord, with the Blessed Mother and with Mother Church!" So "it would do us good to repeat" the invocation "'O wisdom, O Key of David, O King of all nations, come!'

"And to repeat many times today 'Come!' And try to keep our soul from becoming a soul that says: 'Do not disturb.' No! That it may be an open soul, that it may be a great soul, to receive the Lord in these days, and that it may begin to feel what the Church will tell us in the invitatory antiphon: 'Today you will know the Lord is coming, and in the morning you will see his glory.'"

December 23, 2013   *Malachi 3:1–4, 23–24* ✤ *Luke 1:57–66*

149

Putting our hearts to the test to listen to Jesus

Remain in the Lord": this is the exhortation of the apostle John. A "life lesson," which John repeats in an "almost obsessive" way. The apostle indicates "one of the attitudes of the Christian who wants to remain in the Lord: knowing what is happening in his own heart." So he warns against trusting in every spirit but says to put "the spirits to the test." It is necessary to be able "to discern the spirits," to discern if something helps us to "remain in the Lord or distances us from him." "Our hearts always have desires, wishes, thoughts." But "are these from the Lord, or are some of these driving us away from the Lord?" That is why the apostle John urges us to "put to the test" what we think and desire.

"If this is leading you to the Lord, it's fine, but if it isn't . . . Put the spirits to the test in order to find out if they really come from God, because many false prophets have come into the world. Prophets or prophecies or proposals: 'I feel like doing this!' But this isn't leading you to the Lord, it's driving you away from him. This is why vigilance is necessary. The Christian is a man or a woman who knows how to watch over his heart. And many times our hearts, with the many things that come and go, seem like a flea market: there is everything, you find everything there . . . And no! We must test everything—this is of the Lord and this is not—in order to remain in the Lord."

So what is the criterion for understanding if something comes from Christ or from the antichrist? Saint John has a clear, "simple" idea: "Every spirit that recognizes Jesus Christ, come in the flesh, is of God. Every spirit that does not recognize Jesus is not of God; this is the spirit of the antichrist." But what does it mean "to recognize that the Word has come in the flesh"? It means "recognizing the way of Jesus Christ," recognizing that he, "being God, abased himself, humbled himself" even to "death on the Cross."

"That is the way of Jesus Christ: abasement, humility, even humiliation. If a thought, if a desire leads you on that path of humility, of abasement, of service to others, it is of Jesus. But if it leads you on the path of self-sufficiency, vanity, pride, on the path of an abstract thought, it is not of Jesus. Let's think of the temptations of Jesus in the desert: all three of the proposals that the devil makes to Jesus are proposals intended to lead him away from this path, the path of service, of humility, of humiliation, of charity. But the charity he worked in his life, right? Jesus says no to all three temptations: 'No, this is not my path!' "

The invitation is to really think about what is happening in our hearts. About what we are thinking and feeling, about what we want, testing the spirits. "Do I put to the test what I think, what I want, what I desire, or do I accept it all?

"So often our heart is a highway, everything travels down it . . . Put everything to the test. And do I always choose the things that come from God? Do I know which are the things that come from God? Do I know the true criterion for discerning my thoughts, my desires? Let's think about this, and not forget that the criterion is the Incarnation of the Word. The word came in the flesh: this is Jesus Christ! Jesus Christ became man, God made man, abased himself, humiliated himself for love, to serve all of us. And may the apostle John grant us this grace of knowing what is happening in our hearts and having the wisdom to discern what comes from God and what does not come from God."

January 7, 2014   *1 John 4:7–10 ✠ Mark 6:34–44*

150

Christian love is not the love of the soap operas

There's nothing romantic about Christian love; either it is an altruistic and devoted love, which rolls up its sleeves and looks to the poor, which prefers to give rather than to receive, or it has nothing to do with Christian love. The reflection is prompted by the words of the first letter of John, in which the apostle insists on repeating: "If we love one another, God remains in us and his love is perfected in us." The experience of faith lies precisely in this "twofold remaining.

"We in God and God in us: this is the Christian life. Not remaining in the spirit of the world, not remaining in superficiality, not remaining in idolatry, not remaining in vanity. No, no: remaining in the Lord. And he reciprocates this; he remains in us. But, first, he remains in us. So many times we chase him away and we cannot remain in him. It is the Spirit who remains."

After clarifying the dynamic of the spirit that moves Christian love, we next examine the flesh. "Remaining in the love" of God is not so much an ecstasy of the heart, "a wonderful feeling.

"Look, the love that John is talking about is not the love of the soap operas! No, it is something else. Christian love always has one quality: concreteness. Christian love is concrete. Jesus himself, when he speaks of love, talks to us about concrete things: giving food to the hungry, visiting the sick, and many concrete things. Love is concrete. Christian concreteness. And when this concreteness is not there, we can live a Christianity of illusions, because it is unclear where to find the center of Jesus' message. This love does not succeed in being concrete; it is a love of illusions, like those illusions that the disciples had when, looking at Jesus, they thought he was a ghost."

The "ghost" is what the astonished and frightened disciples saw coming toward them walking on the sea. But their amazement arose from their hardness of heart, because—the Gospel says—"they had not understood" the multiplication of the loaves that had happened just before that. "If your heart is hardened you cannot love, and you think that love is some sort of thing you dream up. No, love is concrete." And this concreteness is based on two criteria.

"First criterion: loving with works, not with words. Words are blown away in the wind! They're here today, gone tomorrow. The second criterion of concreteness is that in love it is more important to give than to receive. The one who loves gives, gives . . . Gives things, gives life, gives himself to God and others. But the one who does not love, who is selfish, always wants to receive, always wants to have things, to have advantages. To remain with our hearts open, not like those of the disciples, which were closed, which did not understand anything. To remain in God and God in us; to remain in love."

January 9, 2014   *1 John 4:19–5:4 ✦ Luke 4:14–22*

151

Half-convinced Christians are Christians defeated

R emain in the Lord," in order to love God and neighbor. This "remaining in the love" of God is the work of the Holy Spirit and of our faith, and produces a concrete effect.

"Whoever remains in God, whoever has been born of God, whoever remains in love overcomes the world, and the victory is our faith. On our part, faith. On the part of God, the Holy Spirit, who does this work of grace. On our part, faith. This is powerful! Our faith can do everything! It is victory! And it would be wonderful for us to repeat this, even to ourselves, because so often we are defeated Christians. But the Church is full of defeated Christians, who do not believe in this, that faith is victory; who do not live this faith, because if this faith is not lived it is defeated and the victory goes to the world, to the prince of the world."

Jesus had great praise for the faith of the woman with the hemorrhage, the Canaanite woman, or the man born blind, and said that one who has faith like a mustard seed can move mountains. "This faith requires two attitudes of us: to confess, and to trust." First of all, "to confess.

"Faith means confessing God, but the God who has revealed himself to us, from the time of our fathers until now, the God of history. And this is what we recite every day in the Creed. It is one thing to recite the Creed with our heart, and another to do it like parrots, isn't it? I believe, I believe in God, I believe in Jesus Christ, I believe . . . Do I believe in what I am saying? Is this confession of faith true, or am I saying it by rote, because it has to be said? Or do I believe halfway? To confess the faith! All of it, not one part! All! And to guard the whole faith, as it has come down to us, by the path of tradition: the whole faith! And how can I know if I am confessing the faith well? There is one sign: the one who confesses the faith well, the whole faith, has the ability to worship, to worship God.

"We know how to ask God for something, how to thank God, but worshiping God, praising God is more than that! Only someone with this strong faith is capable of adoration." "I would dare to say that the temperature of the Church's life is a bit low in this." And this is "because in the confession of the faith we are not convinced, or we are convinced only halfway." So the first attitude is to confess the faith and protect it. The other attitude is "trust.

"The man or woman who has faith in God entrusts himself to God: he trusts! Paul, in a dark moment of his life, said: 'I know well to whom I have entrusted myself.' To God! To the Lord Jesus! To entrust ourselves, and this leads us to hope. Just as the confession of faith leads us to the worship and praise of God, entrusting ourselves to God leads us to an attitude of hope. There are so many Christians with a hope that is watered down, not strong, a weak hope. Why? Because they do not have the strength and courage to entrust themselves to the Lord. But if we Christians believe and confess our faith, guard our faith, and entrust ourselves to God, to the Lord, we will be victorious Christians. And this is the victory that has conquered the world: our faith!"

January 10, 2014   *1 John 5:5–13 ✢ Luke 5:12–16*

152

Our relationship with Jesus saves us from the idolatry of the "god Narcissus"

The first letter of Saint John, where it says that we have eternal life because we believe in the name of Jesus, offers the occasion for priests to ask about their relationship with Jesus, because "a priest's strength is in this relationship. When he was growing in popularity, Jesus went to the Father," he retreated "into deserted places to pray. This is a touchstone for us priests, whether or not we go to find Jesus. What place does Jesus have in my priestly life? Is it a living relationship, of disciple to Teacher, brother to brother, poor man to God, or is it a somewhat artificial relationship . . . that does not come from the heart?

"We are anointed by the Spirit, and when a priest distances himself from Jesus Christ, he can lose the anointing. In his life, no: essentially he has it . . . but he loses it. And instead of being anointed, he ends up being unctuous. And how much harm unctuous priests do to the Church! Those who put their strength into artificial things, into vanity, into an attitude . . . into a pretentious way of speaking . . . But how many times do we hear this said painfully: 'But this is a peacock-priest,' because he is always in his vanities. He does not have the relationship with Jesus Christ! He has lost the anointing; he is unctuous.

"We priests have many limitations. We are sinners, all of us. But if we go to Jesus Christ, if we seek the Lord in prayer—the prayer of intercession, the prayer of adoration—we are good priests, even though we are sinners. But if we distance ourselves from Jesus Christ, we have to compensate for this with worldly attitudes. So we get all of these figures: the businessman priest, the priest entrepreneur . . . But the priest who worships Jesus Christ, the priest who speaks with Jesus Christ, the priest who seeks Jesus Christ and allows Jesus Christ to seek him: this is the center of our life. If we don't have this, we lose everything. And what will we give to the people?

"Our relationship with Jesus Christ, the relationship of the anointed with his people, must grow in us" priests "every day more and more.

"But it is wonderful to find priests who have given their lives as priests, truly, of whom the people say: 'Well, sure, he has a temper, he has this, he has that . . . But he's a priest!' And people have the nose for this! But when the people see priests—so to speak—who are idolatrous, who instead of having Jesus have little idols . . . some of them devotees of the 'god Narcissus,' even . . . When the people see a priest like this, they say: 'Poor guy!' What saves us from the worldliness and idolatry that make us unctuous, what preserves the anointing in us, is our relationship with Jesus Christ."

January 11, 2014   *1 John 5:14–21 ✤ John 3:22–30*

153

God's love straightens our crooked histories

Jesus calls Peter, Andrew, James, and John. They are fishing, but they immediately leave their nets and follow him. The Lord wants to prepare his disciples for their new mission. "It is just like God, like the love of God, to prepare the way. To prepare our lives, for each one of us. He does not make us Christian by spontaneous generation; he prepares us! He prepares our way, he prepares our life, long beforehand.

"It seems that Simon, Andrew, James, John were definitively chosen here, and yes, they were chosen! But in that moment they were not definitively faithful! After this election they made mistakes, they made unchristian suggestions to the Lord, they denied the Lord! Peter in a big way, the others just out of fear; they were frightened and they went away. They abandoned the Lord. The Lord prepares. And then, after the Resurrection, the Lord had to continue this journey of preparation until the day of Pentecost. And after Pentecost, some of them—Peter, for example—went wrong and Paul had to correct them. But the Lord prepares.

So the Lord "has been preparing us for many generations.

"And when things aren't going well, he takes part in history and arranges the situation and goes forward with us. Let's think about the genealogy of Jesus Christ, about that list: this one begets that one, that one begets this one, this one begets that one . . . In the history of that list there are sinners. But what did the Lord do? He got involved, he corrected the course, he fixed things. Let's think of the great David, a great sinner and then a great saint. When the Lord tells us, 'With eternal love I have loved you,' he is referring to this. For many generations the Lord has thought of us, each one of us!

"I like to think that the Lord feels like a couple waiting for a baby; he is waiting. He is always waiting for us in this history, and then he accompanies us in history. This is the eternal love of the Lord, eternal, but concrete! It is even a personalized love, because he goes on making history, goes on preparing the way for each of us. And this is the love of God," who "has always loved us, and never abandons us! Let's pray to the Lord to know this tenderness of his heart." And this is "an act of faith," and it is not easy to believe this.

"Because our rationalism says: 'But with all the people he has, how does the Lord think of me? But he has prepared the way for me!' With our mothers, our grandmothers, our fathers, our grandfathers and great-grandfathers . . . This is what the Lord does. This is his love: concrete, eternal, and even personalized. Let's pray, asking for this grace to understand the love of God. But we will never understand it! We feel it, we weep, but we can't understand it on this side. This too tells us how great this love is. The Lord, who has long been preparing for us, walks with us, preparing others. He is always with us! Let's ask for the grace to understand this great love with our hearts."

January 13, 2014   *1 Samuel 1:1–8 ✠ Mark 1:14–20*

154

Faith is not a weight on our shoulders

We can delineate four models of believers: Jesus, the scribes, the priest Eli, and his two sons, also priests. The Gospel tells us what was "the attitude of Jesus in his catechesis: he taught as one who has authority, and not like the scribes." These latter "taught and preached, but they bound the people with heavy burdens on their shoulders, and the poor people couldn't move forward.

"And Jesus himself says that they didn't so much as lift a finger to move these things, right? And then he tells the people: 'Do what they say, but not what they do!' Inconsistent people . . . But these scribes, these Pharisees, it was like they were always beating the people, right? 'You have to do this, this, and this,' to the poor people . . . And Jesus said: 'But in doing this you close'—he says this to them!— 'the door of the kingdom of heaven. You do not allow others to enter, and you will not even enter yourselves!' This is a manner, a way of preaching, of teaching, of giving testimony to one's faith. And how many there are who think that faith is like this."

In the first reading, taken from the first book of Samuel, we find the figure of Eli, "a poor priest, weak, lukewarm," who "allowed his sons to do terrible things." Eli was sitting in front of a doorpost of the Temple of the Lord watching Hannah, a lady "who was praying in her way, asking for a son." This woman "was praying as humble people pray: simply, but from her heart, with anguish." Hannah "was moving her lips," as "so many good women" do "in our churches, at our shrines." She was praying like this "and asking for a miracle." And the elderly Eli looked at her and said: "But she's a drunkard!" And "he disdained her." He "was a representative of the faith, a leader of the faith, but his heart was not good and he disdained this lady.

"How many times do the People of God feel the disfavor of those who are supposed to give testimony: of Christians, of lay Christians, priests, bishops . . . 'Oh, poor people, they don't understand anything. They need to take a theology course to understand properly.' But why do I feel a certain sympathy for this man? Because in his heart he still had the anointing, because when the woman explains her situation to him, Eli tells her: 'Go in peace, and may the God of Israel grant you what you have asked of him.' The priestly anointing comes out. Poor man, he had it hidden inside of him and his laziness . . . He is lukewarm. And he comes to a bad end, poor guy."

His sons are not mentioned in the first reading, but they were the ones who supervised the Temple; "they were brigands. They were priests, but brigands. They were chasing after power, after money, exploiting the people, profiting from the almsgiving, from the gifts," and "the Lord punishes them severely." This "is the figure of the corrupt Christian, of the corrupt layman, of the corrupt priest, of the corrupt bishop, who profits from his situation, from his privilege of faith, from being Christian," and "his heart ends up corrupted," as happened to Judas. From a corrupted heart comes "betrayal." Judas "betrays Jesus." The sons of Eli are therefore the third model of the believer.

And then there is the fourth, Jesus. And the people say about him: "This man teaches like one who has authority. This is a new teaching!" But where is the novelty? It is "the power of holiness. The novelty of Jesus is that he bears the Word of God with him, the message of God, which is God's love for each of us." Jesus "brings God closer to the people, and in order to do this he gets closer himself: he is close to sinners." Jesus forgives the adulterous woman; "he talks theology with the Samaritan woman, who was no angel." Jesus "is looking for the heart; Jesus draws near to the injured heart of the person. Jesus is interested only in the person, and God." Jesus "wants the people to draw near to him, to seek him, and he is moved when he sees them like sheep without a shepherd." And this whole attitude "is why the people say: 'But this is a new teaching!'" No, "the teaching isn't new; it is the way of doing it that is new. It is evangelical transparency.

"Let's ask the Lord that these two readings may help us in our lives as Christians: all of us. Each of us, wherever we are. Not to be pure legalists, hypocrites like the scribes and Pharisees. Not to be corrupted like the sons of Eli. Not to be lukewarm like Eli, but to be like Jesus, with that zeal of seeking out the people, healing the people, loving the people, and saying: 'But if I do such a small thing, think of how much God loves you, and what your Father is like!' This is the new teaching that God is asking of us. Let's ask for this grace."

January 14, 2014			*1 Samuel 1:9–20 ✢ Mark 1:21–28*

155

Let's give God's people the bread of life

The biblical account of a tough defeat of the Israelites at the hands of the Philistines leads to the observation that the People of God at that time had abandoned the Lord. It was said that the Word of God was "rare" at that time. The elderly priest Eli was "lukewarm," and his "corrupt sons were scaring the people and beating them." In order to combat the Philistines, the Israelites were using the Ark of the Covenant, but as if it were something "magical," "an external thing." And they were defeated: the Ark is taken by the enemy. There is no true faith in God, in his real presence in life.

"This passage of Scripture makes us think about our relationship with God, with the Word of God. Is it a formal relationship? Is it a distant relationship? Does the Word of God enter into our hearts, change our hearts? Does the Word of God have this power or not? Is it a formal relationship, everything fine? But the heart is closed to that word! And it leads us to think about the many defeats of the Church, the many defeats of the People of God simply because they do not listen to the Lord, do not seek the Lord, do not let the Lord seek them! And then after the tragedy comes this prayer: 'But, Lord, what has happened! You have given us up to the contempt of our neighbors. To this scorn and derision of those around us. You have made us a byword for the nations! The people shake their heads over us.'"

Our thoughts turn to the scandals of the Church.

"Are we truly ashamed? So many scandals that I don't want to mention them individually, but we all know what they are . . . We know where they are! Scandals, some that have cost a lot of money. Okay, that's fine, it has to be . . . The shame of the Church! But are we ashamed of those scandals, of those defeats of priests, of bishops, of laypeople? In those scandals the Word of God was rare; in those men and in those women the Word of God was rare! They did not have a connection with God! They had a position in the Church, a position of power, even of comfort. But the Word of God, no! 'But I wear a medal.' 'I wear the Cross' . . . Sure, like these others carried the Ark! Without a living relationship with God and with the Word of God! Our attention finally turns to the People of God.

"Poor people! Poor people! We do not give them the bread of life to eat; in those cases we do not even give them the truth! And we even give them poisoned food to eat, so many times! 'Awake, why are you sleeping, Lord!' This should be our prayer! 'Arise! Do not reject us forever! Why do you hide your face? Why do you forget our misery and oppression?' Let's ask the Lord that we may never forget the Word of God, which is alive, that it may enter into our hearts, and that we may never forget the holy faithful People of God, who are asking us for strong food!"

January 16, 2014   *1 Samuel 4:1–11* ✤ *Mark 1:40–45*

156

A Christian does not neglect the Word of God

The temptation of wanting to be "normal," when instead we are children of God. In essence this means ignoring the word of the Father and following a solely human message, the "word of our own desires," in a way choosing to "sell" the gift of preaching in order to immerse ourselves in a "worldly uniformity." The Hebrew people of the Old Testament faced this temptation more than once. In the episode taken from the first book of Samuel, the leaders of the people ask Samuel himself, who is elderly by this time, to establish a new king for them, when in fact they intend to govern for themselves. At that moment, "the people reject God. Not only do they not listen to the Word of God, but they reject it." And the expression that reveals this separation is the one used by the elders of Israel: they want a "judge-king," so that "they will be like all the other people." What this means is that "they are rejecting the Lord of love, rejecting the election, and seeking the way of worldliness," in a manner similar to that of many Christians today.

"Ordinary life demands that Christians be faithful to their election and not sell it in order to set off toward worldly uniformity. This is the temptation of the people, and also our own. So often we forget the Word of God, what the Lord is telling us, and we latch on to the fashionable word, right? Even if it's something from a soap opera, let's take that, it's more fun! Apostasy is precisely the sin of rupture with the Lord, but it is clear; apostasy can be seen clearly. This is more dangerous, worldliness, because it is more subtle.

"It is true that the Christian must be normal, just as other people are normal, but there are values that the Christian cannot take for himself. The Christian must preserve the Word of God that tells him: 'You are my son, you are chosen, I am with you, I walk with you.'" So this means resisting the temptation—as in the episode from the Bible—of considering ourselves victims of "a certain inferiority complex," of not feeling like "normal people.

"The temptation comes and hardens the heart, and when the

heart is hard, when the heart is not open, the Word of God cannot get in. Jesus said to those on the way to Emmaus: 'Foolish and slow of heart!' Their hearts were hard, they could not understand the Word of God. And worldliness softens the heart, but in a bad way; it is never a good thing to have a soft heart! The good thing is to have a heart open to the Word of God, a heart that receives it. Like the Blessed Mother, who meditated on all these things in her heart, as the Gospel says. Receiving the Word of God in order to keep from falling away from the election."

So let's ask for "the grace to overcome our selfishness, the selfishness of wanting to do my own thing, the way I want. Let's ask for the grace to overcome this and ask for the grace of spiritual docility, which means opening our hearts to the Word of God and not doing like these brothers of ours did, who closed their hearts because they had drifted away from God and for some time had not listened to or understood the Word of God. May the Lord give us the grace of an open heart so that we can receive the Word of God and meditate on it always. And from there take the right path."

January 17, 2014   *1 Samuel 8:4–7, 10–22a ✦ Mark 2:1–12*

157

Ours is the God of surprises; let's welcome the innovation of the Gospel

The Word of God is living and active, discerning the sentiments and the thoughts of the heart." In order to truly receive the Word of God we must have an attitude of "docility. The Word of God is alive, so it comes and says what it wants to say: not what I expect it to say or what I hope it will say." It is a "free" word. And it is also "surprising, because our God is the God of surprises." It is "news.

"The Gospel is news. Revelation is news. Our God is a God who always does new things and asks us for this docility to his news. In the Gospel, Jesus is clear about this, he is very clear: new wine in new wineskins. God brings the wine, but it must be received with this openness to the new. And this is called docility. We can ask ourselves: Am I docile to the Word of God, or do I always do what I believe to be the Word of God? Or do I put the Word of God through a still so that it comes out as something completely different from what God wants it to be?"

If I do this, "I will end up like a piece of rough cloth on an old garment, so that the tear becomes worse." And "adapting ourselves to the Word of God in order to receive it" is "an entirely ascetical attitude.

"When I want to get electricity from the outlet, if the appliance I have doesn't fit, I look for an adapter. We must always seek to adapt ourselves, to adjust ourselves to this news of the Word of God, to be open to the new. Saul, who was the chosen of God, the anointed of God, had forgotten that God is surprising and new. He had forgotten, he had closed himself off in his own thoughts, in his schemes, and so his reasoning was merely human."

In Saul's time, when someone won a battle he would take the spoils and perform a sacrifice with part of them. "These animals, so beautiful, will be for the Lord." But Saul "reasoned with his thoughts, with his own heart, closed off in his habits," while "our

God is not a God of habits; he is a God of surprises." Saul "did not obey the Word of God, he was not docile to the Word of God." And Samuel reproves him for this; "he lets him know that he has not obeyed, he has not been the servant, he has put himself in the place of the Lord. He has taken charge of the Word of God. The rebellion, the disobedience to the Word of God, is the sin of divination." And "the obstinacy, the lack of docility in doing what you want and not what God wants, is the sin of idolatry." This is a reminder of "what Christian freedom is, what Christian obedience is.

"Christian freedom and Christian obedience are docility to the Word of God; they mean having the courage to become new wineskins, for this new wine that is continuously coming. This courage to discern always: to discern, I say, not to relativize. To discern always what the Spirit is doing in my heart, what the Spirit wants in my heart, where the Spirit is taking me in my heart. And to obey. To discern and to obey. Today let's ask for the grace of docility to the Word of God, to this word that is living and active, that discerns the sentiments and thoughts of the heart."

January 20, 2014   *1 Samuel 15:16–23* ✠ *Mark 2:18–22*

158

Let's preserve our smallness in order to dialogue with the Lord

The Lord's relationship with his people is a personal relationship"; it is "always person to person." He "is the Lord, and his people has a name, it is not a dialogue between the ruler and the masses." It is a "personal" dialogue.

"And in a people, everyone has a place. The Lord never speaks to the people like that, as a mass, never. He always speaks personally, by name. And he chooses personally. The account of the Creation is a figure that shows this. It is the Lord himself who with his own hands, like a craftsman, makes man and gives him a name: 'You are called Adam.' And so begins that relationship between God and the person. And there is something else, there is a relationship between God and us, who are small: God the great and we the small. When God has to choose persons, including his whole people, he always chooses the small."

God chooses his people because they are "the smallest," they have "less power" than the other peoples. There is a true "dialogue between God and human smallness." Even the Blessed Mother would say: "The Lord has looked upon my humility." The Lord "has chosen the small." In the first reading "we see this attitude of the Lord, clearly." The prophet Samuel stands in front of the oldest of the sons of Jesse and thinks that this is "the anointed, because he was a tall man, big." But the Lord tells him "not to look at his appearance or stature" and adds: "I have rejected him, because what man sees does not count. In fact, man sees the appearance, but the Lord sees the heart. The Lord chooses according to his criteria." And he chooses "the weak and meek, in order to confound the powerful of the earth." In the end, then, "the Lord chooses David, the smallest," who "did not count for his father. He was not at home"; he was "keeping watch over the sheep." And yet it was precisely David "who was chosen.

"In Baptism, we have all been chosen by the Lord. We are all chosen. He has chosen us one by one. He has given each of us a name, and he watches us. There is a dialogue, because this is how the Lord loves. David later became king and went wrong. He may have made many mistakes, but the Bible tells us about two big mistakes, two of those mistakes that really have an impact. What did David do? He humbled himself. He returned to his smallness and said: 'I am a sinner.' And he asked for forgiveness and did penance."

And after the second sin, David said to the Lord: "Punish me, not the people. The people are not to blame, I am guilty." David "preserves his smallness, with repentance, with prayer, with weeping. Thinking about these things, about this dialogue between the Lord and our smallness, I ask myself where Christian faithfulness is.

"Christian faithfulness, our faithfulness, is simply in preserving our smallness, so that we may dialogue with the Lord. Guarding our smallness. This is why humility, meekness, gentleness are so important in the life of the Christian, because they preserve the smallness that the Lord likes to see. And there will always be that dialogue between our smallness and the greatness of the Lord. May the Lord give us, through the intercession of Saint David—and also through the intercession of the Blessed Mother, who sang to God with joy, because he had looked upon her humility—may the Lord give us the grace of preserving our smallness before him."

January 21, 2014   *1 Samuel 16:1–13* ✢ *Mark 2:23–28*

Jealousy, envy, and gossip divide Christian communities

The victory of the Israelites over the Philistines takes place thanks to the courage of the young David. The joy of victory soon turns into sadness and jealousy for King Saul, in whose presence the women are praising David for having killed Goliath. So then, "great victory begins to become a defeat in the king's heart," which is infiltrated, like Cain's, by the "worm of jealousy and envy." And like Cain with Abel, the king decides to kill David. "This is what jealousy does in our hearts; it is an evil form of disquiet that does not tolerate that a brother or sister should have something that I don't have." Saul, "instead of praising God for this victory, as the women of Israel were doing, prefers to close himself off, grumbling to himself" and "cooking his sentiments in the broth of bitterness.

"Jealousy leads to murder. Envy leads to murder. This was the very door, the door of envy, by which the devil entered into the world. The Bible says: 'It was through the envy of the devil that evil entered into the world.' Jealousy and envy open the doors for everything that is evil. They also divide the community. When a Christian community is suffering—some of its members—from envy, from jealousy, it ends up divided, one against the other. This is a strong poison. It is a poison that we find on the first page of the Bible, with Cain."

In the heart of a person struck with jealousy and envy, "two very clear things" happen. The first is bitterness.

"The envious person, the jealous person is a bitter person. He can't sing, he can't praise, he doesn't know what joy is, he always looks at 'what that guy has that I don't have.' And this leads to bitterness, a bitterness that is spread through the whole community. These are sowers of bitterness. And the second attitude that leads to jealousy and envy is gossip. Because this one doesn't tolerate that the other one should have something. The solution is to knock him down, so that I can be a little bit higher. And the tool is gossip. If you look you will always see that behind gossip is jealousy and envy.

And gossip divides the community, it destroys the community. It is a weapon of the devil.

"How many wonderful Christian communities" were getting along just fine, but then one of the members got the worm of jealousy and envy, and with this, sadness, resentment of heart, and gossip. "A person who is under the influence of envy and jealousy kills," the Scriptures say. "He who hates his brother is a murderer." And "the envious person, the jealous person, begins to hate his brother.

"Today, at this Mass, let's pray for our Christian communities, that the seed of jealousy may not be sown among us, that envy may not take root in our hearts, in the heart of our communities, and that we may go forward with the praise of the Lord, praising the Lord, with joy. It is a great grace, the grace of not falling into sadness, into being resentful, into jealousy and envy."

January 23, 2014   *1 Samuel 18:6–9; 19:1–7* ♣ *Mark 3:7–12*

160

Always build bridges of dialogue

I break but I don't bend, the popular saying goes. I bend so that I will not break, Christian wisdom suggests. Two ways of understanding life. The first, with its hardness, easily devoted to raising walls by cutting communication among persons, degenerates into hatred. The second tends to lay down bridges of understanding, even after a disagreement, a fight. But this is on the condition of seeking and practicing "humility." At the center of the reflection is still the clash between King Saul and David. At one point, the latter has the opportunity to kill the former but chooses "another way: the way of reaching out, clarifying the situation, explaining himself. The way of dialogue in order to make peace.

"Dialogue requires meekness, with no shouting. It is also necessary to think that the other person has something more than I do, and this is what David thought: He is the Lord's anointed, he is more important than I am. Humility, meekness . . . In order to dialogue, we need to do what we have asked today in the prayer at the beginning of Mass: to become all things to all men. Humility, meekness, becoming all things to all men and also—although this is not written in the Bible—we all know that in order to do this we have to swallow a lot of humble pie. But we have to do it, because this is how peace is made: with humility, humiliation, always trying to see the image of God in the other.

"Dialogue is difficult," but worse than trying to build a bridge with an adversary is allowing rancor to build up in our hearts toward him. In this way we remain "isolated in this bitter broth of our resentment." A Christian, instead, has for a model David, who overcomes hatred with "an act of humility.

"To humiliate oneself, and always build the bridge, always. Always. And this is being Christian. It is not easy. It is not easy. This is what Jesus did: he humiliated himself to the end; he showed us the way. And we can't let too much time go by. When there's a problem, as soon as possible, at the moment in which it can be done, after the storm has passed, to reach out for dialogue, because time makes the wall get bigger, just as the weeds grow that block the growth of the wheat. And when the walls grow, reconciliation becomes so difficult: it is so difficult!"

It is not a problem if "sometimes the plates go flying, in the family, in communities, in neighborhoods." The important thing is "to seek peace as soon as possible," with a word, a gesture. A bridge rather than a wall, like the one that divided Berlin for so many years. Because in our hearts as well there is the possibility of becoming Berlin with a wall against others.

"I am afraid of these walls, of these walls that grow every day and foster resentment. Even hatred. Let's think about this young David. He could have gotten the perfect revenge, he could have gotten rid of the king, and he chose the way of dialogue, with humility, meekness, kindness. Today, we may ask Saint Francis de Sales, Doctor of Kindness, to give all of us the grace of building bridges with others, never walls."

January 24, 2014   *1 Samuel 24:3–21 ✢ Mark 3:13–19*

161

Thanks to the many holy priests

The episode that speaks of the tribes of Israel that anointed David as their king offers the opportunity to dwell on the spiritual significance of anointing. "Without this anointing, David would have been just the boss" of "a company," of a "political society, which was the kingdom of Israel"; he would have been a mere "political organizer." Instead, "after the anointing, the Spirit of the Lord" descends upon David and remains with him. And Scripture says: "David grew steadily more powerful, for the Lord God of hosts was with him." This is precisely the difference that the anointing makes. The anointed one is a person chosen by the Lord. In the Church these are the bishops and priests.

"The bishops are not chosen only to perpetuate an organization, which is called the particular Church; they are anointed, they have the anointing, and the Spirit of the Lord is with them. But all bishops, all of us are sinners, all! But we are anointed. But we all want to be more holy every day, more faithful to this anointing. And what makes the Church itself, what gives the Church unity, is the person of the bishop, in the name of Jesus Christ, because he is anointed, not because he was voted in by the majority. Because he is anointed. And in this anointing a particular Church has its strength. And by participation the priests are anointed as well."

The anointing brings the bishops and priests closer to the Lord and gives them the joy and strength "of leading a people, of helping a people, of living in service of the people." It gives them the joy of feeling "chosen by the Lord, looked upon by the Lord, with that love with which the Lord looks upon all of us." So "when we think about the bishops and priests, this is how we have to think about them: as anointed.

"Otherwise the Church doesn't make sense, but not only does it not make sense, there is no explaining how the Church can go forward with human strength alone. This diocese keeps going because it has a holy people, so many things, and also an anointed one who leads it, who helps it to grow. And we know only a tiny portion of these in history, but how many holy bishops, how many priests, how many holy priests have given their lives in service of the diocese, of the parish; how many people have received the power of faith, the power of love, of hope from these anonymous pastors whom we do not know. There are so many of them!"

There are so many "country priests or city priests who with their anointing have given strength to the people, have handed down the teaching, have given the sacraments, meaning holiness.

" 'But, Father, I read in the newspaper that a bishop did this or a priest did that!' 'Yes, I read that too, but tell me, do the newspapers print the stories of what so many priests do in so many parishes in the city and the countryside, all the charity that they do, all the work that they do to lead their people forward?' Oh, no! That is not news. It's the same old story: a tree that falls makes more noise than a forest that grows. Today, thinking about this anointing of David, it would do us good to think about our bishops and priests—courageous, holy, good, faithful—and pray for them. It is thanks to them that we are here today!"

January 27, 2014   *2 Samuel 5:1–7, 10 ✤ Mark 3:22–30*

162

Let's not praise the Lord with coldness

D avid danced with all his strength before the Lord." This is a
joyful image, the one recounted in the second book of Samuel. The whole People of God was celebrating because the Ark of
the Covenant was coming home. David's prayer of praise "led him
to lose his composure and dance before the Lord" with "all his
strength." This "was truly a prayer of praise"! Reading this passage,
our thoughts turn to Sarah, after she gave birth to Isaac: This elderly
woman, like the young David, "danced for joy" before the Lord. "It
is easy for us to understand praying to ask the Lord for something, or
to thank the Lord." Even understanding the "prayer of adoration is
not so difficult." But the prayer of praise "we leave aside, and it does
not come to us so spontaneously.

"'But, Father, this is for those Life in the Spirit people, not for
all Christians!' No, the prayer of praise is a Christian prayer for all
of us! In the Mass, every day, when we sing the Sanctus, this is a
prayer of praise. We praise God for his greatness, because he is great!
And we say beautiful things to him, because it pleases us that he is
like this. 'But, Father, I can't do it . . . I have to do something else.'
So, you can yell when your team scores a goal but you can't sing the
praises of the Lord? You can't come out of your shell enough to sing
this? Praising God is completely gratuitous! We don't ask, we don't
thank: we praise."

We must pray "with all our heart." "This is an act of justice, because he is great! He is our God!" David "was so happy, because the
Ark was coming back, the Lord was coming back; even his body
prayed with that dance.

"A great question that we can ask ourselves today: But how is my
prayer of praise? Do I know how to praise the Lord? Do I know
how to praise the Lord, or when I pray the Gloria or the Sanctus do
I do it only with my mouth and not with my whole heart? What
is David saying to me, dancing here? And Sarah, dancing for joy?
When David enters the city, something else happens: a celebration!

"The joy of praise leads us to the joy of celebration. The celebration of the family." When David returns to the palace, the daughter of King Saul, Michal, reproves him and asks him if he is not ashamed for having danced that way in front of everyone, he who is the king. Michal "despised David.

"I wonder how many times we have despised in our hearts good people who praise the Lord as it comes to them, spontaneously, because they are not sophisticated, they don't follow the formal attitudes? I mean real disdain! And the Bible says that Michal was left sterile her whole life for this! What is the Word of God saying here? That the joy, the prayer of praise makes us fruitful! Sarah danced in the great moment of her fruitfulness, at the age of ninety! The fruitfulness that comes to us from praising the Lord, the gratuitousness of praising the Lord. That man or woman who praises the Lord, who prays with praise to the Lord, who in praying the Gloria rejoices in saying it, in singing the Sanctus at Mass rejoices to sing it, is a fruitful man or woman."

But "those who close themselves off in the formality of a cold, calculated prayer may end up like Michal: in the sterility of their formalism." The invitation is therefore to imagine David dancing "with all his strength before the Lord, and to think how wonderful it is to make the prayer of praise." It would do us good to repeat the words of Psalm 24 that we have prayed today: "Lift up your heads, O gates; rise up, you ancient portals, that the king of glory may enter. Who is this king of glory? The Lord of hosts, he is the king of glory!"

January 28, 2014   *2 Samuel 6:12b–15, 17–19 ✤ Mark 3:31–35*

163

It is an absurd dichotomy to love Christ without the Church

The readings of the day present the figure of King David as that of a man who speaks with the Lord like a child talks with his father and, even if he receives a no to his requests, accepts it with joy. David had "a strong sense of belonging to the People of God." And this leads us to ask about our sense of belonging to the Church, our oneness of heart with the Church and in the Church.

"The Christian is not a person who receives Baptism and then goes his own way. The first fruit of Baptism is to make you a member of the Church, of the People of God. A Christian without the Church makes no sense. This is why the great Paul VI said that it is an absurd dichotomy to love Christ without the Church; to listen to Christ but not to the Church; to be with Christ on the outskirts of the Church. It can't be done. We receive the message of the Gospel in the Church, and we become holy through the Church, our way in the Church. The other way is a fantasy or, as he said, an absurd dichotomy."

The "*sensus ecclesiae* means precisely feeling, thinking, willing inside the Church." There are "three pillars of this belonging. The first is humility," in the awareness of being "incorporated into a community as a great grace."

"A person who is not humble cannot feel along with the Church; he will feel what he likes, as he likes. But this humility is the humility that we see in David: 'Who am I, Lord God, and what is my house?' With that awareness that salvation history did not start with me and will not end when I die. No, it is a whole story of salvation: the Lord takes you, he leads you forward, and then he calls you again, and the story continues. The history of the Church began before us, and it will continue after us. Humility: we are a small part of a big people, which travels the path of the Lord."

The second pillar is faithfulness, "which must be linked with obedience.

"Faithfulness to the Church; faithfulness to its teachings; faithfulness to the Creed; faithfulness to doctrine, preserving this doctrine. Humility and faithfulness. Paul VI also reminded us that we have received the message of the Gospel as a gift, and we must hand it down as a gift, not as something of our own. It is a gift received that we give. And in this transmission to be faithful. Because we have received and we must give a Gospel that is not ours, that belongs to Jesus, and we must not—he said—make ourselves masters of the Gospel, masters of the doctrine received, to use it as we please."

The third pillar is a particular service: "to pray for the Church.

"How is our prayer for the Church? Do we pray for the Church? At daily Mass, but not at home? When we say our prayers?" We must pray for the whole Church, in all parts of the world. "May the Lord help us to walk this path in order to deepen our membership in the Church and our oneness of heart with the Church."

January 30, 2014   *2 Samuel 7:18–19, 24–29 ✠ Mark 4:21–25*

164

If we lose the sense of God, the worst sin seems like no big deal

A grave sin—adultery, for example—can sometimes be downgraded to "a problem to be solved." The choice that King David makes becomes a mirror for the conscience of every Christian. David takes a fancy to Bathsheba, the wife of Uriah, one of his generals. He takes her and sends her husband to the front lines of the battle, causing his death and essentially committing murder. And yet adultery and murder don't bother David very much. "David finds himself before a tremendous sin, but he doesn't feel it as sin. It doesn't come to his mind to ask for forgiveness. What comes to mind is: How do I fix this?

"This can happen to all of us. We are all sinners, and we are all tempted, and temptation is our daily bread. If someone were to say to us: 'But I have never had temptations,' either that person is a little angel or they're a bit thick, right? It's understandable . . . The struggle is part of life, and the devil doesn't rest, he wants his victory. But the problem—the most serious problem in this passage—is not so much the temptation and the sin against the ninth commandment, but it is how David acts. And here David does not talk about sin, he talks about a problem that he has to resolve. This is a sign! When the Kingdom of God starts to fade, when the Kingdom of God becomes less important, one of the signs is that we lose the sense of sin."

Every day, reciting the Our Father, we ask God "your kingdom come," which means "may your kingdom grow." But when we lose the sense of sin, we also lose "the sense of the Kingdom of God," and in its place emerges a "superpowerful anthropological vision," according to which "I can do anything.

"Man's power instead of the glory of God! This is the daily bread. This is why we pray to God every day 'May your kingdom come, your kingdom grow,' because salvation will not come from our cleverness, from our astuteness, from our intelligence in doing business. Salvation will come from the grace of God and from the daily training that we do with this grace in Christian life.

"The greatest sin of today is that men have lost the sense of sin." From this famous saying of Pius XII we move on to Uriah, the blameless man sent to death because of the offense of his king. Uriah therefore becomes the emblem of all the victims of our unconfessed arrogance.

"I confess to you that when I see these injustices, this human arrogance, and also when I see the danger that the same thing could happen to me, the danger of losing the sense of sin, it does me good to think about the many Uriahs in history, the many Uriahs who suffer today from our Christian mediocrity when we lose the sense of sin, when we let go of the Kingdom of God . . . These are the martyrs of our unacknowledged sins. It would do us good today to pray for ourselves, that the Lord may always give us the grace of not losing the sense of sin, so that the Kingdom of God may not crumble in us. And also to bring a spiritual flower to the graves of these contemporary Uriahs, who pay the bill for the feast of the secure, of those Christians who feel themselves secure."

January 31, 2014   *2 Samuel 11:1–4a, 5–10a, 13–17* ❧ *Mark 4:26–34*

165

A leader does not exploit God and his people

Ki ing David flees because his son Absalom has betrayed him. The first reading, taken from the second book of Samuel, tells about this "great betrayal" and its consequences. David is sad because "even the people" were with the son against the king. And he feels "as if this son were dead." But what is David's reaction "in the face of this betrayal by his son"? Above all David, "a man of government, accepts reality as it is and knows that this war will be very" tough and "that there will be many dead." So "he makes the decision not to make his people die." He "could have fought in Jerusalem against the forces of his son," but he determines that Jerusalem should not be destroyed.

"David, in order to defend himself, does not use God or his people, and this signifies the love of a king for his God and his people. David is a sinful king—we know the story—but a king who also has this great love. He is so attached to his God and so attached to his people that he does not defend himself using God or his people. In the nasty moments of life it happens that in desperation one may seek to defend oneself however possible, and even use God or use the people. But he doesn't. The first attitude is this: not to use God and his people."

So David decides to flee. His second attitude is "penitential." He goes up the mountain "weeping," walking "with his head covered and his feet bare." And all the "people who were with him had their heads covered and, climbing, they wept." This is truly "a journey of penance. Perhaps in his heart he is thinking of all the ugly things, all the sins he has committed"; he is thinking that he is not "innocent." He is also thinking that it is not right for his son to betray him, but he recognizes that he is not a saint and "chooses penance.

"This climb up the mountain reminds us of that other climb of Jesus, when he too was sorrowful, barefoot, going up the mountain with his Cross. This penitential attitude. David accepts his mourning and weeping. When something like this happens in our lives, we always seek—this is an instinct that we have—to justify ourselves. David does not justify himself. He is realistic; he tries to save the Ark of God, his people; and he does penance along that path. He is one of the great ones: a great sinner and a great saint. How these two things go together . . . God only knows!"

And on the way another figure appears: Shimei, who throws stones at David and his servants. He is an "enemy" who curses David. One of the friends of the king therefore says that he wants to kill this "wretch," this "dead dog." But David stops him. "Instead of choosing vengeance against so many insults, he chooses to entrust himself to God." Even more, he says that they should let Shimei curse him, because "the Lord has ordained it for him." And he adds: "He always knows what is happening, the Lord permits it." David furthermore thinks, "Perhaps the Lord will look upon my affliction and make it up to me with benefits for the curses he is uttering this day." The third attitude of David is therefore entrusting himself to the Lord. The way David acts can also help us, "because in life we all pass through" moments of darkness and trial. So these are the three attitudes of David: "not to bargain God"; to accept penance and weep for our mistakes"; finally, "not to try to take justice into our own hands, but to entrust ourselves to God.

"It is wonderful to hear this and to see these three attitudes: a man who loves God, loves his people, and doesn't bargain; a man who knows that he is a sinner and does penance; a man who is sure of his God and entrusts himself to him. David is holy, and we venerate him as a saint. Let's ask him to teach us these attitudes in life's darkest moments."

February 3, 2014   *2 Samuel 15:13–14, 30; 16:5–13* ✤ *Mark 5:1–20*

166

Even God weeps

King David, who weeps over the death of his rebellious son Absalom, and Jairus, a ruler of the synagogue who begs Jesus to heal his daughter, are the figures of two fathers at the center of our reflection today. David weeps at the news of his son's death, in spite of the fact that his son was fighting against him to take over the kingdom. David's army won, but he was not interested in victory, "he was waiting for his son! All he was interested in was his son! He was king, he was the head of the country, but he was a father! So when he received the news of his son's death, he was shaken to the core. He went upstairs . . . and wept.

"As he went he said: 'My son Absalom. My son, my son Absalom! If only I had died instead of you, Absalom, my son, my son!' This is the heart of a father, who never gives up on his child. 'He is a brigand. He is an enemy. But he is my son!' And he does not give up on fatherhood; he weeps . . . David wept for a son twice, this time and when the son of his adultery was about to die. That time as well he fasted and did penance to save the life of his son. He was a father!"

The other father is the head of the synagogue, "an important person. But in the face of his daughter's illness he is not ashamed to throw himself at the feet of Jesus. 'My little daughter is dying, come lay your hands on her, so that she may be saved and live!' He is not ashamed," he's not thinking about what the others could say, because he is a father. David and Jairus are two fathers.

"For them what is most important is their son, their daughter! There's nothing else. The only important thing! This reminds us of the first thing that we say to God in the Creed: 'I believe in God the Father.' It reminds us of the fatherhood of God. But this is the way God is. God is this way with us! 'But, Father, God doesn't cry!' What are you talking about? Remember Jesus, when he wept as he looked at Jerusalem. 'Jerusalem, Jerusalem! How many times have I wanted to gather in your children, as a hen gathers her chicks under her wings.' God weeps! Jesus wept for us! And Jesus' weeping is the image of the weeping of the Father, who wants us all to be with him.

"In difficult moments the Father responds. We remember Isaac, when he goes with Abraham to offer the sacrifice. Isaac wasn't stupid; he knew that they were bringing the wood, the fire, but not the lamb for the sacrifice. He had anguish in his heart! And what does he say? 'Father!' And immediately: 'Here I am, son!' The Father responds."

In the Garden of Gethsemane, Jesus says "with that anguish of heart: 'Father, if it is possible, take this cup away from me!' And the angels come to give him strength. This is what our God is like: he is Father! He is such a Father!" A father like the one who waits for the prodigal son who went away "with all the money, with the whole inheritance. But the father waited for him" every day and "saw him coming from afar. That is our God!" And "our fatherhood," that of fathers of families and also the spiritual fatherhood of bishops and priests, "must be like this. The father has something like an anointing that comes from the son; he cannot understand himself without the son! And this is why he needs the son: he waits for him, he loves him, he seeks him, he forgives him, he wants him close to him, like the hen wants her chicks.

"Let's go home today with these two icons: David, who weeps; and the other, the head of the synagogue, who throws himself down before Jesus, without fear of being shamed and being laughed at by others. Their children were at stake: the son and the daughter. And with these two icons let us say: 'I believe in God the Father . . .' And let's ask the Holy Spirit—because it is only he, the Holy Spirit, who teaches us to say 'Abba, Father!' It is a grace! To be able to call God 'Father' with our hearts is a grace of the Holy Spirit. Let's ask him for it!"

February 4, 2014   *2 Samuel 18:9–10, 14b, 24–25a,*
                                       30–19:3 ✦ Mark 5:21–43

167

Asking for the grace to die in the Church

The death of David after a life spent in service of his people allows us to underline three things. The first is that David dies "in the bosom of his people." He lives to the end "his membership in the People of God. He had sinned: he calls himself 'sinner,' but he never left the People of God!

"Sinner yes, traitor no! And this is a grace: to remain until the end among the People of God. To have the grace to die in the bosom of the Church, right in the bosom of the People of God. And this is the first point that I would like to emphasize. For us as well to ask for the grace of dying at home. To die at home, in the Church. And this is a grace! This cannot be bought! It is a gift of God, and we must ask for it: 'Lord, give me the gift of dying at home, in the Church!' Sinners yes, all, all of us are! But traitors no! Corrupted no! Always inside! And the Church is a mother to such an extent that she also wants us like this, so often dirty, but the Church cleans us: she is a mother!"

Second reflection: David dies "tranquilly, in peace, serene" in the certainty of going "to the other side with his" fathers. "This is another grace: the grace of dying in hope, in the awareness" that "they are waiting for us on the other side: our home, our family also continue on the other side"; we will not be alone. "And this is a grace that we must ask for.

"Saint Thérèse of the Child Jesus toward the end of her life said there was a struggle in her soul and that when she thought of the future, of what was waiting for her after death, in heaven, she heard something like a voice that said: 'No, don't be stupid, darkness is waiting for you. All that is waiting for you is the darkness of nothing!' This is what the voice says. It is the voice of the devil, of the demon, who did not want her to entrust herself to God. To die in hope and to die entrusting oneself to God! And to ask for this grace. But entrusting oneself to God begins now, in the little things of life and also in the big problems: to entrust oneself always to the Lord! And so one gets into the habit of entrusting oneself to the Lord and hope grows. To die at home, to die in hope."

The third reflection is on the inheritance that David leaves. There are "many scandals over inheritance, scandals in families, that divide them." David, instead, "leaves the inheritance of forty years of governance" and "a strong, well-established people. According to a popular saying, every man must leave behind a son, plant a tree, and write a book: this is the best inheritance!" So the invitation is to ask ourselves: "What inheritance am I leaving for those who come after me? An inheritance of life? Have I done enough good that the people love me like a father or mother? Have I planted a tree? Have I given life, wisdom? Have I written a book?" David leaves this inheritance to his son, telling him: "May you be strong and show yourself a man. Observe the law of the Lord, your God, walking in his ways and following his laws!

"This is the inheritance: it is our testimony as Christians that we have left for others. And some of us leave a great inheritance. We think of the saints who lived the Gospel with such strength, who left us a path of life and a way of living as an inheritance. These are the three things that come to my heart in reading this passage on the death of David: to ask for the grace to die at home, to die in the Church; to ask for the grace of dying in hope, with hope; and to ask for the grace of leaving behind a wonderful inheritance, a human inheritance, an inheritance built on the testimony of our Christian life. May Saint David grant all of us these three graces!"

February 6, 2014   *1 Kings 2:1–4, 10–12 ✛ Mark 6:7–13*

168

Being Christians is not a privilege

Herod has John killed to satisfy his lover Herodias and the whim of her daughter. John is "a man who had a short life, a short time to proclaim the Word of God." He was the man whom "God had sent to prepare the way for his Son." And John is put to death in the court of Herod, "who was feasting.

"At court everything goes: corruption, vices, crimes. What did John do? More than anything he proclaimed the Lord. He proclaimed that the Savior was near, the Lord, that the Kingdom of God was near. And he did this forcefully. And he baptized. He urged everyone to convert. He was a strong man. And he proclaimed Jesus Christ.

"The first thing that the great John did was to proclaim Jesus Christ." Another thing that he did was "that he did not take charge of his moral authority." He had been given "the possibility of saying 'I am the Messiah,' because he had so much moral authority, all the people were going to him." And the Gospel narrates that John told everyone to convert. And the Pharisees, the scholars saw this strength of his: "He was an upright man." So they asked him if he was the Messiah. And in that "moment of temptation, of vanity, he could have made a holier-than-thou face and said: 'Well, I don't know . . .' with false humility. Instead he was clear: 'No! I am not he! After me comes one who is stronger than I, the straps of whose sandals I am not worthy to untie.'" John "was clear; he did not steal the title. He did not appropriate the role." So this is the second thing that he did, "as a man of truth he did not steal Christ's dignity." The third thing that John did was "to imitate Christ." Even Herod, who had him killed, "believed that Jesus was John." John imitated Jesus "above all on the path of abasement: John humiliated himself, he abased himself to the end, even to his death." They also share "the same kind of death, shameful: Jesus as a brigand, as a thief, as a criminal, on the Cross.

"Humiliating deaths. But John also had his 'Garden of Gethsemane,' his anguish in prison, when he believed he was mistaken and sent his disciples to ask Jesus: 'Are you the one who is to come, or should we look for another?' The darkness of the soul, that darkness which purifies like Jesus in the Garden of Gethsemane. And Jesus replied to John as the Father had replied to Jesus, comforting him. That darkness of the man of God, of the woman of God. I'm thinking right now about the darkness of soul of Blessed Teresa of Calcutta, no? Ah, the woman praised by the whole world, Nobel Prize! But she knew that in one period of her life, a long one, there was only darkness inside.

"Proclaimer of Jesus Christ," John "did not take charge of prophecy"; he "is the icon of a disciple." But "in what was the wellspring of this attitude of the disciple?" In an encounter. The Gospel tells us about the encounter of Mary and Elizabeth, when John leapt for joy in Elizabeth's womb. They were cousins. "Perhaps they met a few times after that. And that encounter filled John's heart with joy, with so much joy that it turned him into a disciple." John is "the man who proclaims Jesus Christ, who does not put himself in the place of Jesus Christ and follows the way of Jesus Christ.

"It would do us good today to ask ourselves about our discipleship: Do we proclaim Jesus Christ? Do we or do we not take advantage of our condition as Christians as if it were a privilege? John did not take command of prophecy. Third: Are we going by the way of Jesus Christ? The way of humiliation, of humility, of abasement for the sake of service? And if we find that we are not firm in this, to ask ourselves: But when was my encounter with Jesus Christ, that encounter which filled me with joy? And to go back to the encounter, to go back to the first Galilee of the encounter. We all have one! Go back there! To encounter the Lord again and go forward on this beautiful path in which he must increase and we decrease."

February 7, 2014   *Sirach 47:2–11 ✢ Mark 6:14–29*

169

The mystery of God in the Mass

In the time of King Solomon, the Lord descends as a cloud upon the Temple, which is filled with the glory of God. The Lord speaks to his people in so many ways, through the prophets, the priests, Sacred Scripture. But with the theophanies he speaks in another way, "different from the word: it is another presence, closer, without mediation, nearer. It is his presence." "This happens in the liturgical celebration. The liturgical celebration is not a social act, a good social act; it is not a meeting of believers to pray together. It is something else. In the liturgy, God is present," but this is a closer presence. In the Mass, in fact, "the presence of the Lord is real, truly real.

"When we celebrate the Mass, we are not giving a representation of the Last Supper: no, it is not a representation. It is something else: it really is the Last Supper. It is truly living once again the Passion and redeeming death of the Lord. It is a theophany: the Lord makes himself present on the altar in order to be offered to the Father for the salvation of the world. We hear or we say: 'But I can't right now, I have to go to Mass, I have to go hear Mass.' Mass is not something that we 'hear,' it is something we participate in, and we participate in this theophany, in this mystery of the Lord's presence among us."

The Nativity scene, the Way of the Cross, those are representations, but the Mass "is a real commemoration, a theophany. God draws near and is with us, and we participate in the mystery of the redemption." Unfortunately, too often we are looking at our watches at Mass, "counting the minutes. This is not the attitude that the liturgy requires of us; the liturgy is the time of God and the space of God, and we must put ourselves there, in the time of God, in the space of God, and not look at our watches.

"The liturgy means truly entering into the mystery of God, allowing ourselves to be brought to the mystery and to be in the mystery. For example, I am sure that all of you come here to enter into the mystery; but perhaps someone may say: 'Oh, I have to go to

Mass at Saint Martha's because in the visitors' tours of Rome there is the visit with the pope at Saint Martha's every morning. It's a tourist spot, right?' You all come here, we meet here to enter into the mystery; this is the liturgy. It is the time of God, it is the space of God, it is the cloud of God that envelops us all."

And here a childhood memory comes in: during the preparation for First Communion, there was a song about how the altar was guarded by the angels in order to give "the sense of the glory of God, of the space of God, of the time of God." And during the practice the hosts were brought and the children were told: " 'Now these are not the ones you will receive. These aren't worth anything, because there has to be the consecration!' " So "celebrating the liturgy is having this willingness to enter into the mystery of God," into his space, into his time, and entrusting ourselves "to this mystery.

"It would do us good today to ask the Lord to give all of us this 'sense of the sacred,' this sense that makes us understand that it is one thing to pray at home, to pray in Church, to pray the Rosary, to pray so many beautiful prayers, make the Way of the Cross, so many beautiful things, to read the Bible . . . And the Eucharistic celebration is another thing. In the celebration we enter into the mystery of God, into that path which we cannot control. Only He is the One, his is the glory, his is the power, he is everything. Let's ask for this grace: that the Lord may teach us to enter into the mystery of God."

February 10, 2014   *1 Kings 8:1–7, 9–13* ✣ *Mark 6:53–56*

170

Humility can unleash faith

The readings today help us to reflect on a twofold journey: "from idolatry to the living God" and the opposite "from the living God toward idolatry." The meditation begins with the Gospel, in which a "courageous woman," a Canaanite, meaning a pagan, asks Jesus to free her daughter from the devil. She is a mother who is "desperate, and a mother, when it comes to the health of a child, will do anything. Jesus explains to her that he has come first of all for the sheep of the house of Israel, but he explains it to her in tough language: 'Let the children be fed first. For it is not right to take the food of the children and throw it to the dogs.' This woman, who had certainly never been to the university, knew how to respond." And she responds "not with her intelligence, but with her instincts as a mother, with her love: 'But even the dogs eat what falls from the table; give me the crumbs, give them to me!'" This woman "was not ashamed," and because of her faith, Jesus "worked the miracle for her.

"She exposed herself to the risk of looking bad, but she insisted, and from paganism and idolatry found help for her daughter and for herself found the living God. This is the journey of a person of goodwill, who seeks God and finds him. The Lord blesses her. How many people make this journey, and the Lord is waiting for them! But it is the Holy Spirit himself who leads them forward to make this journey. Every day in the Church of the Lord there are people who make this journey, silently, to find the Lord, because they allow themselves to be led forward by the Holy Spirit.

"But there is also the opposite journey," that of Solomon. Solomon was "the wisest man on earth," he had received great blessings from God, he had "universal fame, all the power," he was "a believer in God, but what happened?" He liked women, and he had so many pagan concubines that they made him "turn his heart away to follow other gods"; thus he introduced idols into Israel. "And these women weakened Solomon's heart slowly, slowly. His heart did not remain wholly with the Lord, like the heart of David, his father.

"His heart was weakened; it became so weak that he lost his faith. He lost his faith. The wisest man in the world allowed himself to be led on by an indiscreet love, he allowed himself to be led by his passions. 'But, Father, Solomon didn't lose his faith, he believed in God and was able to recite the Bible!' Yes, that's true, but having faith does not mean being capable of reciting the Creed. You can recite the Creed and have lost your faith."

Solomon "was a sinner, like his father, David. But then he went further, and from a sinner he became corrupt. His heart was corrupted through this idolatry. His father was a sinner, but the Lord had forgiven all his sins, because he was humble and asked for forgiveness." Solomon, though, was "very wise," but vanity and his passions led him to corruption. It is precisely in the heart that faith is lost.

"The malignant seed of his passions grew in the heart of Solomon and led him to idolatry. And after the first reading, in the Alleluia, this good advice: 'Accept the Word with docility'—with docility—'the Word that has been planted in you can lead you to salvation.' Let's walk the path of that Canaanite woman, that pagan woman, accepting the Word of God, which has been planted in us and will lead us to salvation. May the Word of God, powerful, preserve us in this path and not allow us to end up in the corruption that leads us to idolatry."

February 13, 2014   *1 Kings 11:4–13* ✢ *Mark 7:24–30*

171

The Christian must overcome the temptation of becoming a wolf

What should a disciple of Jesus be like? A Christian is "sent." The Lord sends his disciples; he asks them to go forward. "And this means that the Christian is a disciple of the Lord who walks, who always goes forward.

"A Christian who stays still is unthinkable; a Christian who stays still is sick in his Christian identity. The Christian is a disciple of movement, of walking. The Lord says: 'Go out into the whole world and proclaim the Gospel.' Go. Walk. That's it: a first attitude of the Christian identity is to walk, and to walk even if there are difficulties, to go beyond the difficulties."

This is what happened with Paul in Antioch of Pisidia, "where there were difficulties with the Jewish community and so it was the pagans who moved forward." Jesus "urges his followers to go to the crossroads" and to invite "everyone, good and bad." This is what the Gospel says, "even the bad! Everyone." The Christian therefore "walks" and, "if there are difficulties, gets past them in order to proclaim that the Kingdom of God is near." A second aspect of the identity of the Christian "is that the Christian must always remain a lamb." The Christian "is a lamb, and must preserve this identity." The Lord sends us "as lambs in the midst of wolves." But some might propose using "force against them." We think of David, "when he had to fight against the Philistine; they wanted to put all of Saul's armor on him, and he couldn't move." So "he wasn't himself, he wasn't humble, he wasn't the simple David. In the end, he took his sling and won the battle.

"Like lambs . . . Don't become wolves. Because sometimes temptation makes us think: But this is hard, these wolves are cunning, so I have to be even more cunning than they are. Lamb. Not stupid, but a lamb. Lamb. With Christian craftiness, but always a lamb. Because if you are a lamb, he will defend you. But if you feel strong like a wolf, he will not defend you, he will leave you alone and the wolves will eat you alive."

The third aspect of this identity is the "style of the Christian," which is "joy." Christians "are persons who rejoice because they know the Lord and bear the Lord with them." And "we cannot walk as Christians without joy, we cannot walk as lambs without joy." Even "amid problems, even in difficulties, even in our own mistakes and sins there is the joy of Jesus, who always forgives and helps." So the Gospel "must go forward, carried by these lambs who have been sent by the Lord, who walks with joy.

"They're not doing any favors for the Lord or for the Church, those Christians who have a slow-dirge tempo, who are always complaining about everything, sad . . . This is not the style of the disciple. Saint Augustine says to Christians: 'Go, go forward, sing and walk!' With joy: this is the style of the Christian. To proclaim the Gospel with joy. And the Lord does everything. But too much sadness, this excessive sadness, even bitterness leads us to live a so-called Christianity without Christ. The Cross leaves only emptiness for Christians who stand before the tomb weeping, like the Magdalene, but without the joy of having found the Risen One."

On the feast of two Christian disciples, Cyril and Methodius, the Church has us reflect on the "Christian identity." The Christian "never stands still; he is a man or woman who is always walking, who walks past the difficulties." And he walks "as a lamb; his own strength is not enough. He is a man or woman who walks with joy." May the Lord "by the intersection of these two brother saints, patrons of Europe, grant us the grace to live as Christians who walk like lambs and with joy."

February 14, 2014   *1 Kings 11:29–32; 12:19 ✠ Mark 7:31–37*

172

It is the patience of the People of God that moves the Church forward

P atience is not resignation, it is something else." The letter of Saint James, where he says: " 'Consider it all joy, my brothers and sisters, when you encounter various trials' seems to be an invitation to become some sort of Oriental ascetic," but that's not true. Patience, supporting trials, "the things we don't like," helps us "to become more mature. Someone who has no patience wants everything immediately, everything in a hurry. Someone who does not know this wisdom of patience tends to be picky, like children who are picky" and nothing is good enough for them. "A person without patience is a person who does not grow, who remains picky like a child, who does not know how to take life as it comes: it is either this or nothing. This is one of the temptations: to become picky. Another temptation of those who have no patience is the omnipotence" of wanting something right away, like the Pharisees who ask Jesus for "a sign from heaven"; "they wanted a spectacle, a miracle.

"They confuse God's way of acting with what a sorcerer might do. And God does not act like a sorcerer, God has his way of doing things. The patience of God. Even God has patience. Every time we go to the sacrament of Reconciliation, we are singing a hymn to the patience of God! But how the Lord carries us on his shoulders, with what patience, with what patience! The Christian life must unfold according to this music of patience, because this was the music of our fathers, of the People of God, those who believed in the Word of God, who followed the commandment that the Lord had given to our father Abraham: 'Walk in my presence and be blameless.' "

The People of God—as we remember from the letter to the Hebrews—"suffered so much, they were persecuted, massacred," but they had the joy of holding steadfast to God's promises. "This is the patience" that "we must have in trials: the patience of an adult person, the patience of God," who carries us on his shoulders. And this is "the patience of our people.

"How patient our people are! Even now! When we go to the parishes and find those people who suffer, who have problems, who have a disabled child or an illness, but go on with their lives with patience. They are not asking for signs, like these in the Gospel who wanted a sign. They said: 'Give us a sign!' No, they don't ask, but they know how to read the signs of the times. They know that when the fig tree blooms spring is coming; they know how to tell that. But these impatient people in the Gospel today, who wanted a sign, they didn't know how to read the signs of the times, and because of this they did not recognize Jesus."

So the people who deserve praise are "our people who suffer, who suffer so much, so many things, but do not lose the smile of the faith, who have the joy of the faith.

"And these people, our people, in parishes, in our institutions, so many people—these are the ones who lead the Church forward with their everyday holiness, day after day. 'Brothers, consider it perfect gladness when you undergo every sort of trial, knowing that when your faith is put to the test it produces patience, and may patience complete its work in you, so that you may be perfect and whole, without lacking anything' (Jas 1:2–4). May the Lord give all of us the patience, joyful patience, the patience of work, of peace; may he give us the patience of God, the patience that he has; and may he give us the patience of our faithful people, which is so exemplary."

February 17, 2014   *James 1:1–11* ✛ *Mark 8:11–13*

173

Temptation: an infection that kills

Temptation presents itself as a bit of harmless fun and ends up turning into a prison, which we often try to make less confining instead of trying to get out of it, deaf to the Word of God. A truth and a process described by Saint James in a passage from his letter. The truth is that it is never God who tempts man, but rather man's passions. The process is the one produced by the passions themselves, which, the apostle says, "[conceive] and bring forth sin, and when sin reaches maturity it gives birth to death."

"Where does temptation come from? How does it act within us? The apostle says that it does not come from God, but from our passions, from our inner weaknesses, from the wounds left in us by original sin. It is from there that temptations come, from these passions. It is curious, temptation has three characteristics: it grows, it infects, and it justifies itself. It grows: it starts off with a calm appearance, and then it builds . . . Jesus himself said this, when he told the parable of the wheat and weeds: the wheat grew, but so did the weeds sown by the enemy. And temptation grows; it grows, and grows . . . And if one does not stop it, it takes over everything."

Moreover, temptation "looks for someone else to keep it company; it is contagious," and "in this growth and contagion, temptation closes us off in a place that we can't get out of easily." This is the experience of the apostles, which sees the twelve blame each other before the eyes of the Teacher for not having brought bread aboard the boat. Jesus, perhaps smiling at this squabble, warns them to be on their "guard against the leaven of the Pharisees and the leaven of Herod." But the apostles kept going, without listening to him; "they were so closed off in the problem of who had forgotten to bring the bread that they didn't have the space, they didn't have the time, they didn't have the light for the Word of God.

"In the same way, when we are in temptation, we do not hear the Word of God. We can't hear. We don't understand. And Jesus had to remind them about the multiplication of the loaves in order to snap them out of it, because temptation closes us off, it gives us tunnel vision, and that is how it leads us to sin. When we are in temptation, it is only the Word of God, the word of Jesus that can save us. Hearing that word which expands our horizons . . . He is always willing to teach us how to get out of temptation. And Jesus is great because not only does he get us out of temptation but he gives us more trust."

This trust is "a great source of strength when we are in temptation: the Lord is waiting for us"; "he trusts us, as tempted and sinful as we are"; "he always opens the horizons." The devil does precisely the opposite, and with "temptation he closes, closes, closes" and "grows" an environment similar to that of the boat of the apostles. And not allowing ourselves to be "imprisoned" by this kind of environment is possible only "when we listen to the word of Jesus.

"Let's ask the Lord, as he did with the disciples, with his patience, when we are in temptation, always to say to us: 'Stop, be calm. Remember what I did with you at that moment, at that time. Remember. Lift up your eyes, look to the horizon, do not shut down, do not close yourself off, keep going.' And this word will save us from falling into sin in the moment of temptation."

February 18, 2014   *James 1:12–18 ✣ Mark 8:14–21*

174

In order to know Jesus we must follow him as disciples

It is the life of a disciple, rather than the life of a scholar, that allows a Christian to know truly who Jesus is for him. A journey in the footsteps of the Teacher, in which there are clear testimonies and also betrayals, failures and new impulses, but not only an approach of an intellectual nature. The model of this is Peter, whom the Gospel simultaneously depicts as a "courageous" witness—the one who, when Jesus asks the apostles "Who do you say that I am?" affirms: "You are the Christ"—and immediately afterward as an adversary, when he thinks he has to object to Jesus for saying that he must suffer and die, and then rise again. "So many times Jesus asks us this question: 'But who do you say that I am?'" obtaining "the same answer as Peter's, the one we learned in the catechism." But that's not enough.

"It seems that in order to answer that question that we all hear in our hearts—*Who is Jesus for us?*—what we have learned and studied in the catechism is not enough. It is important to study this and know it. But it's not enough. In order to know Jesus we have to make the journey that Peter made. After this humiliation, Peter went forward with Jesus, he saw the miracles that Jesus worked, he saw his power, then he paid the taxes, as Jesus had told him, he caught a fish, took out a coin, saw so many miracles of that kind. But at a certain point Peter denied Jesus, he betrayed Jesus, and he learned that science which is so difficult—for rather than science, it is wisdom—of tears, of weeping."

He asks Jesus for forgiveness, and in spite of this, after the Resurrection, he is questioned by Jesus three times on the shore of the Sea of Tiberias, and it is likely that in reaffirming his total love for his Teacher he weeps and is ashamed at remembering his three denials.

"This first question—'Who do you say that I am?'—posed to Peter can be understood only along the way, after a long journey, a journey of grace and sin, a journey of discipleship. Jesus did not say to Peter and his apostles, 'Know me!' What he said was 'Follow me!'

And it is in following Jesus that we get to know Jesus. Following Jesus with our virtues, and even with our sins, but always following Jesus. What is needed is not a study of things, but a life of discipleship."

We need "a daily encounter with the Lord, every day, with our victories and our weaknesses." But this is also "a journey we cannot make alone." We need the help of the Holy Spirit.

"Knowing Jesus is a gift of the Father; it is he who allows us to know Jesus; it is a work of the Holy Spirit, who is a great laborer. He is not a trade unionist, he is a great laborer and he works in us, always. He does this work of explaining the mystery of Jesus and giving us this sense of Christ. Let's look at Jesus, Peter, the apostles, and hear this question in our hearts: 'Who do you say that I am?' And as disciples let's ask the Father to give us the knowledge of Christ in the Holy Spirit, to explain this mystery to us."

February 20, 2014   *James 2:1–9 ✠ Mark 8:27–33*

175

Faith without works is just words

The world is full of Christians who recite the words of the Creed all the time, and hardly ever put them into practice. Or of scholars who pigeonhole theology in a series of possibilities, without this wisdom casting any reflections in their lives. "We must remember, faith without results in life, a faith that bears no fruit in works, is not faith.

"We also get this wrong much of the time. 'But I have so much faith,' we hear someone say. 'I believe everything, everything . . .' And perhaps this person who is saying this has a life that is lukewarm, weak. His faith is like a theory, but it is not alive in his life. The apostle James, when he speaks of faith, is talking about doctrine, the contents of the faith. But you may know all the commandments, all the prophecies, all the truths of faith, but if this does not lead to practice, if it does not lead to works, it is no use. We can recite the Creed in theory, even without faith, and there are so many people who do this. Even the demons! The demons know very well what is said in the Creed, and they know that it is Truth."

Words that echo the assertion of Saint James: "You believe that there is only one God? You do well; even the demons believe, and tremble." The difference is that the demons "do not have faith," because "having faith means not knowing about something" but "receiving the message of God" brought by Christ. In the Gospel there are two signs for identifying someone who "knows what must be believed but does not have faith." The first sign is "casuistry," represented by those who asked Jesus if it was permissible to pay the census tax, or which of the seven brothers of the husband should marry the woman who is left a widow.

The second sign is "ideology." "Christians who think of the faith as a system of ideas, as ideological. Even in the time of Jesus, they were there. The apostle John says of them that they are the antichrist, the ideologues of the faith, of whatever tendency they may be. At that time there were the Gnostics, but there would be so many . . . So these who fall into casuistry or those who fall into ideology are Christians who know the doctrine but without faith, like the demons. With the difference that the demons tremble, but these do not; they feel just fine!"

On the contrary, in the Gospel there are also examples of "persons who do not know the doctrine but have great faith." We think of the episode of the Canaanite woman, who with her faith obtains the healing of her daughter who was a victim of possession, and of the Samaritan woman who opens her heart because "she has encountered not abstract truths" but "Jesus Christ." And again, the blind man who is healed by Jesus and because of this is interrogated by the Pharisees and scholars of the law until he kneels down with simplicity and worships the one who healed him. Three persons who demonstrate how faith and testimony are inseparable.

"Faith always leads to testimony. Faith is an encounter with Jesus Christ, with God; it is from there that it is born and leads you to testimony. This is what the apostle means: a faith without works, a faith that does not pull you in, that does not lead you to testimony, is not faith. It is words and nothing more than words."

February 21, 2014   *James 2:14–24, 26 ✣ Mark 8:34–9:1*

176

Following Jesus means having a home, the Church

A boy is seized by convulsions and is rolling around on the ground foaming at the mouth, in the midst of a stunned and helpless crowd. And his father is practically clinging to Jesus, begging him to free his son from the demonic possession. The chatter of the bystanders, who are talking about what is happening without offering any help. Jesus arriving and being informed, "the uproar starting to die down." The anguished father, who emerges from the crowd and decides against all hope to hope in Jesus. And Jesus, who is moved to pity by the crystalline faith of this father, drives out the spirit and then leans down tenderly to the boy, who seems dead, helping him to get up.

"All that disorder, that discussion ends in one gesture: Jesus leaning down to take hold of the child. These actions of Jesus make us think. When Jesus heals, when he goes among the people and heals a person, he never leaves that person alone. He is not a magician, a sorcerer, a healer who goes and heals and moves on. He brings everyone back to where he belongs, he doesn't leave him by the wayside. And these are beautiful actions of the Lord."

This is the lesson: "Jesus always leads us home, he never leaves us on the road by ourselves." The Gospel is spread by these actions. The raising of Lazarus, the restoration of life to the daughter of Jairus and to the son of a widowed mother. But also the lost sheep brought back to the sheepfold and the lost coin found again by the woman.

"Because Jesus did not come down from heaven alone; he is the Son of a people. Jesus is the promise made to a people, and his identity is also in his belonging to that people, who from Abraham journey toward the promise. And these actions of Jesus teach us that every healing, every act of forgiveness always brings us back to our people, which is the Church."

Jesus always forgives, and his actions even become "revolutionary," or "inexplicable," when his forgiveness reaches those who have gone "too far away," like the tax collector Matthew or his colleague Zacchaeus. Moreover, "when Jesus forgives, he always brings us back home. This is why Jesus cannot be understood" without the People of God. It is "an absurdity to love Christ without the Church, to listen to Christ but not to the Church, to follow Christ on the outskirts of the Church," to paraphrase Paul VI. "Christ and the Church are united," and "every time Christ calls a person, he leads him to the Church." This is why "it is good" for a child "to be baptized in the Church," the "Mother Church.

"And with these actions of such tenderness Jesus makes us understand this: that our doctrine, let's put it that way, or our following Christ is not an idea, it is a continual remaining at home. And if each one of us has the possibility and the reality of leaving home on account of a sin, a mistake—God knows—salvation is coming back home, with Jesus and the Church. They are actions of tenderness. One by one, the Lord calls us like this, his people, inside his family, our mother, the Holy Church. Let's think about these actions of Jesus."

February 24, 2014   *James 3:13–18* ✦ *Mark 9:14–29*

177

The scandal of war

From where do wars and quarrels arise among you? The letter of the apostle James, in the first reading, is a vibrant condemnation of all wars. The squabbles among the disciples of Jesus to determine who was the greatest among them emphasize how when "hearts are divided the result is war. Every day, in the newspapers, we find wars": "in this place they were cut in half, five dead," in another place more victims.

"And the dead seem to be part of a daily tally. We have gotten used to reading about these things! And if we had the patience to list all of the wars that there are in the world at this moment, we would surely fill several pages. It seems that the spirit of war has taken command of us. Commemorations are being held for the centenary of the First World War, so many millions dead . . . And everyone scandalized! But it's the same thing today! Instead of world war, little wars all over, peoples divided . . . And in order to secure partisan interests, they kill and massacre each other.

"From where do wars and quarrels arise among you? Wars, hatred, enmity are not bought at the store; they are here, in our hearts." When we were children, in the catechism, "they explained to us the story of Cain and Abel and we were all scandalized"; we could not accept that someone could kill his brother. "Today, however, there are so many killings among brothers, among themselves. But we have gotten used to it." The First World War "scandalized us, but this great war is spread all around," somewhat "hidden, it doesn't scandalize us! And so many are dying for a piece of land, for an ambition, for a hatred, for a racial jealousy. Passion leads us to war, to the spirit of the world.

"In the face of a conflict, we typically find ourselves in a curious situation: in order to move forward to resolve it, we fight. With the language of war. The language of peace does not come first! And the results? Think of the famished children in the refugee camps . . . Think just about this; this is the fruit of war! And if you want, think about the great gatherings, the parties of the bosses of the arms industries, who manufacture weapons, the weapons that end up there. The child who is sick, starving, in a refugee camp, and the big parties, the good life that the weapons manufacturers are living.

"What happens in our hearts?" The apostle James gives us a simple bit of advice: " 'Draw near to God, and he will draw near to you.' This spirit of war, which drives us away from God, is not only far from us" but "also in our house.

"How many families are destroyed because the dad, the mom are not capable of finding the way of peace and prefer war, going to court . . . War destroys! 'From where do wars and quarrels arise among you? Do they not perhaps come from your passions?' In the heart! I suggest to you today that you pray for peace, for that peace which seems to have become only a word, nothing more. In order for this word to become active, let's remember some sound advice: 'Recognize your misery!' "

That misery from which wars come: "wars in families, wars in the neighborhood, wars all over. Which of us has wept in reading a newspaper, in seeing those images on television? So many dead. 'Let your laughter,' continues the apostle James, 'be turned into mourning and your joy into dejection.' This is what a Christian must do today in the face of all these wars, all over: weep, mourn, humiliate ourselves. May the Lord help us to understand this and save us from getting used to the news of war."

February 25, 2014   *James 4:1–10 ✦ Mark 9:30–37*

178

Inconsistent Christians, a scandal that kills

He who receives the sacrament of Confirmation "is manifesting his desire to be Christian. Being Christian means bearing witness to Jesus Christ." He is a person who "thinks as a Christian, feels as a Christian, and acts as a Christian. And this is the consistency of the life of a Christian." One may say that he has faith, "but if he is missing one of these things, he is not a Christian; there is something wrong, there is a certain inconsistency." And Christians "who live ordinary lives, generally with inconsistency, do so much harm.

"The apostle Saint James, to some of the inconsistent who were boasting of being Christian but were exploiting their hired hands, says this: 'Behold, the wages of the laborers who reaped on your lands and whom you have not paid are crying out; and the protests of the reapers have come to the ears of the Lord Almighty.' The Lord is powerful. If someone hears this, he may think: But it was a communist who said this! No, no, the apostle James said it! It is the word of the Lord. This is inconsistency. And when there is no Christian consistency and someone is living with this inconsistency, it creates scandal. And Christians who are not consistent cause scandal.

"Jesus speaks very strongly against scandal: 'He who scandalizes one of these little ones who believe in me, just one of these brothers or sisters who have faith, it would be much better for him to have a millstone tied around his neck and be thrown into the sea.' An inconsistent Christian does so much harm," and "scandal kills. So many times we have heard: 'But, Father, I believe in God, but not in the Church, because you Christians say one thing and do another.'" And again: "I believe in God, but not in you." "This is because of inconsistency.

"If you find yourself before—just try to imagine it!—before an atheist who tells you that he doesn't believe in God, you can read him a whole library, where it says that God exists and even prove that God exists, and he will not have faith. But if before this atheist you bear witness to the consistency of Christian life, something will begin to work within his heart. It could be your own testimony that will bring him this disquiet in which the Holy Spirit can work. This is a grace that all of us, the whole Church, must ask for: 'Lord, may we be consistent.'"

So we have to pray "because living in Christian consistency requires prayer, because Christian consistency is a gift of God and we have to ask for it": "Lord, may I be consistent! Lord, let me never cause scandal, may I be a person who thinks as a Christian, feels as a Christian, acts as a Christian." And when we fall out of weakness, let's ask for forgiveness.

"We are all sinners, all of us, but we all have the capacity to ask for forgiveness. And he never wearies of forgiving! To have the humility to ask for forgiveness: 'Lord, I was not consistent here. Forgive me!' To go forward in life with Christian consistency, with the witness of one who believes in Jesus Christ, who knows that he is a sinner but has the courage to ask for forgiveness when he makes a mistake and has such fear of causing scandal. May the Lord give this grace to all of us."

February 27, 2014   *James 5:1–6 ⚜ Mark 9:41–50*

179

Let's not condemn those who fail in love

The scholars of the law try to lay traps for Jesus to "take away his moral authority." The Gospel offers a catechesis on the beauty of marriage. The Pharisees come to Jesus with the problem of divorce. Their style is always the same: "Casuistry. Is this permissible or not?

"Always the narrow case. And this is the trap: behind casuistry, behind casuistic thought, there is always a trap. Always! Against the people, against us, and against God, always! But is it permissible to do this? To repudiate one's wife? And Jesus replied, asking them what the law said and explaining why Moses made the law that way. But he doesn't stop there; from casuistry he goes to the heart of the problem, all the way back to the days of creation. What the Lord says is so beautiful: 'From the beginning of creation, God made them male and female. For this reason a man shall leave his father and mother and be joined to his wife, and the two shall become one flesh. So they are no longer two but one flesh.'"

The Lord "refers to the masterpiece of creation," which is precisely man and woman. And God "did not want man to be alone; he wanted him" to have a "companion for the journey." It is a poetic moment when Adam meets Eve. "It is the beginning of love: go forth together as one flesh." The Lord "always takes casuistic thought and takes it back to the beginning of revelation." On the other hand, "this masterpiece of the Lord did not end there, in the days of creation, because the Lord chose this icon to express the love that he has for his people." To the point that "when the people are not faithful, he speaks to them with words of love.

"The Lord takes this love of the masterpiece of creation to express the love that he has for his people. And in one more passage. When Paul needs to explain the mystery of Christ, he also does so in relationship, in reference to his Bride; because Christ is married, Christ was married, he had married the Church, his people. Just as the Father had married the People of Israel, Christ married his people. This is the story of love, this is the story of the masterpiece of creation! And in the face of this love story, this icon, casuistry falls flat and becomes sadness. But when a man leaves his father and mother and is united with a woman, becoming one flesh and going forward, and this love fails, because it fails so many times, we have to feel the sadness of the failure, accompany these persons who have had this failure in their love. Not condemn! Walk with them! And not bring any casuistry to their situation."

When we read this, "we think of this plan of love, this journey of love that is Christian marriage, which God has blessed in the masterpiece of his creation." A "blessing that has never been taken away. Not even original sin has destroyed it!" When one thinks of this, then, "he sees how beautiful love is, how beautiful marriage is, how beautiful the family is, how beautiful this journey is, and how much love and closeness we must show to these brothers and sisters who in their lives have experienced the disgrace of a failure in love." Turning again to Saint Paul, we must finally emphasize the beauty "of the love that Christ has for his Bride, the Church!

"Here as well we must take care that love not fail! Not to speak too much of Christ as if he were a bachelor; Christ married the Church! And we cannot understand Christ without the Church, and we cannot understand the Church without Christ. This is the great mystery of the masterpiece of creation. May the Lord give all of us the grace of understanding it and also the grace of never falling into these casuistic attitudes, of the scholars of the law."

February 28, 2014   *James 5:9–12 ✠ Mark 10:1–12*

180

Let's free our hearts of idolatry

The rich man in the Gospel who throws himself at the feet of Jesus to ask him what he must do to inherit eternal life "was so eager to hear the words of Jesus"; he was "a good man, because from his youth he had observed the commandments. A good man," therefore, "but this was not enough for him. He wanted more. The Holy Spirit was urging him along." Jesus looks at him with love and tells him that he should sell everything and come with him to preach the Gospel. But when he heard these words, the man's face became gloomy and he went away sad because he had many possessions.

"His unquiet heart, precisely because of the Holy Spirit, who had urged him to draw near to Jesus and to follow him, was a full heart, and he did not have the courage to empty it. And he made his choice: money. A heart full of money . . . But he was not a thief, a criminal: no, no, no! He was a good man; he had never stolen, never! Never any cheating, either; his was honest money. But his heart was imprisoned there; it was bound to his money and he did not have the freedom to choose. His money chose for him.

"How many young people hear in their hearts this 'call' to draw close to Jesus, and are enthusiastic; they are not ashamed of kneeling down" before him, of "giving public demonstration of their faith in Jesus Christ"; and "they want to follow him, but when their hearts are full of something else and they are not courageous enough to empty them, they turn back, and that joy becomes sadness." Even today there are many young people who have a vocation, but sometimes there is something "that stops them.

"We must pray that the hearts of these young people may be emptied, emptied of other interests, of other loves, that their hearts may become free. And this is the prayer for vocations: 'Lord, send us sisters, send us priests. Defend them from idolatry, from the idolatry of vanity, from the idolatry of arrogance, from the idolatry of power, from the idolatry of money.' And our prayer is to prepare these hearts to be able to follow Jesus up close."

The man of this Gospel passage is "so good and then so unhappy." There are many young people like this today. This is why we need to raise an intense prayer to God. "It is this prayer: 'Help these young people, Lord, that they may be free and may not be slaves, that they may have hearts only for you,' so that the call of the Lord can come, can bear fruit. And this is the prayer for vocations. We must do so much of this: Pray. But take care to understand: the vocations are already there. We have to help them to grow, so that the Lord may enter these hearts and give this inexpressible and glorious joy that belongs to every person who follows Jesus up close."

March 3, 2014   *1 Peter 1:3–9 ✤ Mark 10:17–27*

181

There are Christians condemned today because they have a Bible

Jesus has just finished speaking about the danger of riches, and Peter asks him what the disciples who have left everything to follow will receive. This exchange, narrated by the Gospel, allows us to emphasize that Jesus "is generous." Truly, the Lord responds, "there is no one who has given up" family, home, fields, who "will not receive a hundred times more." Perhaps Peter thinks that "following Jesus" is a "great business opportunity," because it allows us to earn a hundred times as much. But Jesus adds that alongside this gain there will be persecutions.

"As if he were saying, 'Yes, you have left everything and you will receive here, on earth, many things; but with persecutions!' Like a salad with persecution dressing: always! This is the gain of the Christian, and this is the path of the one who wants to follow Jesus, because it is the path that he walked: he was persecuted! It is the path of abasement. It's what Paul says to the Philippians: 'He abased himself. He became man and abased himself to death, death on the Cross.' This is precisely the heart of Christian life."

It is the same in the Beatitudes, when Jesus says: "Blessed are you when they insult you and you are persecuted because of my name; persecution is one of the Beatitudes." The disciples, "immediately after the coming of the Holy Spirit, began to preach and the persecutions began: Peter went to prison," Stephen was killed, and then "many other disciples down to our own time. The Cross is always on the Christian path! We will have many brothers, many sisters, many mothers, many fathers in the Church, in the Christian community," but "we will also have persecution.

"Because the world does not tolerate the divinity of Christ. It does not tolerate the proclamation of the Gospel. It does not tolerate the Beatitudes. And so the persecution comes: in words, calumnies, the things that were said about Christians during the first centuries, slander, imprisonment . . . But we forget easily. But let's think about the many Christians, decades ago, in the camps, in the prisons of the Nazis, the communists—so many! For being Christian! Even today . . . 'But today we have more culture, and these things aren't around anymore.' They're around! And I'm telling you that today there are more martyrs than in the early Church."

So many brothers and sisters "bear witness to Jesus, offer the testimony of Jesus, and are persecuted." Christians who cannot even have a Bible.

"They are condemned because they have a Bible. They cannot wear the sign of the Cross. And this is the way of Jesus. But it is a joyful way, because the Lord never tests us beyond what we can bear. Christian life is not a business advantage, it is not making a career; it is simply following Jesus! But when we follow Jesus, this is what happens. Let's think about whether we have the desire inside to be courageous in bearing witness to Jesus. Let's also think—it will do us good—of the many brothers and sisters who today—today!— cannot pray together, because they are persecuted; they cannot have the book of the Gospels or a Bible, because they are persecuted."

Let's think of those brothers who "cannot go to Mass, because it is forbidden." So many times "a priest comes secretly among them, and they pretend to be having a meal, to be having tea, and there they celebrate the Mass, so that they cannot be seen. This is happening today." Let's think about whether we are willing "to carry the Cross as Jesus did. To bear persecutions in order to give testimony to Jesus," as "do these brothers and sisters who are humiliated and persecuted today. This thought would do us all good."

March 4, 2014   *1 Peter 1:10–16 ✤ Mark 10:28–31*

182

There is no Christian style without the Cross and without Jesus

In the Gospel, Jesus says to the disciples: "If anyone wishes to come after me, let him deny himself and take up his cross daily and follow me." This is "the Christian style," because Jesus was the first to walk "this road.

"We cannot think of Christian life apart from this path. There is always this road that he traveled first: the road of humility, the road even of humiliation, of annihilating oneself, and then rising again. But this is the way. Without the Cross, the Christian style is not Christian, and if the Cross is a Cross without Jesus, it is not Christian. The Christian style takes up the Cross with Jesus and goes forward. Not without the Cross, not without Jesus."

Jesus "has given the example," and, despite "being equal to God," "he annihilated himself, made himself a servant for all of us."

"And this style will save us, it will bring us joy and make us fruitful, because the purpose of this way of denying ourselves is to bring life; it is against the way of selfishness, of being attached to everything good only for myself . . . This way is open to others, because that way which Jesus walked, of annihilation, that way was meant to give life. The Christian style is precisely this style of humility, meekness, gentleness.

"Whoever wishes to save his life will lose it." Jesus repeats this idea: "Unless a grain of wheat falls to the ground and dies, it remains just a grain of wheat; but if it dies, it produces much fruit." And this journey is to be made "with joy, because it is he himself who gives us joy. Following Jesus is joy, but following Jesus in the style of Jesus, not in the style of the world." Following the Christian style means walking the way of the Lord, "each of us as he is able," "in order to give life to others, not to give life to ourselves. This is the spirit of generosity." Our selfishness pushes us to want to appear important in front of others. Instead, the book *The Imitation of Christ* "gives us a great piece of advice: 'Love being unknown and judged as nothing.' " This is Christian humility, what Jesus was the first to do.

"And this is our joy, and this is our fruitfulness: to go with Jesus. Other joys are not fruitful; they think only—as the Lord says—of gaining the whole world, but in the end they lose and ruin life. At the beginning of Lent, let's ask the Lord to teach us this Christian style of service, of joy, of annihilation of ourselves and fruitfulness with him, as he wishes it."

March 6, 2014   *Deuteronomy 30:15–20* ✢ *Luke 9:22–25*

183

Fasting is also a caress

Christianity is not a heartless set of rules, a list of formal obser-vances for people who put on the good face of hypocrisy to hide a heart empty of charity. Christianity is the very "flesh" of Christ, who bends down without shame to those who suffer. What helps to explain this contrast to us is the dialogue in the Gospel between Jesus and the disciples of John, who are criticizing those who don't respect fasting. The fact is that the scholars of the law had turned the observance of the commandments into a "formality," turning "religious life" into "an ethics" and forgetting its roots, which is "a story of salvation, of election, of covenant.

"Receiving from the Lord the love of a Father, receiving from the Lord the identity of a people and then turning it into an eth-ics means rejecting that gift of love. These hypocritical people are good persons; they are doing everything they have to do. They seem good! They are ethicists, but ethicists without goodness, because they have lost the sense of belonging to the people! The Lord gives salvation within a people, in belonging to a people."

And yet, the prophet Isaiah had already clearly described what fasting is according to the vision of God: "loosing unjust chains, setting the oppressed free," but also "sharing bread with the hungry, giving shelter to the homeless, clothing the naked.

"That is the fasting that the Lord wants! Fasting that is concerned about the life of our brothers, that is not ashamed—Isaiah himself says this—of the flesh of our brothers. Our perfection, our holiness move forward with our people, in which we are chosen and incor-porated. Our greatest act of holiness is precisely in the flesh of our brother and in the flesh of Jesus Christ. Our act of holiness today on the altar is not hypocritical fasting; it is not being ashamed of the flesh of Christ, who comes here today! It is the mystery of the Body and Blood of Christ. It is going to share bread with the hungry, to care for the sick, the elderly, those who can give us nothing in re-turn. That is not being ashamed of the flesh!"

This means that "the hardest form of fasting" is "the fasting of goodness." It is the fasting of which the good Samaritan, who bends down to the wounded man, is capable, and not that of the priest, who sees the same unfortunate man but keeps on going, perhaps out of fear of contaminating himself. And therefore "this is the question the Church asks us today: Am I ashamed of the flesh of my brother, of my sister?

"When I give alms, do I drop the coin without touching the hand? And if I happen to touch it, do I do this [Francis probably rubs his hands on his vestments here] right away? When I give alms, do I look into the eyes of my brother, my sister? When I know that a person is sick, do I go to visit him? Do I greet him with tenderness? There is a sign that may help us, it is a question: Do I know how to caress the sick, the elderly, children, or have I lost the sense of the caress? These hypocrites did not know how to caress! They had forgotten. Not to be ashamed of the flesh of our brother; it is our flesh! As we do to this brother, to this sister, we will be judged."

March 7, 2014   *Isaiah 58:1–9a ✠ Matthew 9:14–15*

184

Mercy is the way of peace in the world

To forgive in order to find mercy: this is the way that leads to peace in our hearts and in the world. "Be merciful, just as your Father is merciful": this is the comment on the exhortation of Jesus. "It is not easy to understand this attitude of mercy" because we are used to judging. "We are not persons who naturally make a little room for understanding and for mercy. There are two attitudes we have to have in order to be merciful. The first is knowledge of our-selves," knowing that "we have done many things that are not good; we are sinners!" And in the face of repentance, "the justice of God turns into mercy and forgiveness." But we have to be ashamed of our sins.

"It is true, none of us has murdered anybody, but so many little things, so many everyday sins, day after day . . . And when some-one thinks: What have I done, how petty can I be? I have done this against the Lord! And to be ashamed! To be ashamed before God, and this shame is a grace; it is the grace of being sinners. 'I am a sinner and I am ashamed before you, and I ask your forgiveness.' It is simple, but so difficult to say: 'I have sinned.'"

We often justify our sins by laying the blame on others, as Adam and Eve did. "Perhaps the other helped me, facilitated the way for doing it, but I'm the one who did it! If we admit this, how many good things there will be for us, because we will be humble!" And "with this attitude of repentance we are more capable of being mer-ciful, because we feel the mercy of God upon us," as we say in the Our Father: "Forgive us as we forgive." So "if I do not forgive, I am out of bounds!"

The other attitude for being merciful is "expanding our hearts," because "a small and selfish heart is not capable of mercy.

"We need bigger hearts! 'But I am a sinner.' 'But look at what this guy did, and that guy . . . I have failed so many times! Who am I to judge him?' This question: Who am I to judge this? Who am I to gossip about this? Who am I? Who am I, who have done the same things, or worse? Bigger hearts! And the Lord says this: 'Do not judge and you will not be judged! Do not condemn and you will not be condemned! Forgive and you will be forgiven! Give and it will be given to you!' This generosity of heart! And what will be given to you? Good measure, pressed down, brimful, and overflowing will be poured out into your lap. This is the image of persons who went to fetch wheat in their aprons, and spread their aprons out to receive more, more grain. If you have a big heart, a great heart, you can receive more."

The great heart "does not condemn, but forgives, forgets," because "God has forgotten my sins; God has forgiven my sins. Expanding our hearts. This is wonderful! Be merciful.

"The merciful man and woman have big hearts, big. They always excuse others and think about their own sins. *But did you see what he did?* But I have enough problems with what I've done, and I'm not getting into it!' This is the way of the mercy for which we must ask. But if all of us, if all peoples, persons, families, neighborhoods, had this attitude, how much peace there would be in the world, how much peace in our hearts! Because mercy leads us to peace. Always remember this: 'Who am I to judge?' To be ashamed, and expand our hearts. May the Lord give us this grace."

March 17, 2014   *Daniel 9:4b–10 ✤ Luke 6:36–38*

185

No to hypocrites "gussied up" as saints

Conversion: this is the key word of Lent, the season devoted to "getting closer" to Jesus. In the first reading, taken from the book of Isaiah, the Lord calls to conversion the two "sinful cities" of Sodom and Gomorrah. This emphasizes the fact that we all "need to change our lives," to look "carefully into our souls," where we will always find something. Lent is therefore precisely this "adjustment of life," getting closer to the Lord. He "wants us close," and he assures us that "he is waiting to forgive us." Nonetheless, the Lord wants "a drawing near that is sincere," and he warns us against being hypocrites.

"What do hypocrites do? They make themselves up, they gussy themselves up as good. They put on holier-than-thou faces; they pray looking up to heaven, showing off, feeling better than others, despising others. 'Well,' they say, 'I am very Catholic, because my uncle was a great benefactor, my family is this, and I am . . . I have learned . . . I know this bishop, that cardinal, this priest . . . I am . . .' They feel better than others. This is hypocrisy. The Lord says, 'No, not that.' No one is just on his own. We all need to be justified. And the only one who justifies us is Jesus Christ."

This is why we have to get closer to the Lord: "In order to avoid being gussied-up Christians, who when this appearance is taken away and the reality is seen, it is clear that they are not Christians." So what is "the touchstone for knowing that we are not hypocrites and are getting closer to the Lord"? The Lord himself gives us the answer in the first reading, when he says: "Wash yourselves, purify yourselves, take away from my eyes the evil of your actions, stop doing evil, learn to do good." This is the invitation. But "what is the sign that we are going the right way?

"'Succor the oppressed, do justice for the orphan, defend the cause of the widow.' Care for your neighbor: the sick, the poor, those in need, the ignorant. This is the touchstone. Hypocrites don't

know how to do this; they can't, because they're so full of themselves that they are too blind to look at others. When someone starts
walking and gets closer to the Lord, the light of the Lord shows him
these things and he goes to help his brothers. This is the sign, this is
the sign of conversion."

Of course, "conversion is not everything"; that in fact "is the
encounter with Jesus Christ," but "the sign that we are with Jesus
Christ is this: caring for our brothers, the poorest, the sick, as the
Lord teaches us" and as we read in chapter 23 of the Gospel of Matthew.

"Lent is for adjusting our lives, getting our lives in order, chang-
ing our lives in order to get closer to the Lord. The sign that we
are far from the Lord is hypocrisy. The hypocrite does not need the
Lord, he saves himself, or that's what he thinks, and he disguises
himself as holy. The sign that we are getting closer to the Lord with
penance, asking for forgiveness, is that we care for our needy brothers. May the Lord give all of us light and courage: light to know
what is happening inside of ourselves, and courage to convert, to get
closer to the Lord. It's great to be close to the Lord."

March 18, 2014   *Isaiah 1:10, 16–20 ✣ Matthew 23:1–12*

186

He who trusts in himself and not in the Lord loses his name, meaning everything

The man who trusts in himself, in his own wealth or ideology, is destined for unhappiness. He who trusts in the Lord, however, bears fruit even in seasons of drought.

"Cursed is the man who trusts in human beings, who seeks his strength in flesh"; he will be "like a tamarisk on the steppe," condemned by dryness to remaining without fruit and dying. "Blessed is the man who trusts in the Lord; he is like a tree planted by a stream of water" that in times of drought "does not stop producing fruit. Only in the Lord is our certain trust. Other forms of trust are of no use; they do not save us, they do not give us life, they do not give us joy." And even if we know this, "we like to trust in ourselves, to trust in that friend, or to trust in that good situation that I have, or in that ideology," and "the Lord is set aside." In this way man closes himself off within himself, "without horizons, without open doors, without windows," and "he will not have salvation, he cannot save himself." And this is what happens to the rich man in the Gospel, who "had everything. He wore purple robes, ate every day, big feasts. He was so content," but "he didn't realize that at the door of his home, covered with sores," there was a poor man. The Gospel tells us the name of the poor man: he was called Lazarus. While the rich man "has no name.

"And this is the strongest curse of the one who trusts in himself or his powers, in the possibilities of man and not in God: losing his name. What is your name? Account number, in bank such-and-such. What is your name? So many properties, so many homes, so many . . . What is your name? The things we have, the idols. And you trust in that, and this man is cursed.

"We all have this weakness, this frailty of putting our trust in ourselves or in friends or in human possibilities only, and we forget about the Lord. And this leads us down the path . . . of unhappiness.

"Today, on this day of Lent, it would do us good to ask ourselves:

Where is my trust? In the Lord? Or am I a pagan, who trusts in things, in the idols I have made? Do I still have a name, or have I begun to lose my name and to call myself 'I'? By me, with me, for me, just me? For me, for me . . . Always that egoism: I. This does not give us salvation."

But "in the end there is a door of hope" for those who trust in themselves and "have lost their names.

"In the end there is always a possibility. And this man, when he realizes that he has lost his name, he has lost everything, everything, he lifts up his eyes and says just one word: 'Father.' And God's response is just one word: 'Son!' If some of us in our lives, from having so much trust in man and in ourselves, end up losing our names, losing this dignity, there is still the possibility of saying this word that is more than magical; it is more, it is powerful: 'Father.' He is always waiting for us to open a door that we do not see, and he will say to us: 'Son.' Let's ask the Lord for the grace of giving all of us the wisdom to trust only in him, not in things, in human strength, only in him."

March 20, 2014   *Jeremiah 17:5–10 ✦ Luke 16:19–31*